D1507979

ISMs

A Compendium of Concepts,
Doctrines, Traits, & Beliefs from
ABLEISM to ZYGODACTYLISM

Alan & Theresa von Altendorf

Mustang Publishing Co.
Memphis, TN

Distributed to U.S. bookstores by National Book Network, Lanham, MD. For information on distributors outside the U.S.A., contact Mustang Publishing.

All illustrations used with permission of Dover Publications, New York, NY.

Interior design by Rollin Riggs.

Library of Congress Cataloging-in-Publication Data

Von Altendorf, Alan 1950-
    Isms : a compendium of concepts, doctrines, traits & beliefs from ableism to zygodactylism / Alan & Theresa von Altendorf.
      p.   cm.
    ISBN 0-914457-64-0 (acid-free) : $9.95
    1. English language--Reverse indexes. 2. Learning and scholarship--Terminology. 3. English language--Glossaries, vocabularies, etc.   I. Von Altendorf, Theresa, 1947-
II. Title.
PE1680.V66   1991   91-52876
423' . 1--dc20   CIP

Printed on acid-free paper.

10 9 8 7 6 5 4 3 2 1

Acknowledgments

Many thanks to Tanya Charter, who gave us a beautiful place to write; Steve Bowers, who gave us a garage, a computer, and a lifetime supply of spiritual jelly donuts; Tom Ruppenthal, friend and ally; F. Bentley Mooney, Jr., the world's nicest lawyer; Mary Louise Mooney, tireless editorial assistant; and Rollin Riggs, whose guidance, encouragement, and effort made this book possible.

Very special thanks to Dover Publications, which publishes the wonderful books that supplied all the illustrations herein.

Also, we are indebted to our principal sources: *Webster's Unabridged Dictionary of the English Language*, *The American Heritage Dictionary*, *Random House Webster's College Dictionary*, *The Concise Columbia Dictionary of Quotations*, *Bartlett's Familiar Quotations*, *The Little, Brown Book of Anecdotes*, *The Portable Curmudgeon* edited by Jon Winokur, *The 1,911 Best Things Anybody Ever Said* edited by Robert Byrne, and *An Uncommon Scold* edited by Abby Adams.

Alan & Theresa von Altendorf

Preface

I first realized the potential of "isms" some five years ago, while participating in the Actor's Institute in London. One particular workshop included, as part of the opening session, a review of words that end in "ism." It was soon apparent that for almost every situation we could conjure, someone had an Ism.

Isms place politics, religion, health, art, science, nature, environment—you name it—into a box from which, when so labeled, it is hard to escape. Can it be that we, the masters of our planet, have encapsulated everything we are into a few thousand multi-syllabic words? Have the great writers, poets, and artists reduced the breadth and diversity of self- and communal-expression into a few hundred terms? Who decided we should shrink the essence of the individual and the spirit of the masses into such relatively few words?

Maybe it is our obsession to explain, our desire to vilify, celebrate, and place everything in order, that has lead us to set all things, from the sublime to the ridiculous, in little Ism-boxes. And yet, as this book amply shows, Isms have become not only a way of life but also, so often, an accepted way to explain who someone is, how someone behaves, how someone feels, and why something happens. We are our Isms.

For the continued endurance of Alan and Theresa, we owe a loud thank you, because the minute this book leaves the printing press, a new Ism will appear—a frustration for these thorough authors, no doubt. So, in reading this work, I suggest you look less for what is missing and more for what is universal, personal, and enlightening.

Finally, allow me to indulge the British fondness for scatalogical humor: I advise you to leave this book in the smallest room of the house and delve into it with regularity. May *ISMs* bring smiles to the pained, relief to the constipated, and joy to the bored. For myself, I have found terrific fun and mischievousness in these pages, and I've even learned a few things. I hope you'll have a similar experience.

Mark Ursell-Smith
London

Notice to Readers, Part 1

Very few Isms are actually beneficial and therefore worth remembering. However, there are at least two good reasons to study every entry, preferably starting with Ableism and patiently chugging along to Zygodactylism:

1. This alphabetical plan of attack will help you appreciate the manifold silliness of humanity in its quest to organize and explain itself; and

2. It's the only way to appreciate all the best jokes, which were inserted at considerable expense by a team of highly qualified humorists.

Do not become alarmed if we occasionally ridicule a sacred cow. Independent research has shown conclusively that cows don't give a hoot about being ridiculed.

The only "ism" Hollywood believes in is Plagiarism.
Dorothy Parker (1893-1967)

Notice to Readers, Part 2

A few words of explanation about the editing process are in order:

First, as you'll quickly realize, almost any word can become an Ism. Rather than turn this into a 12-volume set, we decided to limit the words included to those noted in one of our source dictionaries or used in a recent book, magazine, or newspaper. Plus, we rejected most Isms with prefixes (ex, anti, hyper, etc.) if the root Ism is defined. Also, to amuse and/or annoy, we sometimes coined a few Isms of our own.

Second, we excluded lots of highly technical Isms—terms from chemistry, biology, optics, geology, etc.—because 1. they are boring, and 2. we really didn't understand them. We included a technical Ism when we felt it had appeal broad enough that someone, somewhere might want to use it in a conversation.

Third, we are alarmed at the growing "Ism-ization" of the language. (We're also alarmed at the growing "-ization" of the language, but that's another book.) Shallow thinkers believe they can give credibility to any trendy thought just by adding "ism" to the end of a word. But adding "ism" is too often a short-cut past the hard work of defining concepts fully and describing behaviors thoroughly. This is especially true of the recent "politically correct" accusations in vogue on U.S. campuses. Words like Heightism and Weightism employ our favorite suffix only to make their half-baked concepts sound respectable.

Finally, we welcome your comments, Criticisms, suggestions, and, of course, new Isms, which we hope to add in subsequent printings (for which contributors will receive due recognition). Write to us in care of Mustang Publishing, P.O. Box 3004, Memphis, TN 38173 U.S.A.

A new word ending in "ism" that no one else knew was for him a gift of the gods.

Pio Baroja (1872-1956)

Ableism—a term from the "politically correct" lingo currently in vogue on U.S. college campuses and an extension of Racism and Sexism, Ableism is usually used to accuse a person or group who favors someone with ideal health over someone with a physical or mental defect, especially in employment practices.

While we appreciate the fact that young people today like to think that abililty doesn't count and that the blind, deaf, and paraplegic are as qualified as the robust, the truth is slightly less wonderful. Overweight deaf-mutes make lousy F-16 pilots. People with Alzheimer's Disease make bad reference librarians.

Fortunately, all stand equal before the law. If you try to steal milk from 7-11 because you can run fast, or if you're prevented from buying brownies there because you're fat, or if you're charged twice as much for carrots because you're wearing a "Meat Is Murder" button, you'll get the same hearing in court as any citizen.

We'll call these 7-11 Rights, and they aren't granted by law. Rather, they are naturally profitable to the 7-11 company, in whose interest these rights are promulgated. 7-11 wants to entice the largest number of customers to its stores, and it wants customers to be happy, no matter how blind, fat, old, smelly, cantankerous, or able they are. All will be treated much the same in every store by every clerk.

However, if you press for legally mandated "equality" and forced tolerance and attempt to compel 7-11 to hire people who are clearly not the best candidates for the job, such Interventionism will destroy efficient, friendly service and competitive prices, in direct relation to the number of less-qualified workers you force them to employ. Tragedy is seldom profitable to anyone.

(We apologize to 7-11 for using them arbitrarily in the foregoing example. They'd probably say they were doing their utmost to hire the "differently able." These days, everyone cowers a little before the Politically Correct.)

≥≈

Abolitionism—principles or measures fostering the abolition of slavery. As early as 1835, Abolitionism in the U.S. was perceived as such a threat to Southern society that most states south of Virginia imposed severe penalties for printing or speaking anything that might incite insurrection among slaves. Preventing slaves from reading was also part of the plan: in 1853, a Virginia woman was jailed for teaching blacks to read the Bible. A prominent abolitionist, William Lloyd Garrison, eventually focused national attention with his publication *The Liberator*, which popularized the abolition movement in the North and sparked the Civil War.

≥≈

Absenteeism—1. chronic absence from work or school. 2. protracted absence of an owner from his property. Originally, the term referred to landlords who derived their income from one country but spent it while residing in another. This practice persists in European countries, where tax laws make it advantageous to work in one country and live in another. In America, the landlord usually lives in a better part of town.

≥≈

Absinthism—sickness prompted by the use of the liqueur absinthe, made from wormwood, to excess. Absinthe was said to be addictive and could cause convulsions and hallucinations.

≥≈

Absolutism—1. in philosophy, the concept of a non-relative being. 2. government by an absolute ruler. 3. advocacy of a rule by absolute standards or principles. Generally, it's a form of government that considers itself independent of other causes and has no restrictions or limitations on its powers, which are vested in one or more rulers. Niccolo Machiavelli, Francis Bacon, and Thomas Hobbes were leading lights in favor of absolute authority vested in a monarch. Hobbes probably did more damage than the others, because he propounded the idea of a "social contract" which bound one and all to the absolute state. Today, the notion of a social contract dominates left-wing discussion on the merits of Socialism and Welfare Statism, especially at election time.

In the U.S., it's unclear whether the Constitution confers absolute power on any person or branch of government, because the system of "checks and balances" distributes sovereignty among the states, the Federal government, the executives, legislators, and the judiciary. However, from time to time a sort of *de facto* Absolutism exists (e.g., in times of war or civil disturbance). Pres. Abraham Lincoln, for instance, suspended the constitutional right of *habeas corpus* and commandeered private property without going through the niceties of congressional approval or public referendum during the Civil War, and thus he acted as an absolute ruler for a few years.

On the other hand, ruling by absolute standards has a lot of appeal, if you consider it humanly possible. It would be nice to have absolute justice, fairness, and equality, for instance. See Idealism.

Abstract Expressionism—the practice of painting amorphous shapes and color blobs which supposedly convey the artist's emotions. Begun as an innocent rebellion against Formalism and Realism, it quickly degenerated into a global conspiracy against traditional painting and sculpture. In the old days, one had to be able to draw to be called an artist. Nowadays, you're lucky if you can find anything in a gallery that vaguely resembles a recognizable form on canvas.

Strictly speaking, Abstract Expressionism belongs in the category of decorative arts, along with rug weaving, house painting, and wallpaper design, since the most it offers is a pleasing arrangement of color, line, and form. Perhaps this explains why major corporations have patronized avant-garde painters and sculptors: their splashes of color enliven offices without actually making a statement about anything. "To say that a work of art is good but incomprehensible to the majority of men, is the same as saying of some kind of food that it is very good but that most people can't eat it." (Leo Tolstoy)

Abstractionism—the principles, ideals, or creation of non-representational art. This is a profoundly confusing (and misleading) term, since all art amounts to an abstraction of something from something else. The root of "abstraction" means to take away; when the artist selects certain features to the exclusion of others, he's making an abstract interpretation of the subject. Even a documentary photograph implies a point of view and the photographer's preference for certain subjects, techniques, and outcomes. Taken to logical extremes, some say, it would be possible to depict a subject by a single line, or a dot, or nothing at all. However, since few of us could get much pleasure from a painting that consisted of a line, a dot, or nothing at all, the artist had better heed the limits of ingenuity among his patrons, whatever level of abstraction he chooses to employ. Some of us like to have a few clues as to what the damn thing is all about.

ॐ

Absurdism—music and lyrics which take everything to the extremes of imagination, comic exaggeration, and insight; a term applied (somewhat inappropriately) to the music of Frank Zappa.

ॐ

Academism—1. Conservatism in thought or art. 2. speculative thoughts and attitudes which may not consider the exigencies of the "real world." Even though we commonly think of anyone in college, especially faculty or permanent students, as academics, the term is derived from Academus, a Greek hero who owned the property where Plato taught, and it refers to Platonism. Also, Academicism.

ॐ

Accidentalism—1. the belief that everything happens by chance. 2. in music, a sharp, flat, or natural which does not occur in the clef and implies some change of key or modulation different from that in which the piece began. 3. in medicine, treatment based on the symptoms rather than the cause of the ailment. 4. in philosophy, the term implies that nothing has causes or predictable consequences—which rapidly leads to Nihilism.

ॐ

Achromatism—in optics, the quality of refracting white light without dispersing it into its constituent colors; the state of being colorless. A good many politicians could be so described.

ॐ

Acosmism—denial of the existence of an eternal world and/or a mystical hereafter (i.e., heaven), in opposition to most world religions, which preach the immortality of the soul and a variety of afterlifes.

ॐ

Acrobatism—the skill or feats of a gymnastic performer, a trapeze artist, etc.; any action performed with flair and agility.

ॐ

Acrotism—literally, the absence of beating, and therefore an absence or weakness of heartbeat or pulse. Rare among living things except plants and accountants.

ॐ

Actinism—the radiation of heat or light, specifically referring to the chemical part of the sun's rays. In photography, film reacts chemically to light to create a picture.

ॐ

Activism—1. in philosophy, the theory that reality is an act or process. 2. a doctrine or practice featuring forceful action to achieve a goal. Consumer activists lobby for strict government regulation, expose unreliable goods and services, and counsel consumers. Judicial activists are said to ignore legal precedent and literal interpretation of fundamental laws in favor of theories that spawn freshly minted rights and privileges. Environmental activists (such as Greenpeace) physically confront those whom they oppose—a tactic borrowed from the civil rights and anti-war activists of the 1960's.

If you wish to effect social change, it's hard to see how you can succeed except through Activism of some sort, unless you resort to the old-fashioned method of reading and writing. Activism grew popular largely because of television, which explains why we no longer debate social issues with lengthy philosophical reasoning. Instead, today's activists devise photogenic stunts and create slogans to fit into 10-second "sound bites" on the evening news.

Actualism—the philosophical theory that all of reality is in motion all of the time, not just when you're a little drunk.

Adiaphorism—tolerance of an action or a belief that the Bible does not specifically prohibit. See Indifferentism.

Adoptionism—the doctrine or belief that Jesus of Nazareth became the Son of God only by adoption. This squares some of the logical difficulties in the Virgin Birth story.

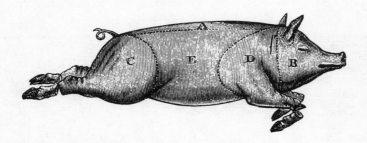

Adventism—the doctrine of the Seventh-Day Adventists which states that Christ's return and the end of the world are near. Just how near, no one knows. From time to time they assemble on mountaintops and get disappointed.

Adventurism—a doctrine favoring defiance of accepted standards of behavior, especially in the conduct of foreign affairs. Oliver North is a recent adventurist, in that he advocated schemes subverting

Congressional authority and standard military procedures to achieve foreign policy goals. Critics first hurled the term at Theodore Roosevelt's policy of Expansionism and Imperialism, which they said was an unlawful or imprudent extension of U.S. military power.

இ

Adwaitism—a doctrine formed by a composite of three sects of Vedantin-Hinduism, founded by Sankaracharya, who was born about 60 years after Buddha's death. (Some believe Sankaracharya was the reincarnation of Buddha.) The basic Adwait doctrine states that Brahmum, the universal Spirit, acts only through Prakrati (matter) and thus is a passive, incomprehensible, unconscious principle, as well as the essence of the universe. This is identical to Transcendental Materialism of Esoteric Buddhism.

The name Adwaitee signifies "not dual," referring to the oneness of the universal spirit. Adwaitees infer that the Buddhist doctrine of karma is completely dependent on the causes each person engenders. The bottom line is a preoccupation with the pathway to salvation—i.e., worship as a means of saving your soul—and so Adwaitees have a lot in common with Christians who believe in Divine Grace.

We often wonder: just what are our souls being saved *from*? So many religious Isms start with the premise that we're divine and then proceed to explain how Ritualism will save us from eternal damnation.

இ

Aeronautism—the ability to sail in the air, like eagles and paper airplanes. Perhaps it also applies to the condition of levitation that some Transcendental Meditators claim to have achieved—a feat that may be the key to air traffic congestion. See Transcendentalism.

Aerotropism—the tendency of some plants to have their growth in-fluenced by air flow.

ஐ

Aestheticism—the principle or doctrine of beauty, art, or morality, often explained in the context of history, psychology, or ethnology. Generally, it's the theory of fine art and the practice of those who value beauty. People who practice Aestheticism can become zealous in their emphasis of beauty and critical or repulsed by works they do not consider beautiful, though cultural differences suggest "beau-ty" is quite relative. The historical connection arises from the in-fluence of Greek civilization on Western culture, and in fact, the origin of the word is Greek (it refers to sense perception).

Clearly, our definitions of beauty change: for example, the recently popular Cabbage Patch dolls, featuring pinched faces and goofy eyes, represent a substantial departure from traditional dolls like Barbie. In fact, Aestheticism may be nearly dead in America, to the extent that society has self-consciously turned from things of exceptional beauty toward the mundane and grotesque. Perhaps the clearest ex-ample is the trend away from glamorous movie stars toward average-looking people doing average things on screen. If the purpose of art is to inspire and uplift, it's difficult to see the art in Cabbage Patch dolls or gritty action films about cab drivers and lunatics. Also, Estheticism.

ஐ

Afrikanderism—a word taken from Afrikaans. Can you think of any? Neither can we.

ஐ

Afrocentrism—promulgation of things centered on Africa and/or Afri-can culture, especially with regard to educational policies. In the current rage to increase self-esteem among black youths in the U.S., schools are adopting Afrocentric curricula which teach that Africa is the cradle of civilization, that Africans discovered the New World 3,000 years before Columbus, and that evil "ice people" (European whites) destroyed the idyllic culture of the "sun people" (African blacks). One question: What will happen to black self-esteem when the kids learn their teachers lied to them all through school? See Revisionism.

ஐ

Afro-Cubanism—early 20th-century trend in Cuban music, litera-ture, and painting which evolved from Avant-Gardism and celebrated primitiveness.

ஐ

Ageism—discrimination against a person or group because of age. From the "politically correct" lingo recently popular on U.S. college cam-puses, the term is usually used to accuse a person or institution of

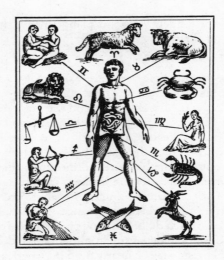

unfairly favoring middle-aged people over the young or the elderly,
especially in employment practices. An extension of Racism and
Sexism. (By the way, "PC" doctrine prefers the term "chronologi-
cally gifted" to "elderly" or "senior citizen.")

Agnosticism—the doctrine or belief that it is impossible to know
whether there is an ultimate reality or God, or how the universe
began. The defect in this type of thinking is that it disqualifies ag-
nostics from further debate, since they have disavowed an ability
to know anything about the subject. Generally, people describe themselves as agnostic when the complexity or abstractness of a question is too much to handle. Some philosophers have labored to prove
we are incapable of answering fundamental questions about reality—
Immanuel Kant being a leader in this field (see Kantianism). "People in general are equally horrified at hearing the Christian religion
doubted, and at seeing it practiced." (Samuel Butler)

Agrammatism—the inability to construct a sentence while retaining
the ability to speak single words. This condition afflicts stroke victims and those with brain injuries and disease. It's also prominently displayed by college athletes in post-game interviews. (No, "Hi
Mom" does not count as a sentence.)

Agrarianism—1. the belief that agriculture is humanity's most noble
and natural relationship with the earth. 2. a movement to inspire
land reform and improve the economic status of farmers. Originally from ancient Roman laws regulating the distribution of land, the
term in America was associated with a romanticized aesthetic of
the rugged pioneers and homesteaders who left Eastern cities in

search of self-sufficiency. In the late 1800's, Western farmers rallied to oppose the railroad and financial interests of the East, as well as gold clause contracts, private grain elevators, payment of Civil War debts, and politicians linked to "money interests." (See Bi-Metallism.) Recently, the legacy of Agrarianism has inspired politicians to court the "farm vote" and Third World peasants to favor Communism.

ε**a**

Alarmism—the annoying practice of publicizing a problem before it becomes an IRREVERSIBLE CRISIS OF DISASTROUS PROPORTIONS!!!

ε**a**

Albigensianism—from the Albigenses, a small religious sect in Albi, France who opposed papal rule and were crushed by Pope Innocent III in the 12th century. They practiced various ascetic rituals to purify themselves and invoke spiritual release. Of all the dualistic Christian sects of the later Middle Ages, this tribe was distinguished by the fact that they were thoroughly rubbed out.

ε**a**

Albinism—the condition of having no pigment, usually characterized by a milky or translucent skin, white hair, and eyes with pink or blue irises and deep red pupils. The ancients thought albinos were either angels or demons. The rare condition is sometimes superstitiously associated with great intelligence or spiritual stature.

ε**a**

Alchemism—the doctrine concerned with transmuting common metals into gold, based on the idea that Nature continually renews her wasted energies by absorption from the Source of all energy, and that humans, by discovering this Source, could extract from the earth the "quintessence" to replenish their own energies. Alchemists studied the secrets of nature and identified three agents said to be a Universal Solvent that unclogs the terrestrial fluids in earth and man, like the Fountain of Youth.

Roger Bacon, Marcus Agrippa, Henry Kunrath, and Jabir Geber were all alchemists. Modern physicists conveniently forget that Democritus (460-370 B.C.), the granddaddy of Atomism, was an alchemist. Transmuting lead into gold also fired the imaginations of Thomas Aquinas, Baptista Porta, and Iraeneus Philaletha Cosmopolita. Imagine naming your first-born Iraeneus Philaletha Cosmopolita.

ε**a**

Alcoholism—an allergy to or an obsession with ethyl alcohol. For years a social stigma, Alcoholism is now considered a disease by the American Medical Association, which says it is a physiological, not a moral, issue. But that does not explain the success of Alcoholics Anonymous, which stresses recovery through abstinence and spiritual growth and encourages drinkers to discover through introspection the causes of their addiction to alcohol. Alcohol itself has a physical action on organ tissues, particularly the liver. In any case, excessive drinking is responsible for thousands of highway deaths, homicides, suicides, and brawls every year. In the first term of George Washington's administration, the federal government levied a tax on whiskey, and ever since, alcohol has been a stable source of tax money, except for a decade of Prohibition, when profits were diverted to bootleggers. "The saloons are reaping a rich harvest that should belong to wives and children." (O. Henry)

Alcoranism—belief in an absolutely literal reading of the Koran; the Muslim equivalent of Biblicism. Of course, hard-line Islamic regimes go even further and make stuff up, then call it Islamic Law. For example, Saudi Arabia claims it's against Islamic Law for women to drive cars. Well, first, there's nothing about driving in the Koran, and second, the book actually describes Mohammad's wives as businesswomen and warriors who piloted their own camels. For something even scarier, check out Wahhabism.

৯

Algorism—the use of Arabic numerals (you know, 1, 2, 3, etc.) which are a lot easier to add than Roman numerals. Let's see, XVII + MCM = ...

৯

Alienism—the scientific study of mental estrangement or insanity. An alienist is one who studies or practices treatments. The term also applies to the state of being an alien—i.e., a being from outer space or a person residing in a country in which he is not a citizen.

৯

Allomorphism—the ability of a substance to assume another form, while the substance remains otherwise unchanged. Water does this when it becomes ice or steam. Also, Allomerism.

৯

Allotropism—similar to Allomorphism: the ability of some substances to exist in more than one form and with different characteristics. Carbon forms both diamonds and charcoal, for example.

える

Alpinism—mountain climbing, especially (but not exclusively) in the Alps. So as not to discriminate against non-Western mountains that have made valuable contributions to humanity's mountaineering experience, we demand the introduction of Himalayanism, Andesism, and Kilimanjaroism.

える

Altruism—devotion to the interests of others, a term coined by Auguste Comte (1798-1857); the opposite of Egoism. When practiced as a concept of morality, Altruism is usually accompanied by a code of behavior imposed by church, state, or culture. To serve God's purpose or your neighbor's welfare, or to please someone beyond the grave, the altruist must surrender his self-interest—and his mind. The opposite of the altruist is one who lives entirely for his own sake (see Egoism, Objectivism). Compare the cynic's view: "No people do so much harm as those who go about doing good." (Mandell Creighton).

える

Amateurism—the pursuit of a sport, art, or profession as a pastime rather than a career; implies a fancy for something (and, often, incompetence) rather than an expert knowledge. In sports, it suggests not so much a lack of skill as a lack of remuneration. Cf. Professionalism. "Hell is full of musical amateurs." (George Bernard Shaw)

える

Americanism—a custom, trait, or tradition originating in the United States, or a preference for things American. Though much of value can be attributed to this extraordinary country, it is often the less-agreeable behaviors of its citizens that catch the attention of the world, probably thanks to American tourists. Further, while most Americans believe in "The American Way" and "The American Ideal," there is vast disagreement in definitions, so specific Americanisms can be controversial. Perhaps we could safely suggest that the American Way is an automobile and the American Ideal is to have a new one. "I have defined the 100% American as 99% an idiot. And they just adore me." (George Bernard Shaw)

える

Amidism—the doctrine of Buddhism turned upside-down. The word comes from the concept of "pure land," a place for the masses who cannot withdraw from the world (as elite religious aristocrats can) and devote themselves to meditation. A popular, democratic religion, it is said to resolve the tension between monastic and lay piety in Buddhist life. Amitabha Buddhism represents a vast evolutionary distance from the historic Buddha, primarily in that it teaches redemption by a supernatural being.

જ

Amorphism—the state of being formless, characterless, with no determinate shape. The term usually refers to crystals or minerals, though it can describe people.

Anabaptism—a ceremony practiced by folks who think it's not sufficient to get water splashed on your head when you're a few weeks old, but suggest you have it done again as an adult, only this time you hold your own nose and go under. Popularized by John the Baptist circa 30 A.D., revived by John Hess in Bohemia circa 1300, and revived again in Zurich in 1524 by radical Christians who allowed only adults in their church and denied the efficacy of Pedobaptism. The Zurich sect practiced holiness, simplicity, and mutual help, and they advocated the separation of church and state. See Baptism. Three anabaptist sects survive today: Amish, Hutterites, and Mennonites.

જ

Anabolism—constructive Metabolism, in which complex substances are synthesized from simpler ones by a living Organism. Cf. Katabolism.

જ

Anachronism—an error in chronology where persons, events, objects, or customs are out of time; something that seems to belong to another age. In Shakespeare's *Julius Caesar*, for example, a clock strikes three, though such an invention was centuries away. The Pee Wee Herman character is an example of deliberate Anachronism, because his character was contrived from the cultural adolescence of America in the 1950's. The fact that Pee Wee is successful is another Anachronism, because it indicates a persistent unwillingness of the American public to grow up.

જ

Anagrammatism—taking words apart and putting them back together in different arrangements to form new words. TV game shows give money, cars, and lovely patio furniture for this.

୨ଛ

Analogism—the art of arguing or reasoning by comparing things or concepts that are partially similar. For example, Groucho Marx had a guest on his TV show *You Bet Your Life* who said she had 22 children. "I love my husband," she said. "I love my cigar, too," replied Groucho, "but I take it out once in a while."

୨ଛ

Anamorphism—1. in geology, the underground process that changes simple minerals to complex minerals. 2. the drawing and presentation of a distorted image of an object which, when viewed from a certain point or reflected by a curved mirror, produces a "normal" view. For example, the Cinemascope process employs an anamorphic lens, which squeezes the image horizontally. The image is "unsqueezed" later during projection, thus giving movie audiences a spectacular panorama.

୨ଛ

Anarchism—political theory that holds all forms of authority unnecessary and undesirable and advocates a society based on voluntary cooperation and free association. Though some anarchists profoundly hate government—to the point of violent overthrow—not all are bomb-throwers. The term came to be associated with a Marxist splinter group prior to the Russian Revolution that believed Communism could not exist without abolishing the state, since government enforced property rights. (See Social Mutualism.) These "classical" anarchists were generally unsuccessful, both in Russia and elsewhere, partly because they could never agree on leaders. Anarchy has its problems.

"Anarchism is the only philosophy which brings to man the consciousness of himself; which maintains that God, the State, and society are non-existent, that their promises are null and void, since they can be fulfilled only through man's subordination." (Emma Goldman)

୨ଛ

Aneurism—a dilation of a weakened blood vessel, often causing it to burst. A stroke is caused by an Aneurism in the brain.

୨ଛ

Anglicanism—the doctrines of the Church of England, the Protestant and Episcopal Church of Ireland, and occasionally the Episcopal Church in the U.S. The originators broke from Catholic control at the insistence of John Knox (1505-1572), a Scottish religious reformer. Anglicans do not believe in Immaculate Conception, although they admit the existence of Original Sin. The movement gained legitimacy in Britain when Henry VIII rejected the Vatican because the Pope refused him a divorce from a queen who couldn't bear a son. Determined to have a male heir, he married Anne Boleyn, who promptly bore a daughter (Elizabeth I). For the rest of this story, watch *Anne of a Thousand Days*, starring Richard Burton. Henry got a son (Edward VI, via Jane Seymour) and England got a Church, which began to make laws governing divorce, succession, primogeniture, and penalties for witchcraft.

Anglicism—see Britishism.

Anglo-Catholicism—the doctrines of the Anglican Church of England which emphasize similarities with the Catholic Church, especially regarding sacramental worship.

Aniconism—a variation of iconoclasm where Anthropomorphism, in the form of the worship of idols, is prohibited, but non-representational objects symbolic of a deity are venerated. Good examples are the veneration of the Torah in Judaism, and the Kaaba in Islam.

Animalism—the theory that human beings are really nothing more than animals, concerned only with the satisfaction of physical pleasure and desire. We usually think of this condition as the aspect of human life without intellectual or spiritual awareness, a life actuated by appetites only. It also refers to buoyant health, uninhibited vitality, and the expression of those traits.

Animal Magnetism—a condition often used to describe the charismatic presence of an individual, but originally it was thought that certain people had an ability to hypnotize others with their piercing stare. Also called Biomagnetism. Mary Baker Eddy, the founder of the Christian Science movement, called it "voluntary or involuntary action of error in all its forms" (whatever *that* means!). Lawrence of Arabia had it. Rudolph Valentino had it. Elvis Presley had it. Jimmy Carter did not.

Animatism—attributing consciousness to inanimate objects. Our car keys, for example, love to play hide-and-seek.

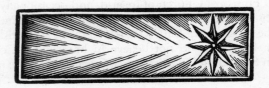

Animism—a primitive theory which holds that all things, including rocks, possess a soul. In the 6th century B.C., Pythagoras and Plato hypothesized that an immaterial force animated the whole universe and was the vital principle of life—a theory featured in the *Star Wars* films, where Luke Skywalker must comprehend "The Force" and its mystical powers. It's pure Platonism, but the same idea occurred in Indonesia without any help from Plato. If you ever travel to Bali, watch out for the rice offerings on the doorstep, placed to appease the hobgoblins who manifest as thunder, lightning, ocean waves, etc.—everything is animated and alive. That stone you just kicked could be somebody's Aunt Betty. Or maybe Elvis.

Anomalism—the state of being a deviation of common forms. In every epoch, the animal, vegetable, and mineral worlds demonstrate many examples of anomaly, such as child prodigies, dwarfs, four-leaf clovers, and Tammy Faye Bakker.

Annihilationism—the doctrine that the souls of the sinful don't even get to go to Hell, but are just obliterated. Ouch.

Antagonism—the condition of being an opposing force. In medicine, it refers to the opposition of physiological forces. (For instance, when one arm muscle flexes, an opposite muscle extends—without which there would be no way to get the arm back to where it started.) Antagonism also refers to the practice of human hostility and active opposition, which tests every fiber of our patience when we are on the receiving end. Good guys are "protagonists;" bad guys are always "antagonists" —unless you are the bad guy, in which case your opponent is literally the antagonist, because he is opposing you. It's possible to avoid all forms of Antagonism by being a com-

plete zero, but most of us have to face the fact that our achievements and characteristics will someday bring us face to face with
one who will resent us, and that breeds Antagonism. "The most
common of Antagonisms arises from a man's taking a seat beside
you on the train, a seat to which he is completely entitled." (Robert
Benchley)

୧**

Antarchism—doctrine similar to Anarchism, but the proponents of
Antarchism are opposed only to government control. They believe
self-rule and self-responsibility should be the only law, and they regard
individual life as the only legal sovereign. Anarchists, on the other
hand, tend toward communistic notions of common property and
shared wealth. If you want to offend a Libertarian, call him an "anarchist" instead of an "antarchist."

୧**

Anthropocentrism—the belief in a human-centered universe, that
mankind is greatest achievement and final aim of existence. "Man
is the measure of all things." (Protagoras)

୧**

Anthropomorphism—the projection of human characteristics onto
non-human entities, especially the belief that the Supreme Being
has human qualities, characteristics, and motivations—like George
Burns in *Oh, God!* or Sir Ralph Richardson in *Time Bandits*. This
makes God far more understandable to people. The Bible suggests
we were created in the image of God, though it's more reasonable
to think the Biblical God was created in the image of us. He even
spoke English in *The Ten Commandments*, which was very helpful
to Charleton Heston during the burning bush scene. Anthropomorphism was common among the ancient Greeks, whose deities had
great virtue *and* very human vices and were forever pursuing human goals, including adultery, incest, and murder. They applied
similar attributes to inanimate objects, natural phenomena, and
animals—although the Greeks were far more interested in the
shenanigans of Zeus and Hera. Television in the 1960's featured Anthropomorphism galore: *Mr. Ed*, *My Mother the Car*, *Lassie*, etc.

Anthropopathism—the attribution of human feelings and passions to non-human objects and animals. For instance, some people believe their dog feels rejection if he loses the annual dog show. "Cats are like Baptists. They raise hell, but you can't catch them at it." (Unknown)

ะล

Antialcoholism—opposition to excessive use of alcohol. Next stop, Teetotalism.

ะล

Anti-Americanism—opposition and hostility to things American. The British resent Americans because they are "over-paid, over-sexed, and over here." In the U.S., the term applies to anyone who questions government policy or refuses to participate in flag-waving Nationalism.

ะล

Anti-Careerism—political strategy of appearing not to want high political office, so that everybody will urge you to accept it. "No longer can a careerist make a career out of Anti-Careerism." (*London Times*)

ะล

Anti-Christianism—description of modern science used in a series of sermons by Father Felix of Notre Dame in the 18th century, quoted in *Isis Unveiled*: "We say revelation; revelation is not scientific. We say miracle; a miracle is not scientific. Thus Anti-Christianism, faithful to its tradition, and now more than ever, pretends to kill us by science.... There were scientists before 1789. If our mysteries are so manifestly absurd and contradictory, how is it that such mighty geniuses should have accepted them without a single doubt?" Um—because it beat being tortured to death?

ะล

Antidisestablishmentarianism—opposition to the disestablishment of a church or religious body, specifically a state church, as in Ireland in 1869, when Gladstone disestablished the Irish Protestant Church to which all the people, including Roman Catholics, had been compelled to pay tithes (10% taxes). George Washington was another noted antidisestablishmentarian. He and Patrick Henry fought to prevent Thomas Jefferson from disestablishing the Virginia Protestant churches, which were supported by taxation. Jefferson prevailed, and the separation of church and state became an Americanism.

ะล

Anti-Federalism—1. opposition to the adoption of the U.S. Constitution in 1787, when many people vehemently opposed surrendering the sovereignty (and economic privileges) enjoyed by the 13 original States of the Confederacy. A great newspaper war between the Federalists and the Anti-Federalists raged for three years before the

State of New York finally ratified the new Constitution. To answer
the fears of unbridled power concentrated in the new Federal Union, proponents of the Constitution promised to add the Bill of
Rights—including an explicit provision in Article X that preserved
common law freedoms and states' rights not pre-empted by the explicit delegation of powers to the national government. The doctrine survived until Roosevelt's New Deal, when the Supreme Court
said the 10th Amendment was kaput—and we got Social Security
whether it was constitutional or not. 2. in Europe, opposition to
expanded powers and trans-national sovereignty in the European
Community. See Euro-Federalism, Federalism.

ᘓᕙ

Anti-Feminism—the theory or practice of those who oppose any
social changes in favor of the emancipation and equal rights of wom-
en. For a quick summary of the War Between the Sexes, rent a video
of *Mary Poppins*. Men generally opposed the emancipation of women
because the Bible had been construed to mean that women were
male property. So long as women believed this, everything sailed
smoothly, as far as the men were concerned. We're still struggling
with it in the 1990's, especially in the context of "equal pay for equal
work." See Feminism. "Nature has given woman so much power
that the law cannot afford to give her more." (Samuel Johnson)

ᘓᕙ

Anti-Intellectualism—hostility toward intellectual pursuits and the
use of reason and scholarship to solve problems, favoring the use
of emotion, tradition, and action. Associated with crude, uneducated people, it exists on the principle that foot-stamping is superi-
or to debate and often arises from sheer envy.

ᘓᕙ

Antinomianism—the dogma of Antinomians, who maintained that
under Gospel dispensation, the moral law set forth in the Bible is
of no use and contains no obligation. Originating with John Agricola
around 1538, the sect believed that the church was subservient only
to the Gospel and that faith is the essential of salvation. The root
word, "antinomy," refers to Antagonism between laws or principles;
any law or rule that has an opposing law or rule in the same code
of morality is invalid. The debate arose during the Reformation and
was more or less quashed by Henry VIII, who created the Church
of England as an alternative to resolving some of these arcane
hubbubs.

ᘓᕙ

Anti-Rationalism—early 19th-century German school of economics which ignored the theory and practical evidence of Capitalism
and extolled the virtues of German hegemony, authoritarian government, and economic stagnation.

ᘓᕙ

Anti-Rentism—the policy or principles of the Anti-Rent Party, an organization (1839-1848) that resisted the payment of rent on certain manorial estates in New York.

‌ॐ‌

Antiquarianism—the study of ancient or old-fashioned relics or things that are out of date, especially books. I guess you could apply it to Civil War buffs or those few of us who persist in the study of philosophy.

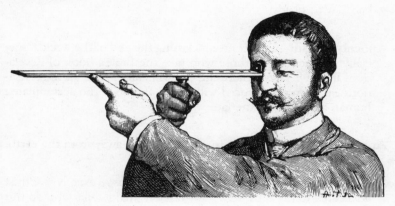

Anti-Semitism—the practice or dogma of persons who hate Semitic people, especially Jews. Not a new idea, Anti-Semitism has fostered oppression of and discrimination against the peoples of Israel for centuries. ("The world is divided into two groups of nations—those which want to expel the Jews and those which do not want to receive them." Chaim Weizmann) Historically, it was not aimed solely at Jews but at all those of Semitic descent, which incorporates many nations of the eastern Mediterranean region, including the Palestinian tribes now being oppressed and discriminated against by Israelis. "In Europe, people used to boycott stores owned by Jews. Now we're doing virtually the same thing to Arabs." (Shimon Amsalen, Israeli greengrocer)

‌ॐ‌

Anti-Smoking, Anti-Drinking Puritanism—an avant-garde American movement devoted to the prolongation of life at all costs and the incessant nagging of those who indulge in "vices" considered harmful (see Busybodyism). Especially exasperating to libertines and ex-hippies, who value the personal freedom to eat, drink, and smoke too much. "Moderation is a fatal thing. Nothing succeeds like excess." (Oscar Wilde)

‌ॐ‌

Antitheism—the belief that no God exists. See Atheism.

‌ॐ‌

Anti-Trinitarianism—denial of the Christian doctrine of the Trinity (the paradox of the Father, Son, and Holy Ghost being one in the same). See Trinitarianism.

৻৶

Aphorism—a brief statement of a principle or tersely phrased truth or opinion. Usually thought of as pithy sayings, maxims, or predigested wisdom, such as "All things noble are as difficult as they are rare" (Spinoza) and "Anyone who hates children and dogs can't be all bad." (W.C. Fields)

৻৶

Apocalypticism—a doctrine concerning the end of the world, especially as practiced by those who take the Bible's Book of Revelations literally. They believe the day will come when all the revelations St. John experienced will occur, and then the accumulated human vice will hit the fan.

৻৶

Apogeotropism—tendency in plants to grow away from the earth.

৻৶

Apostolicism—the practice of preaching the Gospel exactly as Christ advocated to his apostles. Unfortunately, many folks who do this have forgotten that Jesus never advocated building lavish temples, TV networks, or anything else in concrete.

৻৶

Apotropaism—any ritual performed to ward off evil, such as making the sign of the cross.

৻৶

Appropriationism—one of the most heinous Isms, this pertains to stealing elements of another's artwork, calling it your own, and being hailed as a genius in New York: "Last week, George Condo's 'appropriation' paintings could be seen at the Pace Gallery, mainly badly painted echoes of Picasso, though he used ... remembered images by other painters, rather than abstraction." (Geraldine Norman). See Centonism.

৻৶

Apriorism—use of *a priori*, or intuitive, reasoning, rather than knowledge gained from specific experience or experiment.

৻৶

Arabian Polytheism—not many details available, but evidently an ancient Arab religion that worshipped the elements (sun, wind, desert) and dealt exclusively with the present. The belief yielded to Islam. "The unbelievers say there is only our life in this world. We die and live, and only time works our destruction." (The Koran)

৻৶

Arachnotubbism—hydromagnetic principle by which spiders are drawn toward bathtubs and sinks. Once splashed, they can't crawl up the sides of a wet enclosure—which leads to either Arachnorescueism or Arachnoflushism.

ᘓ

Archaism—a word or expression that is out of date or no longer used. "Keen," "groovy," and "I dig you" will strike a familiar chord in older readers—which shows how archaic you've become.

ᘓ

Argyrism—a condition that arises when silver preparations are used on the skin and cause discoloration. Best to be aware of the contents of any medical application, always read the labels, and avoid silversmithing.

ᘓ

Arianism—the doctrines of Arius, a 4th-century Greek theologian who denied that Jesus was of the same substance as God and held instead that Jesus was only the highest of created beings and that his purpose was to create a better world.

ᘓ

Aristocratism—the practice of those who hold that the manners, morals, and tastes of the ruling class are superior. Aristocrats of Europe ruled by privilege or nobility and saw themselves as infinitely better citizens in the feudal system, in view of their chivalry, honor, and loyalty to the crown. They patronized the arts and rode gallantly into battle—which often resulted in their becoming heroes among the peasants. In America, the "aristocracy" consists of rock singers, movie stars, and former movie stars who become presidents—a vastly superior system of privilege, *n'est-ce pas?* "There are bad manners everywhere, but an aristocracy is bad manners organized." (Henry James)

ᘓ

Aristotelianism—the doctrines of Aristotle, Greek philosopher (384-322 B.C.) and student and critic of Plato who developed the theory of the Syllogism. Also refers to empirical investigation or scientific methods and thought, since Aristotle rejected Plato's "intuition" about absolute truths in favor of deductive reasoning and observation. Unfortunately, it was Aristotle—not Plato—who dominated most medieval thinking, and when it came time to renounce dogmatic adherence to tradition, Aristotle's achievements were the proverbial baby thrown out with the bath water. The modern world rediscovered Plato's "higher realm" and transcendental Idealism via Kant and Hegel—and, presto, Aristotle's old-fashioned notion of logic was supplanted by things like Dialectical Materialism.

Among other incisive contributions to philosophy and psychology, Aristotle suggested that imagination was causal in inducing physiological arousal (cf. Interestism), an idea that went out of favor with the introduction of Descartes' Dualism. (Today there is new interest in the use of imagery to activate desired states.) Other Aristotelian notions include an ethic based on moderation, definition of four types of causation, and an elaborate system of aesthetic Criticism. He liked comedies but considered drama a higher form of art. Don't we all.

ॐ

Arminianism—the doctrines of Jacobus Arminius (1560-1609) and his followers, who opposed the Calvinist doctrine of absolute predestination. He maintained that your life is what you make of it and that no celestial script was written prior to your arrival. The Arminian sect flourished at the end of the 16th century and also believed in universal redemption, though none but believers could partake of the benefit of Christ's atonement. Cf. Calvinism.

ॐ

Asceticism—the practice of denying oneself by renouncing the comforts of society and leading a life of extreme austerity, self-discipline, and mortification, often in isolation, to gain purity for a post-mortem reward. "The true ascetic counts nothing his own save his harp." (Joachim of Flora)

ॐ

Ashcanism—an early 20th-century art movement which depicted unattractive aspects of city life.

ॐ

Asterism—1. in printing, three asterisks in triangular form to call attention to a passage. 2. in astronomy, a cluster of stars. 3. in mineralogy, a six-rayed, starlike figure produced in some crystal structures by reflected or transmitted light.

ॐ

Astigmatism—a refractive defect of a lens that prevents focusing of sharp, distinct images. Particularly disturbing when the lens of the eye is involved, since the rays of light do not converge on the retina and result in blurred vision. Spectacles correct the problem.

ॐ

Asylumism—the belief that the world is a ward for the nut cases of the universe. According to newspaper columnist Mike Royko, there's a Church of Asylumism, which preaches that humans "descended from people who were shipped here in spaceships from a distant, highly advanced, peaceful planet... because they had displayed anti-social tendencies, such as becoming politicians, warriors, lawyers, and claiming that God spoke to them. In that planet's language, 'Earth' meant 'loony bin'. " (Royko's kidding, of course, but compare the beliefs of Scientologism.)

❧

Atavism—the reappearance of a characteristic in an Organism after several generations of absence, caused by a recessive or complimentary gene. Examples: baldness in an otherwise hirsute family, where only great-great-grandpa had a chrome dome. In the animal world, it can cause great harm if such a trait reappears, such as separate toes in a duck. Commonly referred to as a "throwback." Ayn Rand used the term to decry the resurgence of orgiastic celebrations, drunkenness, drug use, and Mysticism in 1960's America.

❧

Atheism—disbelief in or denial of the existence of God. The O'Hair family in Texas has made quite a business out of Atheism, publishing books and a monthly magazine on the subject and periodically suing in Federal Court to abolish the motto "In God We Trust" from U.S. currency. "An atheist is a man who has no invisible means of support." (John Buchan) (A dyslexic atheist, of course, does not believe in Dog.)

❧

Athleticism—the practice of training for physical exercises or contests of strength. Once considered an aesthetic practice to honor the human form. We now have behemoths pumped with steroids to remind us how far we've sunk. See Atavism.

Atlanticism—the "special relationship" between the U.S. and England, a term coined by Winston Churchill to express a combination of necessity and mutual interest with respect to political stability in Europe. Churchill knew that America must be involved in something like NATO to prevent European squabbling after World War II. Bankrupt, jealous, and loathe to admit mistakes, Western Europe needed an alliance with the U.S. for several reasons: to rebuild cities and industries, to defend against Soviet aggression, to exorcize Naziism and Fascism, and to promote a standard of household appliances in Europe. The alliance was successful in every respect, with the exception of household appliances (each country still has an unique and non-interchangeable system of plugs and wiring). The American motive for Atlanticism was to export the idea of Federalism as an antidote for European wars. This, too, has succeeded (with the exception of household appliances), as the European Community merges in a grand gesture of Euro-Federalism (although each country will continue to subsidize and protect its own electrical goods manufacturers).

&

Atomism—the ancient theory of Democritus, Epicurus, and Lucretius that proposed simple, indivisible, and indestructible atoms as the basic components of the universe. This means that everything is made up of everything. If we took you and me apart, who knows?—we might recombine as a black velvet painting of bullfighters. Hence, nothing is ever lost, except our dignity.

It was a tremendous achievement for ancient philosophers to conceive of atomic structures, centuries before microscopes and such. From observation of fire/smoke, life/death, sweet/bitter, etc., they deduced that matter could be neither created nor destroyed, thus anticipating Einstein and others. Atomism also accepts that, by virtue of their properties, atoms bring all things into creation without the help of a Creator or God. Plus, it may be the basis for the belief in reincarnation (except that atomists do not say forms will resume their previous form). Atomists also believed social institutions and processes arise solely from the acts of individual people. The word "atom" actually means "indivisible," though modern science has discovered sub-atomic particles.

&

Atonalism—the absence of a tonal center or key as a principle of musical composition. If you think first of heavy metal or rap, you obviously haven't heard any of the so-called symphonies concocted from hammers, scrap metal, and the destruction of pianos. Such things were all the rage in Paris during the heyday of Avant-Gardism.

&

Atropism—poisoning by atropine or belladonna. Also Atropinism.

&

Atticism—devotion to the styles and customs of Athens and its citizens, especially their language. (Athens is located in an area called Attica.) The ancients held Athenian wit in high regard and thought their language the most sophisticated and elegant in the world, because purity and simplicity distinguished their works and culture.

Attitudinarianism—striking poses for effect. Today known as "voguing"—go watch some MTV.

Augustinianism—the doctrine of St. Augustine of Hippo (354-430 A.D.), a member of a monastic order who framed rules of conduct for religious and secular life. Many Catholic orders follow the rules of this monk in their practices—such as vows of poverty, humility, and charity. "Total abstinence is easier to me than perfect moderation." (St. Augustine)

Authoritarianism—the practice of favoring absolute obedience to authority vested in one individual or an elite group that requires blind submission to its policies, with no regard for individual freedom. Practiced today in homes and schools the world over; taken for granted when you enter the military. The root word "authority" simply refers to authorship, and therefore the basic idea is to obey "Because I said so!" Children everywhere should recognize these four magic words.

Autism—in psychology, a mental state characterized by abnormal subjectivity and the acceptance of fantasy over reality. An autistic child tends to alternate between acting out and withdrawing, while remaining mute or uncommunicative. All traditional attempts to reach such children have failed. There is recent evidence that they suffer sensory excitation so intense that they feel pain when they are bombarded by the real world, hence they withdraw. Also, Dereism.

~

Autochthonism—1. the characterists of an aboriginal or indigenous inhabitant. 2. the trait of having ideas that seem to originate outside one's own mind—often called "hearing voices." "If you talk to God, you are praying; if God talks to you, you have schizophrenia." (Thomas Szasz)

~

Autodidacticism—the practice of educating oneself without the benefit of formal schooling. See Didacticism.

~

Autoecism—in botany, the entire life cycle of a parasitic fungus on the host.

~

Autoeroticism—sexual arousal and gratification solely by oneself; experiencing sexual feelings without external stimulation. Arguably, this is more common to women, since men tend to be more interested in external (especially, visual) stimulus. Also, Autoerotism. "Don't knock it—it's sex with someone you love." (Woody Allen)

~

Automatism—1. in philosophy, the theory that all movement arises spontaneously, since the body is a machine without will. That is, only instinctive actions exist, and therefore the body is accompanied by (not controlled by) consciousness. 2. involuntary or unconscious activity, like sleepwalking. 3. in the arts, suspension of conscious control, supposedly to let the unconscious do the creating. Historically associated with Surrealism and Abstract Expressionism. Today, confined to psychotherapy, it's called "art therapy." Its practitioners are still nuts.

~

Automechanism—a device or system that operates automatically, like a thermostat or those silly plastic "tippy birds" that drink water.

~

Automobilism—a word we found in a 1910 dictionary, when automobiles were amazing new technology. But we need a 1990's definition. Um, let's see, how about: psychological displacement of personality in the chassis of a Ferrari or late-model BMW?

~

Automorphism—the attribution of one's own traits to another. Also called "projection," wherein the subject presumes that all people are created equal in deficiencies and stubbornness. Probably more extensive than we realize.

~

Autonomism—the belief in or tendency toward self-governance and freedom. Now playing at an Eastern European theater near you.

ॐ

Autovorism—the practice of eating your own flesh. Coyotes will chew off a leg that's caught in a trap, for example.

ॐ

Avant-Gardism—the practice of inventing and applying new techniques in the arts, the results of which usually produce slightly bizarre and extreme examples of artistic expression, from slightly bizarre and extreme people. Andy Warhol (1930-1987), whose fame rested on tributes to the banality of Consumerism, was considered a leader.

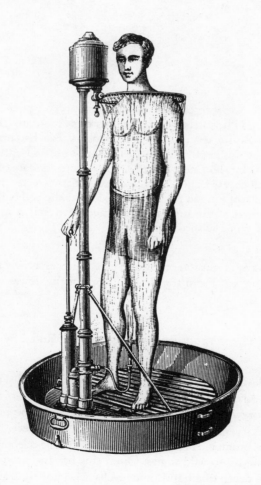

Baalism—the worship of Baal, an ancient sun god of the people of Canaan and Phoenicia whom the Hebrews considered a false idol. In general use, the term connotes any idolatry. Baal had many names: As Baal, he was popular with the Phoenicians. As Belus or Bel, he was served by the priest Berosus, who wrote the famous account of the Deluge. As Babel, he had a tower partly erected to his glory on the plain of Shinar. As Beelzebub, he was the god of flies, which are "begotten of the sun's rays on stagnant water," and thus connected in name with the Devil.

Babelism—any confusion or misunderstanding, especially regarding a word or phrase. From the Biblical story of the Tower of Babel in Genesis 11.

Babism—a 19th-century Persian religion, supplanted by Ba'haism.

Bacchanalianism—the practice of worshipping Bacchus, the ancient Roman god of wine. In general use, the term connotes any drunken feast or orgy. The Bacchanalia celebrated the grape harvest with noisy revelry. An equivalent myth in ancient Greece, in honor of Dionysus, prompted priests and priestesses to stage celebrations which degenerated into wild orgies. Often this behavior resulted in the untimely death of a handsome reveler who was torn apart by sex-crazed females, known as maenads. In seeming contradiction to the

Athenian culture of sobriety and elegance, the bacchanal may have been an institutionalized excuse to go bonkers. Before you start to feel so superior, compare our modern Mardi Gras, rock concerts, and bachelor parties.

ॐ

Bachelorism—the state of being an unmarried man, or the traits thereof. Generally thought to be more fun than Spinsterism. "Bachelors should be heavily taxed. It is not fair that some men should be happier than others." (Oscar Wilde)

ॐ

Bad Art-ism—name of an art revival in Germany, Italy, and the U.S. in the 1970's. Also called Neo-Expressionism.

ॐ

Bagism—a trend in communicating promoted by musicians John Lennon (1940-1980) and Yoko Ono, who held press conferences while inside a big bag. The idea behind Bagism is that if you talk from a bag, people can't determine your gender, race, or appearance, so they'll have to judge you only on what you say. Bagism made a noble point about the problems of discrimination and communication, but it's rather self-defeating, since most people will be prejudiced against someone silly enough to sit in a sack.

ॐ

Baha'ism—a religious sect founded in Iran in 1863 by Bahaullah (1817-1892) and practiced by some Shi'ah Muslims. It emphasizes tolerance and the spiritual unity of mankind. Considered a heresy in Iran, but practiced throughout the world.

ॐ

Balkanism—the practice of dividing one country into several teeny states that fight all the time. Currently happening all over Eastern Europe, including the Balkans.

ॐ

Ballism—see Parkinsonism.

ë

Bantingism—a weight-loss method that stresses a high-protein, low-fat, low-carbohydrate diet. Named, for reasons unfathomable, after a 19th-century London cabinetmaker.

ë

Baptism—a Christian sacrament marked by the symbolic use of water to cleanse Original Sin, resulting in admission into Christianity. The originator, John the Baptist, a cousin of Jesus, declared that all should be baptized in the word of God and that Baptism by fire would follow. (Why the latter rite never caught on is a mystery.) Catholics believe that if you are not baptized you will spend eternity in Limbo—which, on balance, is better than roasting in hell. Baptism is performed with water in two ways: by immersion (dunking the entire body) or by aspersion (sprinkling water on the forehead).

ë

Barbarianism—in ancient Greece, the behavior of a foreigner and/or one whose language was unintelligible (any foreign tongue was just "bar-bar-bar" to their ears). In those days, foreigners were crude and savage, often destitute of pity or humanity, so any offense against the purity and style of the Greek language or manners was called "barbaric." Today, the term refers to a crudeness of taste and a fondness for ostentatious display. Parents may recognize the concept as descriptive of their teenagers, but the term has more to do with Chauvinism, as most tribes or nations tend to view foreigners as inferior and uncultured compared to themselves. Also, Barbarism.

ë

Barbiturism—poisoning caused by a barbiturate like phenobarbital.

ë

Bardism—engaging in the lifestyle of a bard (or poet). In medieval Scotland, bards were wandering minstrels who composed songs to glorify warriors and kings. The ancient Celts held their bards in greater esteem: To be a bard, you followed the teachings of the highly educated men (no women allowed) who recorded the events of their land in song, which they passed to future generations by word of mouth—the writing of poetry was considered a terrible offense against the gods. Today, of course, the writing of poetry is only a misdemeanor, punished by poverty, while the events of the land are recorded by CNN and MTV, who broadcast to a nation of functional illiterates. See?—we've come full circle.

ë

Bauhausism—artistic philosophy founded in 1919 at Weimar, Germany to unify all artistic disciplines and integrate them with the construction industry. The goal was to inspire design based around machine production (and vice versa). The Nazis closed the school in 1933, but it re-opened in Chicago.

❦

Baunscheidtism—named after Karl Baunscheidt, who introduced the method of treating Rheumatism by counter-irritation, pricking the affected part with needles dipped in an irritant.

❦

Beaujolais Bolshevism—a light, fruity variety of Socialism, preferred by orthodontists, book reviewers, and movie stars, and headquartered in the Hampstead suburb of London. Actors Glenda Jackson and Tom Conti are the reigning poobahs. See Champagne Socialism.

❦

Beism—the theory or doctrine that a person must exist and know that he exists in order to actualize himself; to exist in actuality, to make real. In contrast to identity being vested in the "having" or "doing" of a job or role, Beism says one must experience his life without external or imposed definitions of who or what he is. It is the state of detachment from notions, illusions, false ideas, labels, and misconceptions. In that a man lives, so he "be."

❦

Behaviorism—in psychology, the theory that introspection is useless and therefore all investigation of behavior must be objective. Behaviorists concentrate on the influence of environmental conditioning—often to the complete exclusion of moral or genetic factors—to explain why people act in certain ways. The movement was spearheaded by B. F. Skinner (1904-1990), who claimed that positive and negative reinforcement could shape human behavior almost entirely and argued for abolition of civil liberty so that behavioral engineering could be given maximum opportunity to destroy us all.

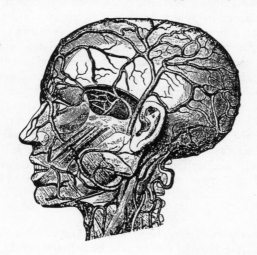

Benedictinism—the practices and organization of the Benedictines, the most famous and wide-spread order of monks, founded at Monte Casino in 530 A.D. by St. Benedict (480-543 A.D.), whose rule the members profess to follow. Called "black friars," because they supposedly wore black robes (which, unfortunately, they did not), the order arrived in the U.S. in 1846. Basically, it's kind of interesting because the word *benedicti* means "Bless you," and the monks supported themselves by making liquor.

જી

Benthamism—the moral philosophy of Jeremy Bentham (1748-1832), who espoused the utilitarian model of man, resting on the notion that the love of pleasure and the fear of pain are the sole motives governing human action. Bentham even devised a utilitarian "calculus" for deciding questions of public policy: a simple formula, with total pain on one side and total pleasure on the other. If more people were pleased by a decision than suffered from it, Bentham advocated sacrificing the minority. (See Utilitarianism.)

Believe it or not, this concept became a cornerstone of the American legal system, as embodied in the doctrines of strict liability, public morals legislation, and the "balancing" of individual freedom with majority wishes. Oliver Wendell Holmes (1841-1935), an influential Supreme Court justice, advanced Benthamism: "The secret root from which the law draws all the juices of life ... is considerations of what is expedient for the community. The law does undoubtedly treat the individual as a means to an end, and uses him as a tool to increase the general welfare at his own expense." The same idea was promoted in Europe by Hitler and Mussolini (see Nazism and Fascism).

જી

Berkeleianism—the philosophy of Bishop George Berkeley (1685-1753), who held that material things exist only inasmuch as our minds perceive them and that the mind is conscious of subjective impressions only and therefore cannot know external things. In a nutshell, if a tree falls in the forest and you didn't hear it, it never happened. Good thing Berkeley didn't organize the Forest Service.

ॐ

Biblicism—the practice of interpreting the Bible literally and without regard to metaphor, allegory, parable, or hyperbole. (So what else is left?) We don't wish to be harsh, but the world was not created in seven days. Period.

ॐ

Bibliophilism—the love of books, and occasionally the love of organizing them according to the Dewey Decimal System. "Outside of a dog, a book is man's best friend. Inside of a dog, it's too dark to read." (Groucho Marx)

Bibliopolism—the business of buying and selling books, especially old or rare volumes.

ॐ

Bilateralism—pertaining to or having two sides. Frequently used regarding diplomatic negotiations: when two parties negotiate, their decisions are equally binding. When the parties happen to be the U.S. and the Soviet Union, the other countries in the world rush to the newsstand to learn who got bound (or freed) by the deal.

ॐ

Bilingualism—knowledge and use of two languages. In Canada, for example, most people speak French and English, except in Quebec, where it will probably become a capital offense to speak English.

ॐ

Bimetallism—a system of currency which recognizes two metals, usually silver and gold, as legal tender. For millennia, humans have regarded gold and silver as suitable "money"—a uniform, easily-divisible, and compact token of value that can be stored, traded, or consumed (as in jewelry). The difference between "hard money" like a metal and paper currency is a basic economic concept. If a metal backs the paper currency, you can print only so many pieces of paper, which are in fact claims to the metal. Perhaps you'll recall that Fort Knox is full of U.S. gold reserves. However, none of this has anything to do with U.S. currency today, because the country is no longer on the "gold standard," and the government can print as much money as it wants without ever paying off in gold or silver.

The question of Bimetallism arose after the Civil War, when Eastern bankers holding U.S. bonds demanded payment in gold rather than paper "greenbacks," which Lincoln introduced to finance the war. Western farmers, who mined silver and hated the New York bankers on principle (no pun intended), agitated for Bimetallism on the theory that a favorable fixed ratio of value between silver and gold would put more money in their pockets and would retire the bonds at a big discount. The bondholders, of course, were infuriated and took the matter to the Supreme Court, demanding payment in gold. We don't remember who won. Eventually, Roosevelt fixed the price of gold during the Depression, and Nixon abolished the gold standard in the 1970's, thus liberating the money supply from the tyranny of reality.

Whenever a region is threatened by coup, gold tends to rise in price and disappear into suitcases in Saudi Arabia, because people know that in times of turmoil it's the only currency that will buy safety. It's still a desired possession and probably always will be. We can't be so sure about the paper dollar. See also Bullionism.

ਵੇ

Biologism—1. any science or doctrine based on biology. 2. a preoccupation with arguing that biology has everything to do with everything when analyzing social situations, such as the argument that men only want to copulate with women and have no interest in them as "persons." The theory is most adamantly defended by those for whom biology is a scary subject.

ਵੇ

Biomagnetism—see Animal Magnetism.

ਵੇ

Biophilism—literally, the love of all life from highest to lowest forms; giving every creature full credit for every power it possesses and proceeding on the assumption that we all have an equal right to live and prosper. Except flies.

ਵੇ

Bipartisanism—the existence of two political parties in a political system. In terms of real power in the government, the U.S. is an example of Bipartisanism, though there are other organized parties besides the Democrats and Republicans.

છ

Biracialism—the belief that it is an acceptable state for two different races to intermingle, whether socially or genetically. Accepted and encouraged in horticulture, but human racial mixing is still taboo to many.

છ

Birchism—the philosophy and practices of the John Birch Society, a group so politically right-wing, they'd call Genghis Khan a bleeding heart pantywaist.

છ

Bisexualism—1. in biology, a hermaphroditic state in which one person has both male and female organs. 2. in psychiatry, the traits of a person sexually responsive to people of either sex. "Bisexuality immediately doubles your chances for a date on Saturday night." (Woody Allen)

છ

Blackguardism—reveling in scoundrel-like behavior. "Oh, better far to live and die under the brave black flag I fly than play a sanctimonious part with a pirate head and a pirate heart." (W.S. Gilbert, *The Pirates of Penzance*)

છ

Black Separatism—racial and political movement championed in the 1960's by Elijah Muhammad, Malcolm X, Stokely Carmichael, and others who believed that separation from whites and violent overthrow of white government was the only acceptable solution to the oppression of black Americans. In 1962, Muhammad declared that integration was impossible because "after giving them 400 years of our sweat and blood and receiving in return some of the worst treatment human beings have ever experienced, we believe our contributions to this land and the suffering forced upon us by white America justifies our demand for complete separation in a state or territory of our own." Today, Black Separatism has not completely disappeared, but black Ethnicism proved to be far more successful.

છ

Bluebeardism—belief in or practice of killing your wives. According to legend, the seventh wife of the Chevalier "Bluebeard" Raoul discovered the remains of her predecessors in a room that was forbidden to her.

છ

Bluestockingism—among women, an interest in scholarly and intellectual pursuits. Originally a term of mockery, from the blue stockings worn by some female members of an 18th-century London literary circle. Today, educational accomplishment and vigorous intellect are as common in women as in men—which is to say, not very.

ॐ

Bohemianism—the practice of living as a wanderer who defies convention, or a bohemian, a term that originally applied to gypsies in France who were thought to be Hussites driven from Bohemia. Today, it applies to people of artistic or literary bent who adopt attitudes conspicuously different from those of the majority. In other words, they lead free and often dissipated lives in pursuit of creativity and unhampered expression—perhaps for good reason, as the creative muse rarely whispers in mundane places. None of this has anything to do with the Bohemian Club in Monte Rio, California, whose members are politicians and captains of industry who meet annually to discuss the price of oil, walk around naked, and other interesting stuff.

ॐ

Boloism—the theories of French financier Paul Bolo, who took many a sucker for a ride to poverty in the early 20th century. Advocating Pacifism and Defeatism for France during World War I, he was convicted of treason for his philosophy, financial treachery, and avarice, and was executed in 1918. Like Ivan Boesky, Bolo was probably in the wrong deal at the wrong time, which put him at risk of public condemnation. Unlike Boesky's feigned remorse, this patron saint of Opportunism never repented and was killed for being terminally unpopular.

❧

Bolshevism—the strategy developed by the Bolsheviks in the Soviet Union between 1903-1917 to seize power and establish a dictatorship of the proletariat. Majority members of the left wing of the Russian Social Democratic Party, Bolsheviks adopted Lenin's thesis on party organization. The passkey to party membership was ancestry: if you came from peasant stock, you qualified for leadership—which put Joseph Stalin's career on the fast track. Cf. Menshevism.

❧

Bonapartism—the policies of Napoleon Bonaparte, who ruled France from 1804-1814 and attempted to conquer the world by playing *Let's Make a Deal* with neighboring countries. By offering them a choice between immediate destruction or alliance, the self-proclaimed Emperor was able to parlay his army into a combined force of almost 1,000,000 men. Britain, his sole opponent, defeated the scheme by naval blockades and a decisive battle at Waterloo.

❧

Boosterism—the act of promoting something, especially a civic cause. Often used snidely, the term can connote unwarranted Optimism, Hucksterism, and shrillness.

❧

Boswellism—the practice of following someone around and recording their every utterance, as James Boswell (1740-1795) did to Dr. Samuel Johnson (1709-1789), who apparently never shut up. See Sycophantism.

❧

Botulism—a virulent, often fatal food poisoning caused by botulin and characterized by vomiting, abdominal pain, coughing, muscular weakness, and visual disturbance. Originally thought to be caused exclusively by bad sausages. Precautions include never eating the contents of damaged cans that have been pierced or leftovers stored in open cans, with or without refrigeration.

❧

Bourbonism—1. extreme Conservatism. 2. adherence to the doctrines of the Bourbon Family, who ruled in France, Spain, Naples, and the Sicilies and were renowned for their obstinate Conservatism.

❧

Bowdlerism—the practice of omitting passages considered indelicate or offensive from an author's published works. Named for Thomas Bowdler (1754-1825) who, in 1818, published an edition of Shakespeare with all the good parts cut out.

❧

Braggartism—the practice of those who have no one else to sing their praises, so they boast ostentatiously. "Noise proves nothing. Often a hen who has merely laid an egg cackles as if she laid an asteroid." (Mark Twain)

ॐ

Brahmanism—the doctrine of the Hindu mystic Brahma and his followers, who claim they are issued from the breath of Brahma and are therefore descendants of a deity of the Trimurti, the Hindu trinity. They are known especially for their minute religious observances, abstemiousness, severe penances, and devotion to divine science, impersonal divinity, and the absolute, self-existent, eternal Universe.

In India, Brahmans were distinguished for mental and spiritual superiority, but they gradually gained power over public worship and became a strictly hereditary class, zealously maintaining the ministry of holy things. They even became inviolable objects of worship themselves. Curiously, paintings and photographs show they had Aryan features and light, golden skin. It is believed they migrated from the Scythian plains, never intermarried with the native Indians, and therefore maintained their "purity." Although they are now found in many walks of life, they retain much of their former dignity and exclusiveness. See Secularism. Also, Brahminism.

ॐ

Braidism—the practice of James Braid (1795-1860), a Scottish surgeon noted for his ability to hypnotize people. Braid coined the term "Neurohypnotism" to express his theory that Hypnotism involved the nerves. See also Mesmerism.

ॐ

Brigandism—the behavior of the plundering sailors of the fast, two-masted sailing ships called brigantines. The crews, notorious pirates, ruthlessly robbed less-protected and slower ships on the high seas. "Brigand" comes from the Italian word *brigare*, which means to fight.

ॐ

Britishism—a word, phrase, or idiom particular to the British people and the English language as spoken in England. For instance, "fag" in Britain means a cigarette, while in America it's a Vulgarism for homosexual males. Also Briticism, Anglicism. "The English never smash in a face. They merely refrain from asking it to dinner." (Margaret Halsey)

ॐ

Broadcast Journalism—television or radio news reporting—a profession dedicated to covering car wrecks and fires and repeating short, misleading statements by public officials, which the reporter introduces with a recital of yesterday's headlines and ends with a cynical smirk to emphasize how little we all understand anything.

ॐ

Brood Parasitism—the practice of ignoring chicks as soon as they are out of the egg. Often observed in cuckoos, a bird known for its parental neglect. The term can also refer to dwelling for a long time uninterruptedly on a subject, or "brooding." Most often it applies to remaining steadfastly settled on something for the purpose of hatching an egg or an idea.

Bruxism—habitual teeth-grinding, especially during sleep. A leading cause of wealthy orthodontists.

Buchmanism—theory propounded by Frank Nathan Daniel Buchman (1878-1961), an American evangelist who believed that the only way the world could change for the better was if humanity changed for the better. Buchman's lectures at Oxford in 1921 evolved into the principles embodied in the Twelve Steps of Alcoholics Anonymous.

Buddhism—religion founded in northern India by the ascetic Siddhartha Gautama (566-480 B.C.), who became Buddha, "the enlightened one." From an aristocratic family, Gautama left home to search for final redemption from suffering and, after much futile Asceticism, he sat under a tree in deep concentration and—presto!—saw the truth of salvation. His teaching of the Four Noble Truths and the Eightfold Path is somehow condensed into five rules for living: do not kill, do not steal, avoid sexual excess, do not lie, and abstain from intoxicants. Eschewing salvation from supernatural deities, the Buddha taught that people could achieve bliss (indeed, godhood) through meditation and the elimination of desire. Formerly a religion found only in India and Asia, Buddhism has spread throughout the world.

ॐ

Buffoonism—the practice of acting the clown by clumsy humor and coarse, practical jokes. In medieval courts, the jester used Buffoonism to absorb nasty comments against the monarch. Jesters also got to mock the king, on the theory that it was better to pay someone to do it than have people do it behind your back.

Bullionism—1. advocating that currency be convertible to a precious metal like gold or silver. 2. a 16th-century belief that treasure like gold and silver is the most valuable thing to possess under any circumstances because one can trade it for anything else. Today we call this "100% liquidity preference." What makes Bullionism rather absurd is the implicit confusion about money versus capital. In the 16th century, a shortage of coin raised its value and inspired hoarding. Not until two centuries later did anyone suspect that the most profitable thing to do with money is spend it on capital equipment (i.e., invest it). It took the Industrial Revolution, the Reformation, the American War of Independence, and Adam Smith's *Wealth of Nations* to convince people that money is not an end in itself. (Sez you. Try telling a teenager that!) See Bimetallism and Protectionism.

ॐ

Bunburyism—the use of an imaginary, deathly ill friend as an excuse to get out of social obligations. From a character discussed in *The Importance of Being Earnest*. It's better to have a fairly young Bunbury than, say, a "sick grandmother," because you can use a young Bunbury for decades. "A man who marries without knowing Bunbury has a very tedious time of it." (Oscar Wilde)

ॐ

Bureaucratism—behavior of and decisions made by bureaucrats, people who rely on rigid policies designed to insulate themselves from responsibility and decision-making. This does not, however, prevent them from making decisions—affecting life, liberty, and property—whenever they feel like it. Elaborate rules and baffling procedures allow them to delay a decision indefinitely, unless it is desirable to issue sudden, unexpected orders, in which case elaborate rules and baffling procedures allow them to delay administrative review of the decision indefinitely, unless it is desirable to reverse the decision suddenly and unexpectedly, provided that any such decision, revision, or delay is made according to the elaborate rules and baffling procedures desirable to the bureaucracy. "Bureaucracy is a giant Mechanism operated by pygmies." (Honore de Balzac)

Bushism—a convoluted, fractured, often hilarious quote from George Bush, 41st U.S. president, who had a penchant for mixed metaphors and non-sequiturs. Made famous by the book *Bushisms*, compiled by editors of *The New Republic* magazine, who immortalized such gems as "It's no exaggeration to say the undecideds could go one way or another," "I've got to run now and relax. The doctor told me to relax. The doctor told me to relax. The doctor told me. He was the one. He said, 'Relax.'" and "Please don't ask me to do that which I've just said I'm not going to do, because you're burning up time; the meter is running through the sand on you, and now I'm filibustering." Cf. Goldwynism.

Busybodyism—the custom of meddling with or prying into the affairs of others.

Byzantinism—the trait of extreme complexity and intrigue; being so intricate as to be unfathomable to outsiders. The term comes from the Byzantine Empire, founded in 330 A.D. in Constantinople by Constantine, who wanted an Eastern capital for the Roman Empire. But the Empire suffered an East-West Schism in 395 A.D. and never reunited. Today, the term often describes Washington politics, filled with lobbyists, schemers, and bureaucrats angling for power. See also Caesaropapism.

Cabalism—an occult theosophy of rabbinical origin, widely transmitted in medieval Europe and based on an esoteric interpretation of Hebrew scriptures. Adherents believed the scriptures contained hidden meaning that could be revealed by a select group or "cabal" if studied enough. The term now applies to the behavior of any small group united to promote its views via secretive intrigues. See Kabalism.

Caciquism—the practices and customs directed by the Indian chiefs of the Spanish West Indies and other parts of Latin America during colonial and post-colonial times. Known today as Arawaks, the people who practice Caciquism live chiefly in the Guyanas, and their leader or "cacique" instructs their behavior and philosophy. The most notorious custom of these tribes was Cannibalism.

Caesarism—the philosophy of military or imperial dictatorship and political Authoritarianism, as established by early Roman emperors. From Augustus to Hadrian, all emperors were called "Caesar." The procedure for delivering a baby through the abdomen—"Caesarian section"—gained its name from the belief that Julius Caesar (100-44 B.C.) was delivered in such a fashion.

Caesaropapism—the practice of a secular ruler presiding over both the state and the church. Also, Byzantinism.

Calvinism—the religious doctrines of John Calvin (1509-1564), a Swiss Protestant theologian who, in 1536, became Professor of Divinity and minister of the church in Geneva. He emphasized an omnipotent God, predestination, and the salvation of a chosen few by God's grace alone. We know Calvinists today by their dedication to hard work and sacrifice in the pursuit of salvation, despite the total depravity of the rest of us. Calvin made his name in Holland, where his doctrine of predestination (or fate), Original Sin, and the irresponsible sovereignty of God were strongly opposed by Jacobus Arminius, another Dutch theologian. See Arminianism.

ॐ

Cameralism—1. pertaining to a judge's chambers and to the judicial affairs which occur there. Judges hear some matters "in camera" and not in public. (The word "camera" has little to do with Polaroid and Nikon. It means vault or office.) 2. pertaining to public finance and state business or to a council that manages such matters. 3. in 18th-century Germany, an economic theory of Protectionism mixed with Feudalism. Cameralists admired Edmund Burke, an English exponent of Conservativism.

ॐ

Campbellism—principles of the Disciples of Christ, an American church founded by Alexander Campbell (1788-1866) and his father Thomas (1763-1854). Followers reject all creeds in favor of strict Biblicism and baptize by immersion.

ॐ

Canadianism—1. devotion to Canada. 2. a custom or idiom peculiar to Canada, such as "take off, eh." For a thorough grounding, see the movie *Strange Brew*, a dopey comedy based on *Hamlet* that's funny only if you are very, very drunk.

Cannibalism—the practice of eating one's own species, whether human or animal, as recorded by Christopher Columbus (1451-1506) when he discovered the Caribs of Cuba and Haiti, who were of Arawakan origin. (See Caciquism.) Among insects, the praying mantis and the black widow are famous cannibals. In general, the term is a synonym for savagery and Barbarism. "Whenever (cannibals) are on the brink of starvation, Heaven in its infinite mercy sends them a nice plump missionary." (Oscar Wilde)

ॐ

Capitalism—an economic system characterized by open competition in a free market, in which people own the means of production and distribution privately, and in which economic development is proportionate to increasing accumulation and reinvestment of profits. Historically, Capitalism is a new kid on the economic block, arising in the 18th century when the first large-scale industrial enterprises required speculative private investment. Other forms of political economy, such as Mercantilism, Feudalism, Socialism, and Communism, came from the ancient concept of state enterprise, in which individuals work at tasks organized by a government authority, and which produced exactly as much wealth as can be expropriated from slave labor.

Capitalism proceeds from the idea that all people are created equal, with an inalienable right to pursue individual happiness. In 19th-century America, this translated into a legal right to own and control the fruits of one's labor and ingenuity, at a time when taxation was almost non-existent. The results were broad incentives to think and grow rich, as entrepreneurs, inventors, farmers, traders, and workers moved from one locality to another, seeking more profitable opportunities. The freedom to accept or quit a job, to hire someone or do it yourself, to save your money or spend it, to take risks or play it safe—all are characteristic of a capitalist economy. When such decisions are taken from private hands by government edicts or tax policies, the "market" function of free trade is distorted, and the economic winners and losers are not determined solely by the merit of their enterprise but by which players government policy favors. Tragically, government policy—through land grants and monopoly privilege—actually created the alleged tyranny of the 19th-century "robber barons," who inspired popular resentment against all capitalists.

But Capitalism was doomed to fail for reasons other than Congressional tinkering. Most of our moral history is based on the notion of social (rather than individual) welfare, and our standard of "justice" has rarely risen above that of a kangaroo court convened to penalize the able and subsidize the slothful. In Capitalism, you get what you pay for—in terms of effort, risk, and the value of the goods you bring to market. If no one wants what you're selling, you walk home empty-handed. Hence, those who cannot build, sell, or equal the achievements of their Capitalist neighbors seem irresistibly drawn to oppose free trade. In this coalition of envy, it's common to find wealthy heirs funding the hysterics of the "downtrodden." Frederick Engels, for instance, used his daddy's fortune to bankroll Karl Marx.

Since 19th-century industrialists had no moral example to follow, except the murky Mysticism of Christianity or a misplaced faith in the inherent value of progress, their wealth and freedom were rapidly transmuted into something Eisenhower called the "military-industrial complex," over which the Federal government firmly presides. If you've ever wondered why your grandparents could go from rags to riches but you have trouble making a mortgage payment, now you know the reason: less economic freedom=less prosperity.

Careerism—the practice of seeking one's professional advancement by all means possible.

Cargo Cultism—the practice of a milleniarist religious movement in the South Pacific, based on the belief that the cargo in crashed airplanes is a gift from the gods. Believers often build huge airstrips in the jungle, hoping to persuade the gods to send more stuff.

Carnalism—indulgence in worldly, sensual appetites, as opposed to spiritual concerns. "For truth is precious and divine—Too rich a pearl for carnal swine." (Samuel Butler)

છ

Carnivorism—the practice or advocacy of eating meat, as opposed to Vegetarianism. Eating other people's flesh is Cannibalism. Eating your own flesh is Autovorism.

છ

Cartesianism—the philosophy of René Descartes (1596-1650), a French mathematician who summed up his idealistic philosophy by the words "*Cogito, ergo sum*" ("I think, therefore I am"). His philosophy of Dualism became the basis of medical theories accepting the separation of mind and body, and the world has never been the same since.

છ

Castroism—the governmental and socio-economic principles and policies of Cuban leader Fidel Castro, who has ruled Cuba since 1959. It boils down to economic dependence on the Soviet Union, compulsory "education," and suppression of all dissent.

છ

Casualism—the practice or science of dealing with ethics, conduct, or conscience by applying principles drawn from Scriptures, and the use of specious reasoning and fallacious argument on matters of morals. It originated from the idea that all things happen by chance without any intelligent cause or design. Advocates believe that nothing is predictable and all is left to accident or luck. Cf. Scripturalism.

છ

Catabolism—see Katabolism.

છ

Catastrophism—a view or belief that all geologic changes are due to sudden, violent physical events rather than gradual forces. See Cosmic Catastrophism.

છ

Catechism—a short book that gives, in question-and-answer form, a summary of the basic principles of any science or art, but especially of a religion. The term originates from "catechize," which means to teach by word of mouth—a method used on children by Roman Catholics, Lutherans, and other sects. The Anglican *Book of Common Prayer* serves the same purpose.

છ

Catharcism—a figurative "cleansing" or release of emotion or tension, especially through the use of art like tragedy. It also refers to the act of cleansing the body with a medicinal cathartic, which means to purge or purify.

❧

Catholicism—the faith, doctrine, system, and practice of a Catholic church, especially the Roman Catholic Church. The word "catholic" means "universal" and so refers to the all-embracing faith of all true Christians. The Christian church originally viewed itself as comprehensive, open-minded, impartial, and free of prejudice. Indeed, Christ's apostles addressed their Catholic Epistles (letters) to *all* the faithful. Now Catholicism is restricted to the Church of Rome, and each church that claims to be catholic has its own creed outlining doctrines approved by its leaders.

Causationism—the doctrine that every event or phenomena is the result of some previous event or phenomena, without which no event could have occurred. It is also a belief that the world had to have a "first cause" to exist today. In other words, it couldn't be nonexistent one day and then exist the next without a cause. Though this is advanced by some as proof of the existence of God, it begs the question: who or what caused God?

❧

Celticism—a fondness for the customs and language of the Celts, an ancient people of western and central Europe, including the Britons and Gauls. Customs include the Maypole ceremony and the Beltane Fires to honor fertility gods. The Celtic language was Indo-European in origin and includes the Brythonic and Goidelic branches. Celts now speaking a distinctive language are the Bretons, Welsh, Scots Highlanders, and some Irish. Descendants of these races still retain many of their ancient characteristics, and there's considerable interest in their language. The two major divisions of the Celtic Britons are the Gaels of Ireland and northern Scotland, and the Cymri of Wales—which we know today as Gaelic.

❧

Cenobitism—the practice of living as a member of a religious convent or community or sharing a common life; being a cenobite. This is an attractive way of life for many: away from the world and providing companionship and the pursuit of enlightenment without modernity's distractions.

ཀ

Centonism—the practice of piecing together a poem made from a patchwork of other poems, or a work—literary or musical—made from selections of the works of various composers or authors. The finished piece is called a "cento." In modern music, rap artists call this procedure "sampling," and the finished piece is called, oh, noise.

ཀ

Centralism—the assignment of power and authority to a central leadership in an organization, as in a political system. See Democratic Centralism.

ཀ

Ceremonialism—characterized by or involved in ceremony, which is an act or set of acts performed as prescribed by ritual, custom, or etiquette.

ཀ

Chaldaism—the occult practices of the ancient sect of Semites called Chaldeans, who ruled in Babylonia and the Euphrates area of Asia (referred to in the Bible as Shinar).

ཀ

Champagne Socialism—a theory of government based on caviar, a cure for AIDS, and concern for the poor. There are two schools: the Traditional, practiced by Soviet commissars and diplomats, and the Orthodox, practiced by Hollywood has-beens and socialites. Though it's widely believed Charlie Chaplin invented the practice of sipping bubbly and toasting the downtrodden, there was probably a merry trip to the cellars when the Romanovs were evicted in 1917, long before the Little Tramp became a pinko multi-millionaire.

ཀ

Charism—a rare quality or power attributed to people who can win mass devotion with their Magnetism and charm. Formerly believed to be a divine gift; some saints are credited with performing miracles with this power. See Animal Magnetism.

ཀ

Charlatanism—the behavior of one who claims knowledge or skill that he does not have, or one who makes unwarranted pretensions to skill; a quack. The word comes from the Italian word *ciarlare* which means "to prattle." "Never waste a lie; you never know when you may need it." (Mark Twain)

ཀ

Chartism—the principles and practices of a party of social and political reformers, chiefly workingmen, active in England from 1838-1848. In their People's Charter (hence the name), they advocated universal suffrage, no property qualification for a Parliament seat, equal representation, annual parliaments, payment by members, and vote by ballot.

ﾞ&

Chasidism—the practices of a sect of Jewish mystics founded in Poland about 1750 in opposition to the formalistic Judaism of the period and to ritual laxity. Their doctrines come from the Old Testament; their practices are severe and ritualistic; and their dress is distinctive: dark suits, fedora hats, and hairstyles in the ancient style of Semitics, with ringlets in front of the ears. Also, Hasidism.

ﾞ&

Chauvinism—militant devotion to and glorification of one's country, with fanatical Patriotism and belief in the superiority of one's group. Named for Nicholas Chauvin, a legendary French soldier and an enthusiastic supporter of Napoleon. Anyone possessed by an absurdly exaggerated Patriotism or military enthusiasm is a chauvinist. Today, Chauvinism often refers to the behavior of a man who treats women in a condescending or flattering manner and who trumpets the superiority of males.

ﾞ&

Chickenism—a sudden, overwhelming desire to hide in the closet, especially immediately prior to the publication of your first book.

Chloralism—a condition caused by excessive use of chloral, a colorless, oily liquid highly irritating to the lungs. In the Jazz Age, people combined chloral with alcohol and developed addiction.

ﾞ&

Chrism—the consecrated oil used in Christian rites; the rite of anointing with this oil.

ﾞ&

Christianism—the doctrines and practices of Christianity, a religious movement numbering over 300 divisions and sects worldwide, with a variety of beliefs as to the origins and meaning of Jesus of Nazareth

(c. 4 B.C.-29 A.D.), a Jewish mystic who was believed to be the Messiah and the son of God (and also God Himself—see Trinitarianism). His actions and teachings, as recorded years later by his followers, are reported in the four Gospels of the Bible.

Christianity was originally a heretical cult of Judaism that became a political movement. Jesus was killed because, unlike other prophets of His time, He had a large enough following to make the Romans and the conservative Jewish priesthood nervous. After Christ's death, His apostles spread the religion around the Mediterranean, and Roman soldiers spread it through the Empire (see also Mithraism).

The early Christians formed the first Communist communities, as recorded in Acts 4-5, and Jesus preached tolerance, forgiveness, and prompt payment of taxes. But He never said a word about sacraments, Bishops, the suppression of literature and scientific knowledge, the persecution of heresy, birth control, or homosexuality. His peaceful teachings have been twisted and misinterpreted to justify such horrors as the Crusades, the Inquisition, and the Holocaust. Yet if you read His actual words, He preached love, unity, and the dignity of all people in a world filled with ignorance, superstition, violence, and ethnic strife: "A new commandment I give unto you, that ye love one another." (Jesus)

Many of Christianity's sacraments and traditions were expropriated from pagan rituals in the lands conquered by Christian armies. Everything from the tonsure of the Catholic monk to the rosary came from Buddhist Tibetans and Chinese. The name "nun" comes from the Egyptian *nunna*, a maiden of the Temple of Isis. Ancient Babylonian artists used the halo symbol to deify a mortal's head. The celebration of Jesus' birth, Christmas, is probably of Nordic origins, either from the Beltane Fires ritual or the winter solstice. And Jesus Himself was likely an initiate of Egyptian "wisdom religion," whose followers (called Gnostics) regarded Him as a philosopher and teacher rather than a deity. Indeed, nothing in the Gospels establishes that Jesus' followers considered Him a god. And though He called Himself a son of God, he took care to say repeatedly that we are all children of God—much as Plato, Hermes, and other sages taught.

"The Christian ideal has not been tried and found wanting; it has been found difficult and left untried." (G.K. Chesterton)

ॐ

Christocentrism—any belief centered around Jesus Christ and His teachings.

ॐ

Churchism—the belief in the congregation of religious worshippers, their principles and forms, especially the state church. In the U.S. there is no national church; however, the Church of England is such an institution.

ॐ

Ciceronianism—following or imitating the doctrines or style of Marcus Tullius Cicero (106-43 B.C.), a Roman statesman, orator, and philosopher. His followers would escort large crowds into cathedrals to hear him speak, and they also showed the faithful antiquities and explained their origin. Hence, they became known as "cicerones."

ॐ

Cicisbeism—the practice of employing a *cicisbeo*, an escort or lover for a married woman, a popular Italian custom in the 17th and 18th centuries.

ॐ

Cinchonism—poisoning by a cinchona alkaloid, the substance derived from tree bark that also yields quinine.

ॐ

Cinquecentrism—a characteristic of the 16th century, especially regarding Italian art and literature.

ॐ

Civism—good citizenship. "The first requisite of a good citizen in this Republic of ours is that he shall be able and willing to pull his weight." (Theodore Roosevelt)

ॐ

Classicalism—1. in art, a classic idiom or style admired by virtue of its antiquity. 2. in economics, the doctrines of Adam Smith and David Ricardo, who championed Capitalism and free trade. Their theory of Economic Liberalism came to be regarded as "classical" because it was the first time in history that political freedom was linked with wealth-creation, competition, and productivity. Some scholars believe that Marxism belongs to the classical tradition, inasmuch as Adam Smith's central thesis was based on a "labor theory of value," which Marx simply elaborated with greater clarity. To avoid the whole mess, Marginal Utilitarianism declared that classical theories of value and virtue were nonsense.

Classicism—aesthetic attitudes and principles based on the culture, art, and literature of ancient Greece and Rome and characterized by emphasis on form, simplicity, proportion, and restrained emotion. It specifically refers to an idiom or style of those authors of ancient Greece or Rome who were from the highest order of the people and were regarded as pure, correct, and refined in their style.

જ

Classism—the favoring of an individual or group based on their societal rank. From the "politically correct" lingo recently popular on U.S. college campuses, the term is used mainly to accuse a person or institution of gross insensitivity toward minorities and is an extension of Racism and Sexism. "The danger is not that a particular class is unfit to govern. Every class is unfit to govern." (Lord Acton)

જ

Clericalism—a policy of supporting the power or influence of the clergy in political or secular matters. In Elizabethan England, it was an accepted function of the clergy to dominate political affairs. In modern America, the Moral Majority and various "Right to Life" groups attempt the same thing. Cf. Laicism, Secularism.

જ

Cliquism—the practice of certain people who regard themselves as an exclusive group and tend to remain aloof from others.

ॐ

Cocainism—symptoms associated with excessive cocaine use, the sniffles being the least of your worries.

ॐ

Cockneyism—the habits, customs, and idioms of a cockney, a person born in the East End of London, technically within the sound of the bells from a tall steeple in the Old Bow, which was the judicial center of London. Since there is no pure source for this term (and no racial or ethnic group called "cockneys"), we must piece together a history of how the term may have evolved: It probably came from the Latin word *coqud* (to cook), since many East Enders were cooks, maids, etc. Another source is the word *cockaigne*, which meant "land of abundance"—the area of London on the Thames River was the major market for produce, fish, and goods from ships. Finally, the Middle English word *cokenei* meant "pampered child." Today, we think of cockneys as those charming Londoners who talk so funny.

ॐ

Collaborationism—to cooperate treasonously, as with an enemy occupying one's country.

ॐ

Collectivism—1. in economics, the principle or system of ownership and control of the means of production and distribution by the people collectively; Socialism. 2. in politics, the direction of public policy and administration based on mob rule. Dating from our most primitive roots, Collectivism is really a fancy word for Tribalism, in which all are bound to all, like a chain gang.

ॐ

Colloquialism—an expression, characteristic of spoken language, or writing that affects speech; an informal, conversational word or phrase. For instance, "catch you later" has nothing to do with catching anyone but implies that you will meet again soon.

ॐ

Colonialism—a policy by which a nation maintains or extends its control over foreign territories by placing its citizens there. The basic purposes of colonization were to transplant undesirables, to export Christianity to "heathen" territories, to obtain trading privileges or monopoly control over certain goods, and to establish overseas bases which enhanced the mother country's geopolitical status. Colonialism seems to be a by-product of exploration, an inherent human trait. Indeed, futurists believe we will colonize the moon, Mars, and beyond.

Colonies were subject to the jurisdiction of the mother country

and often ruthlessly taxed. When the British imposed unbearable taxes on the American colonies in 1765-1775, the Yanks rebelled, and you know the rest. France, Portugal, Spain, and Holland were also colonial powers in the 17th-19th centuries, colonizing chunks of Africa, Asia, and America. Often, colonists found it necessary to displace the indigenous people: In Tasmania, for instance, British settlers eradicated the Aborigines to the last person! But just as often, it was advantageous to enslave the locals or ship them off for service in another part of the world.

Colonialism sounded like a good idea in the beginning, but it seldom paid off. The Dutch consistently lost money on their colony in Java, for example; the British were humiliated by the Americans. Since the whole thing rested on royal patronage, there was considerable inequity in the monopoly charters granted to merchants. By the 18th century, Europe was aflame with Liberalism and the concurrent development of Capitalism. It didn't take much of an intellectual push to decry the waste, fraud, and unearned privilege that lined the pockets of colonial traders at the expense of ordinary merchants and consumers.

Colonialism died slowly, because the European settlers who brought technical, commercial, and administrative skills to less-advanced cultures found themselves shouldering "the white man's burden" of keeping the peace and providing for socio-political development. At the end of World War II, European nations divested themselves of most of their colonies, mainly because they could no longer afford overseas troops. The result was a sudden rush among educated Africans, Asians, etc. for citizenship in the mother countries, since political independence fostered tribal warfare in nearly all of the new Third World "democracies."

A few colonies remain. Portugal maintains Macao, and England holds Hong Kong, but not for long. The American colony of Puerto Rico has agitated for independence, statehood, and continuation as a Federal Territory—each of which has certain benefits and certain liabilities. As the 51st state, for instance, they'd start paying Federal income tax. As an independent nation, they'd have to fend for themselves. And as a Territory with little opportunity for self-government, the Puerto Ricans remain stuck in the 19th-century mud of Colonialism.

Commercialism—the practices, aims, and spirit of commerce or business, emphasizing tangible profits or success. The term often connotes excessive interest in profit and sales. For example, the "commercialization of Christmas" is bemoaned every December, as retailers rake in 25% of their annual sales in celebration of a pagan holiday hijacked by early Christians to mark the birth of Jesus (who was probably born in the spring). This, in itself, would not be so bad, but a horde of spoiled brats clambering for expensive gifts each year, rather than seeking moral or spiritual enlightenment, is enough to make people hate the whole charade of Season's Greetings and thus blame K-Mart. On the other hand, retailers who pander to the mob are disqualified from moral or spiritual leadership and deserve all the Christmas chaos we inflict. "The low level which commercial mentality has reached in America is deplorable. We have God-fearing Christian men among us who will stoop to do things for a million dollars that they ought not to be willing to do for less than $2 million." (Mark Twain)

ॐ

Commodity Fetishism—a Marxist term that ridicules the way classical economists attributed value to the products of labor. Karl Marx said labor has a dual character: use-value and exchange-value. Marx believed that, in the hands of a baker, bread was "the carrier of an economic relation," whereas in the hands of a consumer it was a commodity (i.e., food). Since his agenda was the violent overthrow of Capitalism, he denounced commodity value and urged his followers to ponder the mysteries of Dialectical Materialism. After careful study of these concepts, one quickly appreciates the enormous amount of time and trouble Marxists expend trying to talk sense (and with such little success).

ॐ

Communalism—a theory or system of government in which virtually autonomous communities, loosely bound in a federation, own property in common and have strong devotion to the interests of an ethnic group rather than those of the society as a whole. Communalism began in France in 1789, when a revolutionary committee replaced the municipality of Paris during the French revolution, and again in Paris in 1871 after the evacuation of German troops. Thus, small "communes" or territorial districts arose under the leadership of a Mayor.

ॐ

Communism—a social system characterized by government ownership of the means of production and organization of labor by a coercive bureaucracy. Communists do not acknowledge any social contribution by entrepreneurs, speculators, or capitalists and favor the elimination of private property for the common good, over the interests of a hereditary or capitalist aristocracy. On its face, it would seem compatible with democracy, because collective decision-making is typical of a communist society. However, the communist state is often admittedly authoritarian, organized to create a "higher" social order in which all goods are shared equally by the people, but which frequently suppresses all debate and dissent in pursuit of that objective and finds it necessary to distribute wealth and privilege according to seniority or rank in the political hierarchy.

Historically, Communism appealed to people living in feudal conditions, where the landed gentry enjoyed long-term privilege and peasants were unable to rise socially or economically. In the U.S., Communism has remained unattractive because most people revere the national heritage of immigration, self-improvement, and upward mobility. Immigrants arrived virtually penniless; second-generation Americans worked hard and went to high school; third-generation citizens grew up to be lawyers, doctors, politicians, and businessmen. The fly in the ointment is the fourth generation—many of whom were so spoiled by the accumulated wealth inherited from their forebears that they became confused about the source of that wealth.

The reason that "capitalist" America is far richer and happier than the whole Communist Bloc put together is that Americans are free to compete, bargain, travel, save, and invest according to individual conscience, rather than being enslaved by one-party rule and central economic planning. Similarly, the reason that Communist countries are so destitute is because they forbid almost all competition, individual initiative, and private property. The distinction, however, is easily lost on punkrockers and overfed university professors, who see Communism as a way to vent their hatred for anyone who has earned or saved a dollar more than they have.

Few are willing to attack Communism on moral grounds: they say they agree with the ideal, though they disagree with the means to the end of "share and share alike." But to agree with the ideals of Communism is to hasten its victory over freedom, and that tacit agreement has done more to keep the communists in power than Lend-Lease, subsidized grain sales, and the United Nations.

After 75 years of forced labor and collectivization of agriculture, the Soviet Union cannot feed its own people, and most political debate there today involves how quickly to re-introduce a market economy, profit incentives, and private property. Such developments are not new in the U.S.S.R.—Lenin himself had to tolerate a brief season of free enterprise, called the New Economic Plan, shortly after his party expropriated every factory and storefront in the country. This is typical of Communist regimes, because the economics of Communism are abysmally wrong, and therefore Red governments are repeatedly forced to tolerate a degree of private enterprise. But whenever they "liberalize" their economies, they rekindle a thirst for more freedom, which requires a massive crackdown on "counter-revolutionaries"—and the whole pretense of progress has to start all over again.

If you agree with the notion that your body is or should be the property of the state, you qualify as a Communist. Millions of Chinese women have had forced abortions; millions of Soviets were starved to death by Stalin's policies; and nearly two billion people today have no right to travel any farther than to and from their place of work—all in the name of "equality." Perhaps it's true: they are all equally enslaved.

"Communism avoided the whole question of its viability by killing everybody who wouldn't do things its way." (Ian Shoales)

Communitarianism—1. the belief in the primacy of the general community over Individualism, and the right of society to dictate individual behavior. 2. the belief that being a member of a communist society or group is a good thing. "Send your son to Moscow and he will return an anti-Communist; send him to the Sorbonne and he will return a Communist." (Felix Houphouet-Boigny)

Comtism—see Positivism.

Conceptualism—a philosophical doctrine pertaining to the theory of knowledge, intermediate between Nominalism and Realism, which holds that "universals" or abstract concepts exist only within the mind and have no external or substantial reality, and that the mind alone has the power or function of forming general conceptions. The issue arises in explaining how an absent object of perception enters our consciousness and becomes a "concept" that subsumes not only the concrete, daily encounters we have with dogs, trees, etc., but all the dogs and trees in the world, as well as intangible things like God, freedom, shape, and culture. A concept is like a file folder which holds the universal attributes of a class of objects (or ideas). The concept of "human," for instance, is sometimes defined as "a rational animal," and thus states that humans belong to another, wider class of things called "animals," and that mankind is distinguished from the rest of that category by virtue of the ability to reason.

The pertinent and crucial aspects of defining a concept, therefore, are statements of 1. the genus to which this concept belongs, and 2. the defining characteristics which make it a viable and useful thing that deserves to be remembered by a word to express it. Some adherents of Conceptualism, in rebellion against Nominalism and Realism, declared that what we think is a precursor to its being brought into objective reality, which echoed Descartes' maxim "I think, therefore I am" and which has encouraged hucksters to fleece the public with the quasi-mystical Power of Positive Thinking. Not coincidentally, there's a school of philosophy called Positivism.

≈

Conceptual Realism—the philosophical doctrine that universals exist independently and in reality.

≈

Concettism—an ingenious thought or turn of expression with emphasis on the affected wit. Conceited people do this to declare their own cleverness. So why it is called Concettism? Because *concetto* is the Italian word for conceit. The best example comes, not surprisingly, from Oscar Wilde. Going through customs upon entering the U.S., Wilde said, "I have nothing to declare—except my genius."

≈

Confessionalism—the advocacy of a formal confession of faith, declaring acceptance of dogma, before being admitted into a church. Similarly, Roman Catholics and Episcopalians recite the Apostles' Creed as a part of their services.

≈

Conformism—1. obedient living in harmony with the dogma, customs, and codes of a group, especially the Church of England. 2. the practice of trying to bring opposing views into compliance and to obtain agreement.

≈

Confucianism—pertaining to or characteristic of the Chinese philosopher and educator Confucius (551-478 B.C.), whose system of morality focused on developing virtue without worshipping a god. He believed that one should act honorably and that concerns about how or why we are here or where we are going are of little value. Systematically denied a high position in the Chinese government— no doubt because the leadership would have found his virtue intolerable—he died a sad and lonely man, whose dream of honorable government by honorable men was never realized. "Hold faithfulness and sincerity as first principles." (Confucius)

≈

Congregationalism—a type of church government in which each congregation is self-governing; especially applicable to Congregational churches, which are usually Protestant churches who regulate the details of their own worship, discipline, and Sunday School picnics.

ॐ

Connectionism—the psychological theory that all mental processes can be described in terms of stimulus and response.

ॐ

Conservationism—the policy or practice of resisting change and protecting anything threatened with extinction, reduction, or rearrangement, especially natural resources. Antarctica, rainforests, and "wetlands" (formerly "swamps") are currently in vogue among conservationists. At the rate Communist countries are vanishing, we wouldn't be surprised to hear pleas for a Communist "refuge," complete with a working gulag, "Please Don't Feed the Bears" signs, and the *People's Heroic Five-Year Plan for Tractor and Cabbage Production* on sale in the gift shop.

ॐ

Conservatism—generally, the belief and practice of those who wish to preserve the status quo, prevent radical change, and delay innovation. In politics, it applies to those who work to support and preserve the existing institutions of a country and to oppose change. It also applies to civil and ecclesiastical institutions as well.

The basic impulse behind Conservatism is fear. Without progress and growth, institutions stagnate and decay, and thus the conservative clings with futile persistence to the established order without sufficient courage to improve the situation by undertaking positive action.

In American politics, Conservatism is a recent movement, gaining popularity under Presidents Truman, Eisenhower, Kennedy, and Nixon, all of whom saw America as the best darn place in the world and thought it proper to send the Marines into Cuba, Korea, Vietnam, etc. to stop the spread of Communism—a major disaster for conservatives, since the U.S. lost every foot of ground the Marines tried to hold by force. Soundly beaten in the global arena (and disowned by their own children in the 1960's), conservatives refocused their agenda to preserve what was left of their cherished domestic

institutions. Under Ronald Reagan, the most "conservative" president ever elected, they managed to preserve the Social Security System, the Chrysler Corporation, 200 bankrupt Texas savings banks, and the cushy jobs of each member of the Federal bureaucracy—at a cost of $2 trillion in new debt. Pretty funny way to implement the conservative agenda of "less government."

What remains of the hard-core conservative movement in America is dissolving into political splinter groups, most of whom fight for single-issue outcomes like outlawing abortion. Indeed, one could say the old-line Democrats like Ted Kennedy are today's real conservatives, as they fight to preserve discredited social programs like welfare and subsidized housing against innovative change proposed by young Republicans like Jack Kemp.

Conservatism as a political concept was inspired by Edmund Burke, an 18th-century English champion of tradition and a bitter critic of the French Revolution. For more on British conservatives, see Toryism and Thatcherism.

"A Conservative government is an organised hypocrisy." (Benjamin Disraeli)

"I've been told that since the beginning of civilization, millions and millions of laws have not improved on the Ten Commandments one bit." (Ronald Reagan)

Constitutionalism—a form of government with a system of fundamental rules, principles, and ordinances for governing. The U.S. Constitution created the Federal system of government with specific powers, duties, and functions of the three branches (executive, legislative, and judicial). The British constitution, rather than a written document, is a series of precedents and long-standing principles which define the rights of British citizens and the privileges of Parliament. Thus, a constitution consists primarily of a social contract between the rulers and the ruled, rather than a written charter.

Another distinguishing characteristic of Constitutionalism is its focus on fundamental structures, processes, and principles, instead of detailed rules or policies. The delegation of broad powers in the U.S. Constitution enables Congress to make war, conclude peace, levy taxes, regulate commerce, etc.—but the actual law-making and implementation of policy varies according to the needs of the day and the results of democratic voting (another system established by constitutional articles and amendments). In the absence of fixed, basic rules for electing government officials—and specific duties/limitations by which they enjoy power—a society is helpless to restrain abuse of that power. And, historically, Constitutionalism ended most absolute monarchy, tyranny, and arbitrary government.

The goal of Constitutionalism is "a nation of laws, not of men" — which means that questions of public policy, justice, and procedure are decided according to enduring and well-established principles, rather than the pressure of the loudest mob or the whim of today's top banana.

Constructionism—the practice or belief in interpreting something, especially the law, in a certain manner, as in a "strict constructionist," as Judge Robert Bork supposedly was.

Constructivism—1. in law, the practice of putting an interpretation on a law, a paper, or public document, or the advocacy of a particular interpretation. In the early 20th century, the term implied advocacy of "strict" construction of the U.S. Constitution, particularly with regard to Federal and states' rights, favoring a limitation of the former to the powers enumerated in the Constitution. 2. in art, a concept that arose in Soviet Russia shortly after the Revolution. The main idea was to create things of a utilitarian and propagandistic nature, and thus overcome the anti-social isolation of being an artist by entering the field of Soviet industrial design.

Consubstantialism—belief in the Christian doctrine that, when blessed, the items of the Eucharist (usually, bread or bread wafers and wine or juice) co-exist with the body and blood of Jesus Christ. As Jesus was said to be both man and God, so wine is said to be both wine and blood. Cf. Transubstantiationism.

Continentalism—1. an attitude or expression characteristic of "the Continent," i.e., Europe. 2. Favoritism by or toward a particular continent. Since Australia is both a continent and a nation, Aussies could be accused of Continentalism and Nationalism simultaneously.

Consumerism—the practice of affluent nations in the consumption, waste, or dissipation of commodities, as distinguished from those who produce the commodities. Consumerism is rampant in the Western world, and one wonders where the mania for "stuff" will end. The term has also come to mean advocacy of the rights of consumers versus producers—which has had the net effect of discouraging manufacturing and innovation, since it has eroded incentives for production and rewarded mainly lawyers and bureaucrats engaged in "consumer protection." Of all the trends in American law, the rush to make life idiot-proof is the most worrisome, because it promotes over-production of idiots. "The ultimate result of shielding men from the effects of folly is to fill the world with fools." (Herbert Spencer)

Contrabandism—the practice of importing or exporting goods prohibited by law; smuggling. Once a common practice on the high seas, it is still practiced today, especially in the Strait of Malacca between Singapore and Sumatra, along the U.S.-Mexico border, in the Soviet Union, and everywhere people have incentive to defy the law. Smuggling drugs and weapons is big business in the West, whereas East Bloc daredevils engage in the cloak-and-dagger importation of Levi's jeans and Marlboro cigarettes.

Conventionalism—phrases, forms, ceremonies, or concerns, both political and ecclesiastical, agreed upon or tacitly understood among parties. The Geneva Convention, for instance, establishes the rules of "civilized warfare" —which amounts to a contradiction in terms, of course, and typifies the hollowness of most such agreements.

Copperheadism—support for the Confederate cause among Northerners during the U.S. Civil War. See Secessionism.

Coprophilism—obsession with or sexual attraction to feces. Eeeeuuuww, gross. See also Stercoranism.

৵

Corporatism—1. the system of organizing political units, like cities, into corporations. 2. a British political concept derived from Statism, which attributes economic progress to the involvement of government in the direction of industry and support for Trade Unionism, especially as advocated by the Labour Party during the 1960's and 70's. 3. the advocacy of centering absolute authority in one corporate body consisting of representatives of major industries, as employer/employee groups, each of which controls all phases of its own field of endeavor; specifically, the Italian system of state enterprises, in which governmental activity is carried on by such bodies. Also, Corporativism.

৵

Corporealism—the belief that all matter is without spirit or spiritual substance; that all matter is dead or lifeless. Now there's a cheery Ism.

৵

Cosmic Catastrophism—the belief that two cosmic catastrophes occurred 26 and 34 centuries ago, causing change in Earth's orbit and hence the length of the day and year, the position of the terrestrial axis, and the planet's rotation. Polar regions shifted, and polar ice became displaced. All these events are said to be the consequences of electrical discharges between Venus, Mars, and Earth. If necessary, this theory can conform with the celestial mechanics of Newton.

Religious scripture and folklore testify to common legends all over the world, often expressed in the deification of planets. The Hebrew prophets, the *Iliad*, and Toltec and Aztec myths all share a similar theme—which, adherents say, could only have originated from a common cosmic experience. It would also account for the frozen mammoths in Siberia, Atlantis tales, and fossilized sea creatures on mountaintops. Try reading Exodus with Cosmic Catastrophism in mind. Very interesting stuff.

৵

Cosmism—the philosophy of the evolution of the universe.

৵

Cosmopolitanism—the condition of people who never feel like strangers, no matter where they are. At home in every place, they are free from local, provincial, or national prejudices and are "citizens of the world." We commonly think it refers to someone well-traveled, and to some extent that's true, since travel tends to enlarge perspectives and diminish churlish views.

৵

Cosmopolitism—the theory that to be without national borders is desirable for all countries and people.

৵

Coueism—the practice of psychotherapy as taught by Emile Coue (1857-1926), a French chemist who counseled his patients to recite "Every day in every way I am getting better and better." The efficacy of such affirmations is dubious. Modern practitioners advocate highly specific "visioning" outcomes instead.

Creationism—1. the religious doctrine that God creates from nothing a soul for each person born. 2. the educational doctrine that God created the world 6,000 years ago, exactly as described in Genesis, complete with all the life-forms that exist today. According to this view, God was something of a prankster, since he created fossils that indicate the existence of extinct species millions of years ago and abundant evidence of animal and human evolution from lower forms.

❧

Credentialism—alleged discrimination based on favoring those whose credentials and achievements reflect the supposed standards of white males over those whose backgrounds are more diverse or colorful. The term is part of the recent "politically correct" agenda on U.S. college campuses. In interviewing applicants for a professorship at a law school, those who shun Credentialism would favor, for example, an inexperienced Hispanic woman lawyer who had taught Yoga over a white man who had graduated with high honors from Harvard Law School and clerked for a Supreme Court Justice.

❧

Creeping Spanish-English Bilingualism—the trend toward official recognition of two languages in the U.S., which proponents see as a necessary tool for education and democracy in an increasingly bilingual society. Opponents note that few people speak one language very well.

❧

Cremationism—preference for or advocacy of cremation over burial. "O grave, where is thy victory?" (I Corinthians 15:55)

❧

Cretinism—a medical condition which involves thyroid deficiency and produces deformity and idiocy. The term inspired the epithet "cretin" to describe a stupid or obnoxious person.

৯

Criticism—passing judgment on the worth of something, especially the values and faults of a literary or artistic endeavor. Literally, it has nothing to do with verbal abuse leveled at your behavior, habits, or moral stature, though the term is associated with harsh, personal comment. I suggest you steer clear of all helpful souls who deem themselves qualified to criticize you, unless you're interested in Masochism. "Asking a working writer what he thinks about critics is like asking a lamp post what it feels about dogs." (Christopher Hampton)

Cronyism—the practice of distributing favors and advantages to friends, employees, and colleagues to retain political or economic control of the resulting power structure. Typical of absolute rulers who gain power by marshaling a cadre of like-minded opportunists, who must then be repaid by sharing the spoils of victory. Cronyism also refers to a group of intimate acquaintances who stay pals though they are withered in their thinking and actions—which increases their mutual dependence—year after year.

৯

Cryptorchidism—the condition of having undescended testicles. Also, Cryptorchism.

৯

Cubism—the doctrine of a school of painters who sought to reduce all forms to geometric shapes and said art should be an expression of the artist's "soul," denying any representation of nature or human form. Based on their paintings, we can presume their souls looked like cubes.

≥●

Cubist Realism—an abstract style of 20th-century American painting which tried to straddle the fence between Cubism and Realism. The outcome was the exemplar of all such compromise. The subject matter—urban and industrial architecture—was depicted in completely unrecognizable shapes but with realistic hard edges. Also, Precisionism.

≥●

Cullyism—the practice of the people of Romany (gypsies), who wandered the countryside in gaily colored caravans and duped gullible people. Traditionally, they told fortunes and read cards, tea leaves, and crystal balls—but nowdays you'll find them selling aluminum siding, hair growth potions, and New Age books. If you are easily tricked, imposed upon, cajoled, or lied to, you stand a good chance of being cullied sooner or later. "Never give a sucker an even break." (W. C. Fields)

≥●

Cultism—the system of rituals and ceremonies used in worship, religious rites, and formalities in honor of some person or thing which receives extensive attention and admiration. The devotion to Adolf Hitler and Rev. Jim Jones are infamous examples of Cultism, while those who revere Elvis Presley and sell Amway products are more benign cultists, to the extent that ceremonies or totems are involved. "A cult is a religion with no political power." (Tom Wolfe)

≥●

Cultural Imperialism—a term first used to criticize the Peace Corps by left-wing intellectuals, who saw American foreign-aid programs as "an opiate to calm the potentially revolutionary masses" (James MacGregor Burns). Presidents Kennedy and Johnson, eager to implement these programs, were quick to reassure critics that the Peace Corps would respect the socialist aspirations of aid recipients. So, the U.S. Information Agency, charged with explaining America to the world, reported in 1963 that "Capitalism is evil. The United States is the leading capitalist country. Therefore, the United States is evil." The solution: omit all references to the U.S. economic system and nod approvingly at any nonsense preached in the Third World. Today, the charge of Cultural Imperialism is leveled anew at the U.S. because of the popularity of American culture abroad.

≥●

Cyclonism—the theory that describes cyclones as storms of immense force, revolving at high speed around a calm center and advancing at 20-40 miles per hour. They rotate clockwise in the northern hemisphere, counterclockwise in the southern. Cyclone-prone areas are usually in the tropics. The tornadoes of the Mississippi Watershed, which are also considered cyclones, are smaller and more violent. The wind velocity around the center of a tornado may reach 500 miles per hour.

Cyclotourism—the practice of traveling in a region by bicycle. Especially popular in Luxembourg, Lichtenstein, and Andorra—European countries you can explore from border to border and be back in time for lunch.

❧

Cynicism—1. doctrine of a sect of ancient Greek philosophers who prided themselves on their contempt for riches, arts, science, and amusements. They were surly, sneering, and morose and probably not on the "A" list for parties. (The term is derived from Greek and means "dog.") Diogenes (412-323 B.C.), the best-known Cynic, was genuinely admired by Alexander the Great. Once, when the young conqueror found Diogenes sunbathing, he asked if he could do anything for him. Diogenes said, "Get out of the way—you're blocking the sun." 2. the exhibition of contemptuous, sarcastic, and generally pessimistic traits by people who believe humans are irredeemiably selfish. "It is a sin to believe evil of others, but it is seldom a mistake." (H. L. Mencken)

❧

Czarism—a dictatorial or autocratic government; support for and belief in such a system. Also Tsarism, Tzarism.

Dadaism—artistic movement begun in Zurich in 1916, moved to Paris in 1920, and subsequently became Surrealism. Dadaist painters and poets spent their time dreaming up provocations, promoting Nihilism, and demanding "the right to urinate in different colours." A real happy-go-lucky bunch of guys.

Daltonism—the condition of color blindness. Named after John Dalton (1766-1844), English scientist, chemist, and philosopher, who suffered from this malady.

Dandyism—the practice of men who pay excessive attention to their dress and behave in a foppish manner. The word is derived from the French word *dandin*, which means ninny. "Distrust any enterprise that requires new clothes." (Henry David Thoreau)

Darwinism—the theories of Charles Darwin (1809-1882), a British naturalist, pertaining to the origins and modifications of species of animals and plants, based on observations he made during an extended study of tropical birds. His principal points: there is a tendency to variation in organic beings; descendants may differ widely from their forebears; animals and plants tend to multiply rapidly and, if unchecked by change, would soon overstock the globe; since there is a continual struggle for existence among all living beings, the strongest, most adaptable, and best-fitted for particular surroundings survive, and the others die out; and from a few forms (perhaps even one), sprang all existing species, genera, orders, etc. See Evolutionism, Social Darwinism. "Man with all his noble qualities ... still bears in his bodily frame the indelible stamp of his lowly origin." (Darwin)

?❧

Deathism—the belief that when you're dead, you're dead, and it's a good thing to stay dead once you are dead. Condemned as narrow-minded by Immortalists, who believe that death can be avoided (the current hope is cryonics) and is, basically, a waste of time. For the record, death is not a waste of time, though Deathism is, unless you're dead, in which case you probably don't have much else to do. See Immortalism. "Those who welcome death have only tried it from the ears up." (Wilson Mizner)

Decaphonism—in music, a system of ten notes.

?❧

Deconstructionism—1. in theater, a drama without action, story, characterization, or plot. See Minimalism. 2. the practice of avoiding analysis or speculation, especially in literature, on the assumption that there are no stable references and that language cannot represent reality. According to deconstructionists (led by the French thinker Jacques Derrida), texts have no intrinsic meaning, there should be no hierarchy in literature, and, historically, literary interpretation is simply a way for those in power (i.e., white males) to impose their views on the oppressed masses. Therefore, the only books worthy of study are those with "politically correct," egalitarian views. Shakespeare, Dickens, Twain—all trash. Instead, read *Stars in My*

Pocket Like Grains of Sand, a recent novel about a homosexual affair in which one of the men is part space-alien.

ॐ

Deconstructivism—modern architectural movement that rejects Classicism and promotes asymmetry and oblique angles.

ॐ

Defeatism—an attitude of expecting the failure of one's country, one's work, or life itself, on the grounds that defeat is inevitable. Anyone who has ever tried to write a book knows what this is all about. Has nothing to do with surgical removal of feet. See Pessimism.

ॐ

De Gaullism—the policies, purposes, and militancy of former French president Charles de Gaulle (1890-1870), who withdrew from the postwar Western alliance and led his country on a path of autonomy, favoring neither America nor the Soviets. See also Gaullism. "How can anyone govern a nation that has 240 different kinds of cheese?" (de Gaulle)

ॐ

Deism—the doctrine or creed of one who believes in the existence of a Supreme Being but denies revealed religion, basing this belief on the light of nature and reason. Deism generally implies Antagonism to Christianity, which is largely based on Mysticism. A similar term—Theism—applies to Jews, Muslims, Christians, and all who believe in "one God" and oppose Atheism or Pantheism.

ॐ

Demagogism—the practices and principles of a leader who arouses passion and prejudice. In antiquity, a demagogue was a professional speaker who swayed people with oratory. Today, the term implies an unprincipled, factious orator—one who acquires influence with the populace by pandering to their prejudices or playing on their ignorance; specifically, an agitator for political or mercenary purposes. "A plausible insignificant word in the mouth of an expert demagogue is a dangerous and deceitful weapon." (Robert South)

ॐ

Democratic Centralism—a Communist dictatorship, as advocated by Lenin and practiced in the Soviet Union. In theory, leaders are chosen by democratic principles, whereupon they enjoy absolute power. In practice, after one election, it's winner take all—in perpetuity.

ॐ

Democratic Socialism—the modern, more palatable name for Communism.

ॐ

Democratism—the principles by which "the people rule." Several variations have been tried throughout history, beginning in ancient Greece, the birthplace of direct democracy. To decide issues, the Greeks made a few speeches and called for a show of hands, and the majority did whatever it felt like—such as ordering Socrates to drink hemlock. The New England "town meeting" still functions this way, with each member having an opportunity to say his piece before the majority does whatever it feels like.

Parliamentary procedure (codified in *Robert's Rules of Order*) exemplifies what's worthy in Democratism: that decisions may not be taken in secret, that objections may be heard and considered, that amendments may be offered to achieve compromise, and that a system of rules keeps things calm during debate.

What's wrong with Democratism is the fact that justice is not a matter of arithmetic. Popular passions and prejudices tend to make democracy an unstable, irrational mess. The 18th-century cure for this problem was Republicanism, which interposed a system of representatives elected by the people to vote on their behalf. Serious students of democracy should examine *The Federalist Papers* by James Madison and Alexander Hamilton and then spend a month or two pondering the history of the U.S. Congress from 1789 to the present. We defy anyone to prove that republics make more sense than democracies, since representatives invariably share their constituents' passions and prejudices. See Populism and Pragmatism.

It is often said, tongue in cheek, that democracy is the worst possible form of government—except for all the others. This is like saying hepatitis is the worst disease you can have except cancer—a rather disingenuous argument that assumes we are forever doomed to disease (or wicked governments) and that we can only choose between evils. The comparison is most frequently made by Americans, who rightly feel freer and more prosperous than the victims of other forms of government.

However, the unique feature of the American system is neither Democratism nor Republicanism—both of which are features of the Soviet system, too. The remarkable achievement in the U.S. was an iron-clad Constitutionalism that protected civil liberties and common law rights, largely preserved from legislative interference or usurpation. Thus, whatever Americans think they mean by "democracy" is, in fact, a constitutional barrier which puts certain things off-limits to the majority and guarantees to each individual certain inalienable rights which no government may lawfully abridge. Indeed, democracy inspired most of the waste, fraud, aggression, and injustice perpetrated in the name of "the people."

You'd think people would be sick of democracy by now and more willing to explore the Rights of Man pioneered in 1776. This, however, is not the case. Being the most free and prosperous nation on earth is not exactly an urgent impetus for change. And so, in the hope that Conservatism will somehow balance the wreck-

age of Welfare Statism, most Americans are happy to wave the flag
and sing the praises of a "democratic system" that continues to whittle
away the Economic Liberalism which made 19th- and 20th-century
prosperity possible. Democratism teaches one thing: The blessings
of liberty are not fit to submit to majority rule.

"Democracy: An institution in which the whole is equal to the
scum of the parts." (Keith Preston)

❧

Demonianism—the state of being possessed by a demon; in mythology, falling victim to an immaterial being, usually evil, holding a
middle place between men and the celestial beings.

Demonism—a belief in demons, which are spirits for good or evil.
Though we think of demons as wicked, some ancient Greeks felt
the presence of a "daimon" who gave them guidance and was a source
of wisdom and goodness, like a muse. Today, Demonism has been
reduced to movies made to terrify teenagers.

❧

Denominationalism—adherence to a religious sect or a particular
society, class, or collection of individuals, wherein each sect has its
own school and teachings.

❧

Depedestrianism—a theory of crime which holds that the use of cars
has "depedestrianized" cities and caused an increase in assault, robbery, Vandalism, etc. According to Edwin Shaw, a British crimi-
nologist, police officers are unwilling to be pedestrians ("beat cops")
because it's too dangerous. The problem is further exacerbated by
the need to devote police resources to traffic-related duties.

❧

Dereism—see Autism.

જ્

Desmognathism—in ornithology, the union of the maxillo-palatine bones, as exhibited by ducks, hawks, herons, and other birds.

જ્

Despotism—1. the practice of a sovereign, monarch, or master who rules with absolute power and enforces his will in an arbitrary and authoritarian manner, regardless of the interest or feelings of others. 2. arbitrary government which is not limited by constitution or laws and which depends solely on the will of the ruler. See Absolutism.

જ્

Determinism—a system of philosophy which denies the existence or reality of human freedom, holding that the "will" is not free but is determined by biological, environmental, social, or mystical imperatives. In the most innocent version of this theory, determinists conclude that we obviously can't choose freely, because there is no free lunch. If there were, everyone would be choosing it, right? But psychological Determinism is also used to exonerate criminals, fools, and charlatans, on the general assertion that "they can't help themselves." And an extreme version holds that absolutely every event in your life is determined by outside causes.

In the Philosophy Hall of Fame, we should erect a statue (or, better, a gargoyle) in honor of the penultimate determinist, Friedrich Hegel (1770-1831), who said that individuals were merely pawns in service to the destiny of World History and that certain races and nations had been chosen to squash the rest. Hegel concocted and personally preached this drivel to the Prussian army one generation before Adolph Hitler—which eloquently demonstrates that philosophy does indeed "determine" what we do. Choose the wrong one and forfeit your life.

જ્

Deviationism—the practice of turning aside or wandering from the common or right course, either in a literal or figurative sense; to stray from the path or the true course in one's actions; in Communism especially, to depart from the party line.

જ્

Diabolism—1. the belief in or worship of devils. 2. the actions of a devil while in possession of a soul. 3. black arts or sorcery which overpower a victim and exonerate whatever mischief he may commit.

જ્

Diageotropism—the inclination of a plant to form a right angle to the direction of gravitation. A fancy word for the fact that some plants grow sideways rather than up.

જ્

Diaheliotropism—the tendency of a plant or its leaves to assume a transverse (flat) position in relation to the light for photosynthesis.

૨૪

Dialectical Materialism—the philosophy of history that put Karl Marx (1818-1883), a celebrated 19th-century mystic, on the map and kept two billion people enslaved a century longer than the rest of us. Marx declared that matter was the sole subject of change, and all change was the product of a constant conflict between opposites arising from internal contradictions inherent in all events, things, and movements. Thus, the "materialist" aspect of Marx's theory stressed the notion that ideas, religions, and morality were nonsense, while the alleged "dialectical contradictions" inherent in economic history produced irresistable outcomes.

Marx predicted that Capitalism would result in the systematic impoverishment of the working class and that Communism was the historically mandated antidote for wage slavery. He was exactly wrong on both counts. As Capitalism raised the prosperity of the "working class" at an astounding rate, Socialism and Marxism achieved little beyond mass repression and chronic want.

As a final rebuke to Marx's materialistic outlook, the spread of Communism depended entirely on propaganda and wishful Idealism—the sum of his contribution to the material world.

૨૪

Dialogism—use of the third person or an imaginary counterpart in a narrative. Usually applied when a direct statement by the writer would be boring or too self-serving. Thomas Jefferson's admired *Dialogue Between My Head and My Heart* typifies the Dualism implied in such efforts. Dialogues usually proceed from competing premises the writer finds difficult to resolve, which thereupon become personified.

૨૪

Diamagnetism—the phenomena of a class of substances (e.g. bismuth and copper) which, when magnetized and freely suspended, take a position at right angles to the magnetic meridian. (That is, they point east and west instead of north and south.)

૨૪

Diastrophism—in geology, the process by which internal forces develop the configuration of the earth's crust, producing continents, ocean beds, mountains, etc. This is the opposite of Catastrophism, which explains the same outcome by blaming external elements (earth, wind, fire).

૨૪

Diathermanism—the state of being freely permeable by heat. Certain substances, such as rock salt, conduct heat.

૨૪

Diatropism—the tendency of certain plants to arrange themselves at right angles to the line or force of a stimulus.

Dichroism—the property of certain crystals to appear in two distinct colors depending on the direction in which light is transmitted through them. Dichroic mirrors and prisms are used to separate colors in television cameras, for instance, and the process of polarization utilizes similar stuff. Also, Dichromaticism.

Dichromatism—1. a vision defect in which the eye sees only two primary colors. 2. the state of having two colors; specifically, in zoology, two colors unrelated to characteristics of sex or age and occurring at different times. Applied to animals such as the screech owl, which exhibits gray plumage one season and red the next.

Dicrotism—1. having two arterial beats for one heartbeat. 2. a pathological doubling of the pulse with each beat of the heart.

Didacticism—1. the manner of speaking as a teacher. 2. speech containing doctrines, precepts, or rules. Some people tend to address others in this annoying manner, especially when writing books on Isms.

Die-Hardism—the belief in resisting to the last or in defending a hopeless cause. "I disapprove of what you say, but I will defend to the death your right to say it." (Voltaire)

Digitalism—condition resulting from an overdose of the heart stimulus digitalis. Warning: Do not eat foxglove leaves!

Dilettantism—the practice of dabbling in the fine arts as an admirer for amusement and without deep appreciation or understanding. Today, this has extended to many professions (especially book reviewing) and is not exclusive to the fine arts. Typically, dilettantes have more money than brains. Also, Dilettanteism.

૨ઙ

Dimorphism—1. in mineralogy, the property of some minerals to crystalize into two distinct bodies that do not appear to be derived from each other. 2. in biology, the property of plants of the same species to appear in two dissimilar forms (e.g. two oak trees with different leaves), or of offspring of an animal species to appear to be totally different, in apparent contradiction of genetic theory. Today, biologists investigate the theory of "gene imprinting" to solve the mystery.

૨ઙ

Diorism—the practice of producing things for scenic contrivance, as in a diorama.

૨ઙ

Disismism—horror at the discovery of yet another Ism that, by virtue of its historical or political significance, cannot possibly be excluded from a compendium of Isms without risking the accusation of slipshod research.

Dispensationalism—the interpretation of history as a series of divine arrangements. For example, the defeat of the Spanish Armada was described thusly: "God blew, and they were scattered." (The Armada was disabled by storms.) The modern equivalent is people who say they will win a war because God is on their side, or those who claim that AIDS is God's punishment for homosexuality. Generally, a viewpoint that rejects Rationalism and appeals to the ignorant and superstititous.

೮

Disraelian Conservatism—the act of resigning political office gracefully and devoting oneself to the good of the party by supporting a former opponent whom one loathes; after Benjamin Disraeli (1804-1881), British prime minister. "Though I sit down now, the time will come when you will hear me." (Disraeli)

೮

Dissenterism—the principles of one who argues or differs in opinion. We have an in-house dissenter—our editor—whose silly prejudices occasionally interrupt this otherwise error-free intellectual production. "In all matters of opinion, our adversaries are insane." (Mark Twain)

೮

Distributionism—a watered-down version of 19th-century Capitalism which advocated free-market principles as a means of production but sought to share the wealth according to need, "fairness," or perceived welfare. Regarded as economic folly in its day, you will no doubt recognize it as the progenitor of modern Welfare Statism and the cornerstone of contemporary politics. The Soviets are trying to adapt their hopeless economy into "a middle way" between Socialism and Capitalism, although the prognosis is gloomy. Once the means of production have been seized by the proletariat, it's difficult to explain why they should be returned to greedy capitalists.

೮

Disunionism—see Secessionism.

೮

Disyllabism—the state of a word with two syllables, like "birdbrain," "bonehead," and "nitwit." Also, Dissyllabism.

೮

Ditheism—the doctrine of the existence of two gods, as expounded by the ancient Persian religion; includes the opposition of the two (good versus evil), otherwise known as Manicheism. (See also Dualism.)

   Without much exaggeration, it could be said that all understanding and political belief proceeds from the perception of two opposing forces—which, among other things, fuels the doctrines of Christianity (Jesus vs. Satan), superpower rivalry (USA vs. USSR), and class war between the "haves" and the "have nots." Taken to extremes, it leads to silly notions of a metaphysically necessary and literal existence of the opposing forces, as in Demonism and Dialectical Materialism.

In reality, Ditheism stems from our ability to do right and wrong at will, plus a corresponding mental capacity to isolate and define perceptual material into categories that help us differentiate the world for the purpose of remembering that some things are hot and others cold. In morality, some things promote life and others lead to ruin, and in primitive societies these perceptions gave rise to the proposition of two competing gods who tempted, ruled, or inspired mankind.

~

Divisionism—a branch of Neo-Impressionism in which colors are divided into their components and mechanically arranged so that the eye organizes the shape. The technique was used by the Pointillists.

~

Docetism—the doctrines of the Docetae, a heretical sect of early Christians who believed that Christ's body was a mere phantom or, if real, of celestial origin, and therefore the Incarnation, Crucifixion, and Resurrection were illusions.

~

Doctrinairism—1. the practice of someone who advocates a policy without regard to reality and practicality. 2. a doctrine of French politicians after the Restoration of 1815 which argued that important change in political or social matters is inept without sufficient regard to practical considerations.

~

Dogmanism—the practice of "an army of beings who were once men. Even yet they go upright upon two limbs and retain human form and speech; but you will observe that they are behind animals in progress. Each of these beings follows a dog, to which he is fastened by an artificial ligament... Circe, instead of turning them into animals, has kindly left the difference of a six-foot leash between them." (O. Henry)

Dogmatism—a quality in those who assert opinions with arrogance or blind obedience to institutional ideas, especially regarding religious doctrine or philosophy. The issue arose in the Middle Ages, when the church held a monopoly on reading and writing and religious doctrines determined the legitimacy of civil institutions. Today, the term is used to condemn anyone who adheres to a philosophy or belief, on the assumption that all conviction is heresy. Thus, the new dogma is "Anti-Dogmatism," or pure Pragmatism. "Dogmatism does not mean the absence of thought, but the end of thought." (G.K. Chesterton)

Dolichocephalism—a condition where the head is unusually long from front to back (compared with side to side). Found in West African Negro tribes.

Donatism—the principles embraced by Donatists, African schismatics of the 4th century; from Donatus, their leader. They considered theirs the only true church and believed ordinances administered in other churches were invalid.

Do-Nothingism—the policy or practice of opposing change by inaction; deliberate Obstructionism.

Donutism—the doctrines of a vaguely religious group of radio listeners in San Francisco sometimes called The Church of the Holy Donut. Led by Bernie Ward of KGO Radio on his Sunday morning program, the group believes that all religion is based on dough.

Doukhoborism—beliefs of the Doukhobors (Russian for "spirit wrestlers"), a sect which split from Russian Orthodoxy in the 18th century. Exiled to Siberia for defying taxes and conscription laws, they emigrated to Canada in 1898 and are still there, where they practice Communism, Pacifism, and Egalitarianism. Doukhobors reject the divinity of Christ and the establishment of a church in favor of the supremacy of the inner voice: "The letter killeth, but the spirit giveth life" (Aylmer Maude). They have had several charismatic leaders whom they revere as demigods, and they have a history of public Nudism to protest Materialism. Not related to Dukeofearlism, the quality of being a nonsense song from the early days of rock-n-roll.

Druidism—the doctrines and ceremonies of the Druids, a pre-Christian order of priests who oversaw morality and religion and served as judges among the Celtic nations in Gaul, Britain, and Germany. The monument of Stonehenge is thought to be a place where the Druids worshipped at certain times.

Reminds us of a London cab ride in which our companion, a Dutch mystic, became enamored of our Lebanese driver because he thought the driver said he belonged to this arcane cult—an extraordinary claim, which prompted my friend to explain his commitment to the pursuit of higher mysteries and his encounter with the reigning Druid priestess at a party. The conversation abruptly ended when the cab driver more carefully pronounced the fact that he was a Druze, which is an entirely different Fanaticism.

ᎋᎧ

Dualism—1. the belief in two antagonistic, supernatural beings, one good, the other evil; or the general belief that both good and evil co-exist and are necessary. "You cannot have power for good without having power for evil, too. Even mother's milk nourishes murderers as well as heroes." (George Bernard Shaw)

2. a philosophical principle articulated by Rene Descartes (1596-1650), who believed that matter and spirit are two distinct substances—in opposition to traditional Idealism. A variety of sub-Isms flowed from this mind/body split: Metaphysical Parallelism says that these two realms of reality are independent but perfectly correlated and synchronized; Epiphenomenalism states that mental events are just phenomena of physical events; and Interactionism assumes that there is a complex interaction between mental and physical events and that they influence each other.

Such theories were particularly unhelpful as medical science sought to understand somatic, nervous, and psychological illness, but the worst of Descartes' legacy was the fundamental split that divided Western philosophy into two camps—the Rationalists, who were committed to reason, divorced from material reality; and the Materialists, who abandoned reason in the name of science.

All of this could have been avoided simply by rejecting Mysticism and revealed religion, of course, but the Age of Enlightenment never rose to that challenge, and thus we inherited a compromise intended to reconcile man's immortal soul with the awkward fact of his mortality, especially in the theories of Kantianism and Pragmatism, which preached our inability to figure out *anything*. Chief heir to the "rational" side of the dualist doctrine was Friedrich Hegel (1770-1831), who claimed that nothing exists except ideas, while David Hume (1711-1776) championed the "material" view and denied the existence of causation since it could not be isolated or perceived independently of physical events. By the time this debate arrived on college campuses in the 20th century, so-called thinkers were arguing about the metaphysical significance of pronouns.

To put the question to rest, we implore you to remember that you are indeed a physical entity and that your ideas are generated in the course of living, in direct proportion to the effort you expend thinking. This does not mean you are guaranteed an unerring or spontaneous result—and that sober fact suggests the importance of reason and logic when attempting to do something in the physical world, like making breakfast or choosing a mate or burning your draft card. If you accept any part of Dualism, you split yourself in half and commit to a civil war between mind and body, which neither side can "win" since they are merely two attributes of the same animal. And if you don't believe you are indeed an animal, nothing we can say will save your butt when you meet a predator.

&

Dwarfism—a condition in which an animal or plant is much below the ordinary size of its species. In humans, Dwarfism may be caused by a defect in the pituitary gland and its secretion of growth hormone in the early phase of fetal development. For reasons known only to those of convict descent, Australians indulge in a contest called Dwarf Tossing.

&

Dynamism—1. the power or principle of sufficient force to accomplish significant action or change. 2. the theory which states that all substance involves this force. Dynamism has been divided into statics and kinetics. The former deals with forces that compel rest or prevent action (like friction), the latter with forces that cause motion or change of motion (like heat). In physics, it's used to express a unit of work equal to a weight of one pound raised one foot in one second (a foot-pound). We commonly think of Dynamism in conjunction with a vigorous personality or with the impetus driving an economy or sector while others remain stagnant.

&

Dynasticism—the practice of rule by a family for many generations; applies to the Nehru-Gandhi family in India and the Kennedys in Massachusetts. See Nepotism.

&

Dysbarism—the condition that results when the atmospheric pressure and the pressure of bodily gases is different. An example is "the bends," which can happen to scuba divers who ascend too rapidly.

&

Dyscrinism—a condition caused by defective glandular secretions, like Dwarfism and Hirsutism.

&

Dysphemism—the substitution of a harsh word or phrase for a term more neutral; the opposite of Euphemism.

Ecclesiasticism—adherence to the strict principles of the church and whatever privileges so designated. In the Old Testament, the book of laws placed between the Book of Proverbs and the Song of Solomon was written by Solomon of Jerusalem, son of King David and a noted wit, who ruled with judicious insight. Solomon describes correct behavior and gives his opinion on many subjects. One of the few humorous books in the Bible, it bashes the vice of Ecclesiasticism.

Echoism—also called onomatopoeia, an Echoism is a word that sounds like its meaning, like "murmur" or "Whap!" "Bam!" "Pow!" —a familiar concept to fans of the old *Batman* TV show.

Eclecticism—1. in art, philosophy, and general behavior, the practice of selecting techniques or styles from a variety of sources. Rather than adhere to one system, some philosophers of antiquity felt it wise to consider several shrewd principles, perhaps assuming that one person was unlikely to get everything right. The difficulty with Eclecticism, of course, is that you're often unable to resolve contradictions or organize the parts into a whole, since eclectics reject the need for fundamental principles or axioms. See Pragmatism.

Economic Colonialism—a phrase describing the hysterical belief that the Japanese are colonizing the U.S. by buying hotels, golf courses, and factories. Racism has nothing to do with it (although in France it does). The basic beef with Japan is an objection to reality: They worked; we played. They studied; we watched *Laverne & Shirley*. They saved; we bankrolled Jimmy Swaggart. But who wants to admit he snoozed while someone else built a better mousetrap? Until Americans learn how to work, study, save, and cut government spending, Japan will continue to outperform the U.S. What the Japanese are doing is not Colonialism, it's competition.

Economic Determinism—the doctrine that economic factors determine all social and political forms and interactions. Therefore, a guy who robs and murders a convenience store clerk should be excused, because poverty drove him to a life of crime.

Economic Liberalism—a term derived from the most fundamental aspect of laissez faire economics: the liberty to make economic decisions without government interference. See Capitalism.

Ecoterrorism—the practices of environmental activists who sabotage, or "ecotage," efforts by the military and business to exploit natural resources which these groups feel should be protected. Methods range from disabling machinery to committing acts of civil disobedience, such as getting between whalers and whales or between chainsaws and trees. The environment may need protection, but people have rights, too, and the ecoterrorists' focus on attacking machinery begins to sound like another movement which used Vandalism to destroy business and express a hatred of technology—see Ludditism.

Ecumenical Fundamentalism—a concept proposed by the All-Faith Conference in 1991, which declared that, since all religions share a piece of the Universal Truth and no single religion has a monopoly, it was possible for a martyr of one faith to die for another religion. Uh-huh.

Ecumenism—a movement seeking to achieve worldwide unity among religions (especially the unification of all the Christian sects) through cooperation and improved understanding—an effort necessitated by the fact that other religions stubbornly refuse to disappear, no matter how many heretics the true believers kill. Also, Ecumenicalism, Ecumenicism.

Edwardianism—a characteristic of the reign of England's Edward VII (1841-1910), especially regarding opulence and self-satisfaction.

Edwardsianism—a variation of Calvinism professed by American theologian Jonathan Edwards (1703-1758), author of the original fire-and-brimstone sermon "Sinners in the Hand of an Angry God." He once described man as "a little, wretched, despicable creature; a worm, a mere nothing, and less than nothing; a vile insect." Edwards was always a big hit at parties.

ᘒᕀ

Egalitarianism—1. the doctrine of equal political, economic, and legal rights for all human beings, regardless of their abilities. 2. the hysterical claim that all people are equal in every respect, regardless of individual traits. "The defect of equality is that we only desire it with our superiors." (Henri Becque)

ᘒᕀ

Egocentrism—the state of being totally self-centered, dwelling upon one's own interests to the exclusion of all else, including the impact of other egomaniacs and the crushing weight of world history. To the egocentric, nothing exists or has a valid purpose in the world except his own whims.

ᘒᕀ

Egoism—1. a philosophical doctrine which asserts that all knowledge derives from the phenomena of personal existence; specifically, the opinion of one who thinks everything is uncertain except his own existence. 2. a passionate love of self—which is decried by every traditional form of religion, philosophy, and ethics except Objectivism.

ᘒᕀ

Egotheism—love of self elevated to deification. This madness strikes the afflicted with predictable regularity, marking the apogee of a mystic's death wish and immediately preceding its implementation. Adolph Hitler and Rev. Jim Jones were notable proponents. Sadly, egotheists always take vast numbers of gullible followers to the grave with them.

ᘒᕀ

Egotism—an attitude of exaggerated and passionate (and obnoxious) reference to oneself and one's opinions and of seeing the world only as it relates to one's interests and importance; selfishness. Egotism often requires extreme magnification of one's achievements, especially in the presence of others. Egotists are usually people of low taste, more interested in themselves than in external examples of dignity or achievement. They're easy to spot and tiresome to behold. "The last time I saw him he was walking down Lover's Lane, holding his own hand." (Fred Allen)

૨૦

Eleaticism—characteristic of the school of philosophy founded by Xenophanes and Parmenides, 6th century B.C. Greek philosophers who believed that immutable being is the only knowable reality and that change is mere opinion (!). The name is derived from the region of Italy called Elea, where they taught.

૨૦

Electromagnetism—1. that portion of physics which examines various actions and relations between magnets and electrical currents. 2. the magnetic properties exhibited by electrical currents.

૨૦

Electrotropism—see Galvanotropism.

૨૦

Elementarism—the artistic successor to Neo-Plasticism. Its big improvement was the freedom to use inclined planes in a painting.

૨૦

Elitism—1. rule by a select group. 2. a practice of selecting only the best in one's friends, food, clothes, and ideas—and the mistaken belief that they are indeed the best. Country clubs and Ivy League schools are often condemned for Elitism. The pursuit of excellence is not *per se* pernicious, but it often amounts to snobbery when it works to the deliberate disadvantage of the rest of us. For example, TV program producers, while busily preoccupied with the concoction of crowd-pleasing garbage, often sneer at the mob of unsophisticated "Tommy T-Shirts" and "Bobby Beer-Drinkers" who pay for the luxury homes, sports cars, and cocaine habits that distinguish these television executives from ordinary whores.

૨૦

Embolism—1. the practice of relating historical or personal accounts in exact days, years, or months. 2. in the Communion service, the prayer after the Lord's Prayer. 3. in medicine, a condition in which a clot obstructs a blood vessel.

૨૦

Emotionalism—the cultivation of emotions, usually extreme and unwarranted, by persistent encouragement; the tendency to yield to

or exalt the emotions and to view matters more from the stand-
point of feeling than of reason or morals. Cf. Rationalism. "The
advantage of the emotions is that they lead us astray." (Oscar Wilde)

ૐ

Empirical Materialism—the scientific theory championed by Francis Bacon (1561-1626) and others, who saw science as an observable
pursuit of knowledge about the material world. In economics, Sir
William Petty (1623-1687) led the crusade for statistical measurement,
as opposed to theoretical speculation, on the causes of wealth.

ૐ

Empiricism—the dependence of a person on his own experience or
observation as a source of knowledge, often in disregard of theory
or deductive reasoning. Applied in medicine to make judgments
based upon practical experiences and not on scientific theory, and
therefore pertains to Pragmatism.

   The debate between proponents of empirical and deductive
reasoning is actually a false issue stemming from the ancient war
between Platonism and Aristotelianism. Plato proposed the existence of an abstract realm of ideas, said to be the "real" reality, of
which our world was only "an imperfect shadow." Aristotle emphasized the role of observation and (paradoxically) pure logic.

   In reaction to this fundamental split, modern thinkers divided
into opposing camps along similar lines. The Empiricists, led by John
Locke (1632-1704), demanded the right to observe nature and learn
from what they could measure. Rationalists clung to the "logical"
proofs advanced by Thomas Aquinas (1225-1274) for the existence
of God and the tenets of Catholic faith. What a mess! Those who
saw value in what we now call "the scientific method" (careful observation and repeatability of experiments) rejected any form of *a
priori* logic, since deductive reasoning was a weapon used against
them by defenders of the Church. Those committed to the supremacy of the Syllogism, meanwhile, had to reject all empirical research
to keep their jobs at the church-dominated universities. In fact, the
empirical scientist implicitly relies on deductive reasoning every time
he conducts an experiment or draws conclusions on the basis of
test results. Likewise, the most stubborn ivory-tower thinker must
taste a pie before he declares he likes it.

   The whole war between Idealism and Materialism was fought for
nothing, just because the Church had a monopoly on science during
the Middle Ages and anyone who questioned its doctrine was a
heretic. Today, we're still pulled in opposite directions by idiots who
claim TV ratings and popularity polls are infallible standards of public
good, while evangelical tub-thumpers proclaim abortion is murder
by definition—the former being undiluted exponents of Social Empiricism; the latter Born-Again Rationalists.

ૐ

Employeeism—the quality or state of not giving a damn because "I just work here."

ᓬ

Encyclopedism—the practice of making encyclopedias, which are extensive works on the range of human knowledge, or dictionaries of things instead of words. It also refers to extensive learning and possessing a wealth of information. During the Age of Enlightenment, Denis Diderot (1713-1784) led the crusade to broaden knowledge by collating as much as he could.

ᓬ

Endemism—the trait of being indigenous or arising from local sources, something by which people are likely to be affected and to which they are peculiarly susceptible. Often refers to diseases from local air or water, but could also refer to genetic phenomena, prejudices, or even Isms.

Endomorphism—1. in geology, the Metamorphism of igneous rock as it cools, resulting from contact with and assimilation of wall rock. 2. in mathematics, a Homomorphism that maps a mathematical set into itself.

ᓬ

Energism—the theory that the ultimate good is self-realization.

ᓬ

Entryism—the Trotskyite tactic of subverting an opposing regime by gaining a few seats in government, from which "agitprop" (agitation and propaganda) activities can be effectively deployed. Used by the Militant Tendency faction to gain power over Liverpool's city government in the 1970's. See Proletarianism.

ᓬ

Environmentalism—moral and political creed which emphasizes concern for and humanity's dependence on flora, fauna, air, water, and other natural resources. Extremists have much in common with Ludditism and have been known to call humans a "cancer on the planet."

ᔕᗷ

Epicureanism—the philosophy that pleasure and pain are the chief good and evil respectively. Epicurus (342-270 B.C.), a Greek devoted to sensual enjoyment and culinary delights, found no valid argument that one should suffer. He therefore decided that the full use of all the senses for pleasure was a good and proper thing. The problem, of course, lies in defining the terms. Often, a little pain yields enormous pleasure—a pleasure that would not exist if the early pain had been avoided. Also, Epicurism. Cf. Egoism, and see also Benthamism, Sensualism.

ᔕᗷ

Epigonism—practice of those who are second-rate followers of leading members of the arts and philosophy. In Greek mythology, the term refers to the Epigoni, the descendants of those who fought against Thebes—inferior successors who tried to imitate the first and best.

ᔕᗷ

Epigrammatism—a style of Greek literature consisting of poetic inscription on a tomb, public monument, or temple. In a restricted sense, an epigram is a short poem with one subject and a witty or ingenious turn of thought. In a general sense, it is an interesting thought expressed cheerfully in a few words.
    "What is an epigram? A dwarfish whole,
    It's body brevity, and wit its soul."
    (Samuel Taylor Coleridge)

ᔕᗷ

Epilogism—the practice of reconsidering or reckoning over. In drama, the Epilogue is the speech or short poem at the end of a performance, stating the play's theme for the dumbbells in the audience. In oratory, it's the closing part of a discourse, enumerating the high points.

ᔕᗷ

Epiphenomenalism—the doctrine that mental activities and consciousness are simply perceived effects of the physical processes of the brain. The classic way of explaining this is to say that thought is like smoke from a fire—a by-product of the brain's chemical and/or mechanistic activities, over which we have no real control. To paraphrase Descartes: "I think, therefore my body must be doing something to my brain." See Dualism.

ᔕᗷ

Episcopalianism—1. the doctrines and practices of the Protestant Episcopal Church. 2. a system of religion or ecclesiastical government in which bishops are distinct from and superior to priests. Bishops lead the Episcopal Church and have no superiors—unlike Catholics, who, in addition to bishops, employ monsignors, cardinals, and popes, all higher in rank. Also, Episcopalism.

Epizoism—a condition in which parasitic animals live externally upon the living body of another (e.g. fleas and ticks, but not tapeworms). Some live on the skin and some in the skin, but both types feed and breed on their hosts. See Parasitism.

Equalitarianism—1. the belief that no person, thing, or quantity is inferior or superior to another, specifically in regard to rank or talents. 2. the political philosophy espoused by Herbert Marcuse, which proposes there should be no legal, political, or economic distinction made among "comrades." See Egalitarianism.

Equestrianism—the trait or practice of skilled horsemanship. In ancient Rome, equestrians were a rank of knights who performed feats of agility on horseback. Today, it applies to riders in a circus or any group or person who demonstrates ability with horses. "Nothing does as much for the insides of a man than the outsides of a horse." (Ronald Reagan)

Equiprobabilism—in Roman Catholic theology, the doctrine that if you don't know whether an action is lawful or not, either choosing the action or dismissing it is acceptable. In this case, ignorance of the law is a good excuse. See Probabilism.

Erastianism—the doctrine that the state should be in control of the church. Thomas Erastus (1524-83), a Swiss-German physician, theologian, and philosopher, first proposed such control. In the U.S., separation of church and state prevents Erastianism.

Eremitism—the practice of living in seclusion, often in the wilderness, and indulging in radical ascetic practices to purify the spirit. Practitioners are called eremites. "Happiness seeks obscurity to enjoy itself. A good-looking milkmaid might have kept Alexander the Great from conquering the world." (Mark Twain)

Erethism—a high degree of irritation or stimulation in an organ or tissue.

Ergotism—the disease condition that develops when humans consume rye or other grasses infected with ergot fungus. In the 18th and 19th centuries, Ergotism epidemics baffled doctors, who discovered normally modest people cavorting, undressing, and doing all sorts of odd things in public. We now know that the afflicted were "tripping," and, in fact, the hallucinogen LSD was developed from this fungus. Before you rush to the nearest rye field, note that Ergotism also causes painful cramps and a form of gangrene.

Eroticism—a sexual theme or quality of behavior that is highly insistent on physical passion; any interest in sexual activities or sexual objects pursued for the sake of gratification, often in defiance of social, political, or religious taboos. Also, Erotism. "Nine-tenths of the appeal of pornography is due to the indecent feelings concerning sex which moralists inculcate in the young; the other tenth is physiological, and will occur in one way or another whatever the state of the law may be." (Bertrand Russell)

ਟੈ

Erraticism—1. the state of being a wanderer, of having no fixed course or destination, or of deviating from the standard course. 2. in geology, boulders or rocks that apparently were transported from their original sites by ice in the Pleistocene period.

ਟੈ

Erythrism—excessive or abnormal redness resulting from Dichromatism, which describes certain birds who have an excess of red pigment in the plumage.

ਟੈ

Erythroism—a term used by Baron Jons Jakob Berzelius (1779-1848), a Swedish chemist, to describe the red coloring of fruits and leaves in autumn.

ਟੈ

Escapism—1. avoiding reality and life's challenges and the fact that we can't have our cake and eat it, too. The movies are considered a pleasant form of Escapism; alcohol and drugs more insidious forms. 2. a manic stabbing of the "Esc" key to stop the computer from destroying a full day's work.

ਟੈ

Esoteric Buddhism—a primeval doctrine of spiritual science (articulated by A. P. Sinnett, who claimed to have received it from the esoteric teachers in the Himalayas), which outlines the origin of the world (cosmogenesis). First published in 1883 by the Theosophical Society, it claims to present absolute truth concerning nature, humanity, and the origin of the universe. See Theosophism.

ਟੈ

Esotericism—beliefs or systems of thought which are abstruse, secretive, and deliberately occult. The ancient philosophies were of two kinds: "exoteric," which philosophers themselves could partly understand, and "esoteric," which nobody could understand. It is the latter that have most profoundly affected modern thought and found greatest acceptance in our time.

ਟੈ

Esperantism—1. advocacy of Esperanto, a language invented by Russian philologist L. L. Zamenhof (1859-1917), based on the most common words in the "most important" European languages. A lost cause, since language difference is something Europeans cherish, a vital component of their nationalist Chauvinism. Besides, it would probably be condemned as Eurocentrism today. 2. a word or term from Esperanto, something that doesn't really exist, since Esperanto is comprised of words from other languages. If you want to hear a sample, the musical group Cocteau Twins sings in Esperanto.

ॐ

Essentialism—the idea that everyone should be taught the skills and concepts essential for functioning in society, regardless of individual ability. An obviously sensible belief apparently abandoned in U.S. public schools, where many students are just passed through the grades until they graduate—illiterate, ignorant, and lacking the basic skills to get a job or otherwise function as adults and full participants in society. With our schools churning out grown-up, stupid children, it's no wonder Paternalism rules government policies.

ॐ

Etacism—the pronunciation of the seventh letter of the Greek alphabet, like the long "a" in "fate."

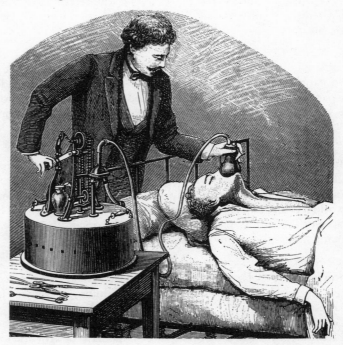

Etherism—the practice of using ether, a light, volatile fluid obtained from alcohol, for anesthesia. Obtained by replacing the hydrogen of organic acids by alcohol radicals, ether is lighter than alcohol, has a strong sweet smell, is susceptible to great expansion, and has a pungent taste. A mixture of ether vapor with air is extremely explosive. A few drops on a clean cloth pressed against the face and *zap!* you're out cold, hence the term "knock-out drops." Its use must be monitored carefully to prevent sudden death. Don't try this at home, kids!

ॐ

Ethnicism—1. the state of being a pagan or heathen, whose form of worship is considered idolatrous. 2. the political philosophy or policy of giving legal privileges to ethnic groups based on their color, religion, or national origin. In their zeal to rectify the sins of past generations, many politicians are eager to cash-in on the ethnic differences which are supposedly irrelevant under the "equal protection" clause of the U.S. Constitution. Thus, Americans insure that blacks, Hispanics, Native Americans, Asians, etc. preserve their racial identities and cultural heritage, while providing educational and employment quotas to compensate them for their racial identities and cultural heritage.

   If you live in a city that has not renamed a street or public school "Martin Luther King, Jr." or "Malcolm X," your community is one of the few remaining pagan enclaves whose forms are hopelessly ethnic under definition 1., and it behooves you to get in line with definition 2. if you want any Federal money.

❧

Ethnocentrism—belief in the superiority of one's own ethnic group, usually accompanied with a contempt for other groups; practices associated with such a belief. See Afrocentrism, Eurocentrism.

❧

Eudemonism—the philosophy which espouses human happiness as the highest object and declares that virtuous actions produce this happiness. See Epicureanism. Also Eudaemonism.

❧

Euhemerism—the philosophy described by Euhemerus, 4th-century B.C. Greek philosopher who said Greek mythology arose from the deification of dead heroes. It's a system of mythological interpretation which reduces gods to the level of distinguished men, and so regards myths as stories based on real histories.

❧

Eunuchism—the practice of castrating men during the eras when kings kept harems of women and needed servants who would pose no sexual threat; the state of being a castrated man. The word *ennuchi* means to keep charge of the bed, and so eunuchs were the chamberlains in the royal household, supervising the women's needs. Some rose to great power and were usually privy to all the palace intrigue.

❧

Eunuchoidism—a medical term describing a man with reproductive organs not fully developed and female characteristics like a high voice and lack of body hair.

❧

Euphemism—the substitution of mild or vague words that are more palatable than a curse or explicit words; the use of an auspicious word for an inauspicious one, or when a harsh or indelicate word is substituted or softened. "He passed away" is a Euphemism for "He died." "When red-headed people are above a certain social grade their hair is auburn." (Mark Twain)

Euphuism—an elegant, excessively refined, and affected language used by the hero in two of the works of British writer John Lyly (1554-1606). His strange and elaborate speech was fashionable among the court of Elizabeth I.

Eurocentrism—1. doctrines or opinions having Europe as the focal point or arising exclusively from European concepts. 2. the chauvinistic view that Europe and Europeans contributed all that is of value to the modern world in art, literature, science, philosophy, politics, etc., and the deliberate exclusion of contributions made by Africans, Asians, etc. Taken to extremes by multiculturalists, who see Eurocentrism as pervasive and pernicious and criticize anything from "dead, white, European males," especially in literature. Cf. Afrocentrism. "Europe and the UK are yesterday's world. Tomorrow is in the United States." (R.W. Rowland)

Eurocommunism—a watered-down form of Communism once popular in Western Europe. People who advocated Eurocommunism claimed to be independent of the Soviet Communist Party, for all the good it did them.

Euro-Federalism—the political and economic cooperation of the nations of Europe. An Ism of recent coinage, it received an enormous boost lately by Jacques Delors, Helmut Kohl, and the defeat of Margaret Thatcher.

In 1957, the European Community (EC) was a fairly simple concept: a free-trade zone in which member states would dismantle tariffs and trade barriers. Thirty years later, this has evolved into an "EC superstate" with sovereign jurisdiction over European agriculture, commerce, aspects of foreign affairs, and taxation. In 1992, the EC

becomes a single market governed by Brussels, and the next item
on the political agenda is monetary union. If the French and Germans get their way, national currencies will be replaced by the "ecu"
regulated by a central bank accountable to none of the member
states. Spain has advocated a pan-European passport, because it
would allow her paupers to find work (and welfare benefits) in Germany and Britain.

The basic issue is Socialism. Euro-Federalists are eager to merge
their bankrupt economies and admit as many new members as possible, on the implicit theory that a pan-European superstate will
employ far more politicians and bureaucrats who could not otherwise find a job.

ᝐ

Europeanism—1. a trait or practice of Europeans. 2. advocacy of or
affection for a unified Europe or a pan-European society, economy,
or culture. After fighting with each other for centuries, the nations
of Western Europe are trying to be un-French, un-German, un-
British, un-Italian, and un-everything else. The prospects for
achieving this lofty ideal are approximately zero. See Racism.

ᝐ

Evangelicalism—the doctrines of Protestant churches that give special prominence to the idea of the corruption of human nature by
the "fall from grace" in the Garden of Eden and of human redemption through Christ by free and unmerited grace. In Germany, this
applied to Protestants and not Catholics, and more especially to
the National Protestant Church formed in Prussia in 1817 by a union of the Lutheran and Calvinist branches. The term also refers
to the preference for Scriptural teaching and personal revelation
over institutional authority.

ᝐ

Evangelism—the zealous preaching and dissemination of the Gospel
through missionaries, principally on TV, which God created to tor-
ment mankind.

ᝐ

Evolutionism—belief in the theory of biological or metaphysical change
and development. In biology, the theory of evolution states: 1. the
seed of a new Organism pre-exists in the parent; 2. its parts will
be unfolded and expanded, not by procreation but by a series of
successive stages, through which any individual Organism passes
from the time of fertilization of the ovum to maturity; and 3. all
existing Organisms have arisen as morphological and physiological
modifications of pre-existing forms; they are all genetically related,
and the change resulting in present differences has been gradual,
from the simple and less-differentiated to the complex and more
highly differentiated. An important theory in connection with evolution is that characteristics are inherited, and those acquired through

environment, function, etc. are transmitted to the offspring. The evolution theory of the origin of the species is that later species have been developed by continuous differentiation of organs and modifications of parts from species simpler and less differentiated, and thus all Organisms can be traced back to a single cell. See Darwinism.

In metaphysics, the theory sees in the history of all things, organic and inorganic, a passage from simplicity to complexity, from an undifferentiated to a differentiated condition. "All the evolution we know of proceeds from the vague to the definite." (Charles Sanders Pierce)

ᕒ

Exclusionism—principles or practices of those who seek to shut out others and socially ostracize them; one who would preclude another from privileges. Specifically, in English history, it refers to one of the political parties which sought to exclude the heirs of Charles II from the throne because they were Roman Catholics.

ᕒ

Executive Feminism—the practices of ambitious career women who belong to groups such as LWL (Ladies Who Lunch) in London, the purpose of which is to develop business contacts and find female mentors. Rules involve always having loads of business cards at the ready and always acting interested in everyone. All this schmoozing is designed to create copy-cat "networks" (like men's "old boy networks") to help each other up the ladder of success.

The idea of women creating old boy networks is dismaying, since such things were attacked so vigorously in the early days of feminist Activism. What's worse is the naïveté in the thought that a successful woman is more likely to assist her female colleagues than a man is.

Historical note: Old boy networks have nothing to do with networking, power-breakfasts, or handing out business cards. An "old boy" is a man who attended an English boarding school like Harrow and Eton. The theory is, if you survived the beatings, buggery, and academic pressure at such a place, you are probably a "steady chap" and can be trusted with responsibility. The American equivalent is probably an education at Andover and Choate and then on to Harvard or Yale.

❧

Exemplarism—1. the doctrine that all human knowledge is based on the models of reality in God's mind. See Idealism. 2. the belief that the death of Christ is relevant to man only as the highest example of self-sacrifice and perfect love.

❧

Exhibitionism—a tendency to display that which modesty usually conceals, whether mental or physical.

❧

Existentialism—a 20th-century philosophy that arose in war-ravaged Europe and reduced human thought to an analysis or chronicle of existence, which was said to be impossible to exhaustively describe or understand in scientific terms. It stressed the freedom and responsibility of the individual, the irreducible uniqueness of an ethical or religious situation, and the isolation and subjective experience (such as anxiety, guilt, dread, anguish) of individual life. It is a creed of despair and darkness, devoid of reason or purpose, which quickly conquered the left-leaning elite with its unabashed Subjectivism and exaggerated Emotionalism. "Everything has been figured out except how to live." (Jean-Paul Sartre)

❧

Exorcism—the act of expelling evil spirits thought to control a person. Priests regularly conducted prayers and rites when people appeared to suffer from the influence of bad spirits. Once common among Jews, Exorcism is still part of the doctrine of some faiths: the Greek and Roman Catholic churches use it in the Baptism of both infants and adults and sometimes when individuals are supposedly possessed. See Demonism.

❧

Exotericism—principles or doctrines suitable for public knowledge because they are readily understood. Opposite of Esotericism.

❧

Exoticism—the state of being from a foreign land or having an unusual and exciting effect or appearance. It can refer to a plant, person, word, or practice with an aura of far-away places, and it usually conveys romance or intrigue. It can also refer to the art of strip-tease, practiced by "exotic dancers."

❧

Expansionism—the beliefs and practices of those who favor enlarge-ment of national territory or currency—pretty much a thing of the past, since it was inextricably connected with wars, exploration of the New World, and America's "manifest destiny" to extend its juris-diction from Maine to California. Under Pres. Theodore Roosevelt, the U.S. also dug the Panama Canal, conquered Puerto Rico, and planted its flag in the Philippines—all of which stemmed from the archaic belief that nations grew stronger by grabbing more land. Today, even the Soviets recognize that Expansionism is an expen-sive headache that diverts resources from the domestic population and upsets the geopolitical balance.

Miniature expansionist powers like Israel are driven to occupy ad-jacent lands because they fear the proximity of enemies—but today this is more an exception than a rule. It's a well-settled principle of international law that nations and states may not unilaterally move their borders, as Saddam Hussein attempted with his inva-sion of Kuwait in 1990.

Unfortunately, this is not the case with monetary policy. A na-tion can expand (inflate) its currency at will, which is the fastest and surest way to weaken one's position in the world. Perhaps there is some justice after all, since nations who pursue territorial Expan-sionism are almost always forced to resort to monetary Expansionism—which wrecks their credit and undercuts their ability to wage war.

ஒ

Experientialism—the doctrine that we derive all our knowledge from our experiences and that no knowledge is intuitive or genetically transmitted. Though an appealing doctrine, it fails to explain why babies possess certain behaviors and why twins often pursue simi-lar lifestyles even though they were raised by different parents in vastly different places.

ஒ

Experimentalism—1. the practice of or fondness for experimenta-tion. 2. in philosophy, the theory that experience is the origin and test of all knowledge (as opposed to Idealism or Rationalism), and therefore, empirical methods are the only proper way to determine the validity of an idea. See Empiricism.

ஒ

Expertism—demonstration of a high degree of skill or knowledge as the result of training or education.

ஒ

Expressionism—in art, a theory or practice of seeking to depict not the object as seen in reality, but the emotions and responses which objects and events arouse in the artist. The use of strong colors and distortion of form were typical, with Vincent Van Gogh (1853-1890) as a patron saint.

ஒ

Externalism—regard for or devotion to things that are outward or visible, especially in religious matters, where it connotes a superficial or dogmatic view rather than sincere belief.

୫

Extremism—a policy of radical behavior, unyielding commitment, or pursuit of an objective by all available means, far exceeding the accepted standard and thus perceived as excessive, especially in politics. Modern political consensus, compromise, and mediocrity were spawned by a cowardly refusal to debate fundamental change or basic principles. In defense of the status quo, anyone who holds a radical (i.e., non-mainstream) view is automatically condemned as an extremist. This practice results in condemnation of anyone who remains faithful to a creed. Libertarians, for instance, are just as unacceptable as Totalitarians, because both are "extremist." If you've ever wondered why Democrats and Republicans pursue almost identical policies and why both parties are supported by labor unions and corporations, now you know. "Extremism in the defense of liberty is no vice.... Moderation in the pursuit of justice is no virtue." (Barry Goldwater)

Fabianism—the policy of the Fabian Society of England, a late 19th-century socialist group which proposed to win by a long process of political education and indirect methods like sabotage. Such a strategy was first devised by Quintus Fabius Maximus (275-203 B.C.), a Roman general who fought Hannibal by declining to risk a battle in the open field but harassing his troops with marches and ambushes.

Factualism—devotion or adherence to fact. "Get your facts first, and then you can distort 'em as much as you please." (Mark Twain)

Faddism—the practice of whim, fancy, or hobby, adopted and pursued for a time with zeal; devotion to a passing fashion in dress, entertainment, beliefs, etc. The good news is, all fads fade. "Fashions are induced epidemics." (George Bernard Shaw)

Fairyism—the belief in fairies, imaginary beings usually represented as small, dainty humans capable of changing form at will and inclined to play sometimes malicious pranks. A variation of Demonism, popular in Britain in the late 1800's. Arthur Conan Doyle (1859-1930), author of the Sherlock Holmes stories, was especially vocal in preaching the existence of fairies, based on photographs submitted to him by two scheming teenagers who used paper cut-outs to simulate the appearance of ethereal spirits in a garden.

Familism—1. the subordination of individual interests to the desires of a family. 2. the tenets of the Familists, a religious sect in Holland in 1556 who taught that religion consists entirely of love, independent of truth. They lived in family groups, and their social system saw the family as a political and economic model.

❧

Fanaticism—excessive enthusiasm for a cause; wild and extravagant notions, especially about religion or politics. "A fanatic is one who can't change his mind and won't change the subject." (Winston Churchill)

❧

Fantastic Realism—an Austrian art craze in the 1940's which combined Surrealism with elements of Academism.

Faradism—1. the form of electricity produced by an induced current. 2. using such a current for medical therapy. Michael Faraday (1791-1867), an English physicist and chemist, described the laws governing the action of electric batteries and made the first electric generator. A *faraday* is a quantity of electricity which, when passed through an electrolyte, will liberate one gram of a substance. It's measured by a *faradmeter*. A *farad* is the basic unit of measuring the charge held by a capacitor. A *Faraday cage* is an electrified metal box used to isolate a subject from the laboratory environment. And for you die-hard Faraday fans: young Michael used to poke his head through a fence and challenge his chums to debate which side of the fence he was on. Reputedly, Faraday could take either side of the argument and win.

❧

Fascism—the principles, teachings, or government of the Fasciti, an Italian organization founded in Milan in 1919 by Benito Mussolini

(1883-1945) to suppress all other political movements in Italy. The Fascists exercised absolute control over Italian industry, commerce, and finance, advocated nationalist policies, imposed strict censorship, and suppressed dissent. Broadly, the fascist mentality is one which presumes to dispose of the lives and fortunes of others: "For Fascism, society is the end, individuals the means, and its whole life consists of using individuals for its social ends." (Alfredo Rocco) "Because Fascism is a lie, it is condemned to literary sterility. And when it is past, it will have no history, except the bloody history of murder." (Ernest Hemingway)

❧

Fatalism—the doctrine that all things are subject to unavoidable destiny or occur by inevitable necessity; a disposition to accept everything as predetermined and independent of human will. Victor Hugo's novel *Notre Dame de Paris* is a *tour de force* of Fatalism, in which all the major characters are doomed from page one. Most people agree that one's life builds toward an inevitable conclusion, since early choices restrict later possibilities, but pure fatalists insist you never have any choice at any time, not even in the smallest details of living. "What's laid is played." (Charlie Reitzner)

❧

Fauvism—an early-20th-century movement in painting marked by the use of bold, often distorted forms and vivid colors. From the word *fauve*, meaning wild. It gave way to Cubism after a few years.

❧

Favism—acute anemia caused by the ingestion of too much fava bean pollen.

❧

Favoritism—the disposition to aid and promote the interests of one person or one class of people to the neglect of others having equal claims.

❧

Febronianism—a doctrinal system in Roman Catholic theology which is antagonistic to the claims of the Pope and which asserts the independence of national churches and the rights of bishops to unrestricted action in their own dioceses. The author of the doctrine was Justinius Febronius, the *nome de plume* of John Nicholas von Hontheim, archbishop of Treves.

❧

Federalism—the principles of the Federalists, the name given to friends of the proposed U.S. Constitution during its framing and adoption (led by James Madison and Alexander Hamilton) and to the political party supporting George Washington. Federalism argued that a federal government should derive its power from its citizens and not from a compact among the states. A series of newspaper articles, collectively known as *The Federalist Papers*, published between 1787 and 1789, persuaded a majority of states to abandon the loosely organized Confederation under which they had fought the War of Independence and to adopt the new Constitution as drafted by 55 delegates to a secret convention in 1787, which was convened to propose relatively minor amendments to the Articles of Confederation.

Reasons advanced for adopting the new system, which dramatically reduced the autonomy of states and gave the national government broad powers, were 1. the need to adjudicate interstate disputes over Crown Lands, taxation, and Continental debt; 2. the need to strengthen the Union and resist European intrigues; 3. an alternative to potential civil war between Northern and Southern confederacies; and 4. economies and greater strength obtained from having one army instead of 13 separate militias. Moreover, Federalists promised that the national government would not encroach on existing state laws or revenue sources, since the Congress and President would be elected by the same constituencies who chose state officials.

The Federalists succeeded in establishing a new, improved Union, but they failed to keep their promises. In Pres. Washington's first term, they imposed heavy taxes on whisky and sent Federal troops to squash opposition to the tax collectors. Hamilton's plan to establish a national bank monopolized interstate finance and introduced the concept of "implied powers," which came to mean that the Feds could do damn near anything in pursuit of national policy. The First Amendment was nixed by the Alien and Sedition Acts, and within a few generations the U.S. fought a Civil War, despite the Constitution. Not a sterling track record.

However, the Federalists made lasting contribution to the history of Constitutionalism in two notable ways: 1. their advocacy of "checks and balances" among hot-headed legislators, autocratic leaders, and fossilized judges at the Federal level, and among myopic states who felt no compunction about bullying their neighbors, is still regarded as a cornerstone of Liberalism; and 2. the Chief Justice of the first U.S. Supreme Court, John Marshall, enunciated a doctrine of "judicial review" which still gives the courts a role in opposing the will of the people, based on interpretation of what Congress and the states can and cannot do in the context of their constitutional powers. This doctrine waxes and wanes according to the fortitude of the Court, but generally it put forward the notion that written constitutions do in fact mean something, and when it says "Congress shall make no law..." it means there are fixed limits to how much waste and cupidity the bureaucrats can get away with. Cf. Euro-Federalism.

೭ఊ

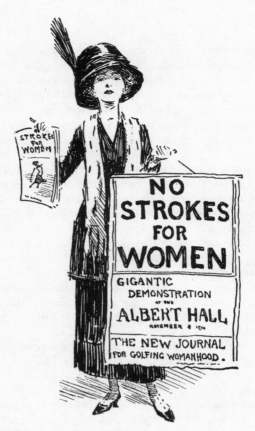

Feminism—1. a theory or movement of those who advocate the rights of women and favor abolishing social, economic, and political restrictions on the female sex. 2. a radical cult which asserts that women are superior to men, or that the sexes have so little in common that we would all be better off without intercourse—figuratively and literally. "People call me feminist whenever I express sentiments that differentiate me from a doormat or a prostitute." (Rebecca West)

❧

Fenianism—the policy of the Fenian Brotherhood, or Old Militia of Ireland, named after Finn (or Fionn), a hero of Irish tradition, and his group of warriors in the 2nd and 3rd centuries, and after Fene, the name of the ancient inhabitants of Ireland. Fenianism was reborn in the mid-19th century in New York City to overthrow British rule in Ireland.

❧

Ferromagnetism—the characteristics of ferrous substances, such as iron, nickel, cobalt, and various alloys, that exhibit the ability to acquire high magnetization in weak or non-existent magnetic fields, with a characteristic saturation point and with magnetic hysteresis. Ask a physicist.

❧

Fetishism—the adoration of fetishes, which are objects—animate or inanimate, natural or artificial—regarded with awe, as having mysterious powers, or as being the representative or habitation of a deity. Among primitives, a tribe may have a fetish in common, and an individual may have one of his own, to which he offers prayers and which, if the prayers are not heard, he punishes, throws away, or breaks. As an aspect of Eroticism, a sexual fetish is a body part, a situation, or articles of clothing that are precursors to arousal and bring profound gratification when contemplated, or which relate to abnormal obsessions. Apparently, many people have a foot fetish, and they often make the news soon after they get a job selling women's shoes. Also, Fetichism.

ॐ

Feudalism—a primitive political organization long in force throughout Europe and Asia, under which persons holding lands in "feud" or "fee" were bound to serve the monarch in all wars and military expeditions. Peasants who lived on the feudal estate were bound to the feeholder and owed their livelihood to his favor. By the rule of primogeniture, first-born sons inherited the father's title and lands; sisters or younger brothers got zilch.

Feudalism was a static legal system that permitted no upward mobility, except in rare cases where the monarch created a new "landed" title of nobility, thus giving a chunk of the dominion to a favored knight or warrior. Concurrent with the king-lord-peasant system of real estate management, Feudalism encouraged a system of craft guilds, wherein the trades (carpenter, bricklayer, etc.) were similarly monopolized by the right to inherit a job from one's father: sons of carpenters became carpenters, period. The practice still exists, to the extent that Nepotism allows family members to obtain jobs in a family business or labor union, but pure Feudalism forbade any career change or "upward mobility" of any kind, because property, employment, and taxation were permanently frozen by the laws of who begot whom.

The whole system was derived from the "Divine Right of Kings," which sprang from the notion that God intended some of us to be serfs and others to be kings, the latter having unlimited power over the former. See Serfism.

ॐ

Feuilletonism—1. the doctrine of a French religious order, an offshoot of the Bernadines, founded by Jean de la Barriere; so called from the convent of Feuillans, in Languedoc, where it was first established. 2. the practice of printing reviews, essays, fiction, etc.—"soft news"—in a certain section of the newspaper, called the feuilleton. In the case of *USA Today*, the whole thing is the feuilleton.

ॐ

Fhrumpfulism—morbid addiction to bakery (pies, cakes, strudels, etc.) and a major cause of being fat. Sufferers are incapable of visiting

Luxembourg without succumbing to the temptation to live entirely on *fhrumpfuls* and strong coffee. We know from experience.

Fifth Columnism—the practice of having an organized group of trai-
tors who, by subversive activities within an area, prepare the way
for an enemy invasion; used by Francisco Franco (1892-1975) in Spain,
who predicted he would conquer Madrid with his four armed
columns and a "fifth column" of conspirators within the city. Prior
to World War II, the German-American Bund was considered a dangerous organization in America, because they paraded in Nazi uni-
forms and preached the wisdom of Hitler's leadership. And during
the war, similar fears and a wave of racist hysteria caused officials
to round-up and imprison Japanese-Americans in "internment
camps."

Filibusterism—the methods or practices of a filibuster, a tactic to defeat
or delay legislation with frivolous questions of order, motions to
adjourn, or simply by holding the floor in a debate, especially in
the U.S. Senate. Employed by the minority to weary the opposition or gain time. Admirably depicted in the film *Mr. Smith Goes
to Washington*, when Jimmy Stewart decides to take on the corrupt
majority.

Fissiparism—a mode of reproduction in certain animals and vegetables that break spontaneously into minute portions, each having
a separate existence and growth.

Flagellantism—the belief that to whip oneself is valid religious discipline and a proper display of religious zeal. It arose from a fanatical sect in Italy, circa 1260, which maintained that flagellation was
of equal value with Baptism and other sacraments. The flagellants
walked in procession, shoulders bare, and whipped themselves until they bled. In the 20th century, this conduct remains part of the
Shi'ite Muslim discipline. See Masochism.

Flapperism—the speech, attitudes, and actions characteristic of a flapper, one of those bobbed young women of the Jazz Age who lived free of traditional social constraints and generally had fun.

ॐ

Floccinaucinihilipilificationism—the practice of habitually estimating things as worthless. The word recently gained fame when Sen. Daniel Patrick Moynihan, in an attempt to coin the longest word in the English dictionary, repeatedly used it in the Senate. But he's not even close, as the *Oxford English Dictionary* lists a 45-letter word describing a lung disease. Perhaps the Senator will be satisfied with gaining an entry in *ISMs?*

ॐ

Fletcherism—the practice of chewing food into a liquified mass before swallowing, advocated by nutritionist Horace Fletcher (1849-1919). I don't need a nutritionist to tell me how to chew my food—my mother already does that. Nutritionists do seem to have a wide streak of Paternalism: A nutritionist named S. Graham (1794-1851) invented the graham cracker because he believed bland snack foods would prevent boys from masturbating. Kellogg created corn flakes for the same reason. Saltines were probably invented to make you wash behind your ears.

ॐ

Flunkyism—1. a belief in the usefulness of being surrounded by servile followers who do menial tasks. 2. the characteristics of a flunky, such as a disposition to cringe to superiors and obsequiousness. It perhaps comes from the French word *flanquer*, which means to flank or run alongside. See Toadyism.

ॐ

Fluxisism—an international art movement founded in 1962 to resurrect Dadaism.

ॐ

Fogeyism—1. the policy of maintaining old-fashioned, conservative habits and outlooks. 2. the beliefs and practices of a person not abreast of the times, usually called an "old fogey." Also, Fogyism.

ॐ

Foreignism—the state of being foreign; any foreign custom, characteristic, or peculiarity, as in dress, speech, or language. Foreigners are people not born in the country in which they reside.

ॐ

Formalism—1. the quality of being formal, especially in matters of religion. A formalist is one who punctiliously observes forms or practices external ceremonies. 2. in religion, one who observes the trappings of religious worship without feeling its deeper spirit. 3. in ethics, the concept that acts are right or wrong *per se*, and consequences do not effect their morality. (That is, good ends do not justify bad means.)

≥●

Formulism—the practice of following procedures, rules, or principles articulated in a book of forms, as in oaths, declarations, prayers, etc. Often considered derogatory, since one who relies on Formulism lacks imagination.

≥●

Fortuitism—the doctrine or belief that natural adaptations occur by chance and not by design.

≥●

Fossilism—1. the organized study of animals or plants of a former epoch. 2. the condition of being a fossil and the process of becoming one. See Fogeyism.

≥●

Fourierism—the political and economic system of F. M. C. Fourier (1772-1837), a Frenchman who recommended the reorganization of society into small, self-sustaining, socialist communities. No relation to French mathematician J. B. J. Fourier (1768-1830), whose "Fourier transform" function is the basis of trigonometry and whose "Fourier transform plane" is the spot where all the rays gathered by a lens are infinitely converged. Just goes to show that you can't judge a political philosophy by its surname.

≥●

Fraternalism—the state or quality of being a brother or brotherly; the practices of fraternal societies, in which members are organized for mutual benefit, social intercourse, and silly rituals. Adult fraternities like the Kiwanis Club offer members business connections, community charities, and tedious luncheons. In college fraternities, rituals often involve beer-chugging contests, community charities, and gang rape.

Freemasonism—the doctrines of the secret fraternity called Freemasons (or Free and Accepted Masons) and all the mysteries connected therewith. According to its public statements, the order is founded on the practice of social and moral virtue and claims the character of charity in the most extended sense, with brotherly love, relief, and truth as principal tenets. George Washington and his cronies were all Freemasons, and it is still believed that Freemasons unduly influence many, if not all, business and political relationships in the Western hemisphere. A parallel group, Eastern Star, gives the wives something to do while the boys are being virtuous at the Masonic Temple.

એ

Freudianism—investigation or study of the causes of mental phenomena based on theories of Sigmund Freud (1856-1939), a Viennese psychologist, especially in regard to the causes and treatment of hysteria and other psychopathic manifestations, based on the interpretation of dreams and a theory of psychology which explains all human behavior in terms of sex impulses and the unconscious mind. Freud's patients were almost exclusively women who had ample reason to fear the repressive, male-dominated society in which they lived. In his spare time, Freud busied himself with cocaine addiction. His nose underwent three operations to repair the damage. "I have found little that is good about human beings. In my experience most of them are trash." (Freud)

એ

Frivolism—behavior that is trivial or trifling; an unbecoming levity of mind or disposition.

એ

Froebelism—a system of kindergarten education outlined by Friedrich Froebel (1782-1852), who thought kids would be better prepared for the rigors of school if they were encouraged to play games and be involved in constructive projects. Naturally, he was denounced by most pedagogues, but "pre-schools" and such today have vindicated his ideas. I remember kindergarten clearly as an important step in learning how to go to school—it was so effective that it took me 10 years to realize I disliked being taught. This is indeed a remarkable achievement: to convince so many of so much by offering graham crackers, juice, and a midday nap.

એ

Functionalism—1. in architecture and design, the doctrine that the function of a building or object should determine its design and materials, stressing purpose, practicality, and utility and reducing or eliminating purely decorative effects. 2. in psychology, the doctrine that emphasizes mental and behavioral adaptability.

એ

Fundamentalism—the belief that the basic claims of the Bible are fundamental to Christianity, that the miracles recorded therein are described without error, and especially that the Virgin Birth, Christ's Resurrection, His atonement for mankind, and His imminent return must not be doubted. The recent fundamentalist movement in the American Protestant church probably has grown in reaction to "modern" Christians who find it embarrassing to insist on literal interpretation of Biblical stories. Fundamentalists spend a lot of time decrying anything they don't like in American society as being due to the influence of Satan and attacking anything resembling rational thought as Secular Humanism. The word "fundament," by the way, means "buttocks." Cf. Islamic Fundamentalism and see Biblicism.

ᥱ᎐

Fusionism—1. in politics, the advocacy of coalitions for the purpose of election. The term was employed recently in Britain when Dr. David Owen achieved the fusion of the Social Democrats with their rivals in the Liberal Party. The resulting constituency promptly ousted Dr. Owen.

2. in physics, fusion describes the process of lighter elements combining to form heavier ones, with tremendous energy released as a by-product. Billions have been spent to develop technology to control atomic fusion and harness the process for power generation, more or less in emulation of the Sun, which produces enough fusion energy to fry an egg on a Dallas sidewalk in July from 93 million miles away.

At present, the only earthly application of fusion is the hydrogen bomb, which has limited prospects for industrial or commercial use. From time to time, some bright spark at the Department of Energy proposes to dig a canal or tunnel with hydrogen bombs, but these proposals are routinely shelved for obvious reasons. A recent scientific tempest involved a claim of "cold fusion," which basically asserted that the Sun was hot for no good reason.

ᥱ᎐

Futilitarianism—the belief in the hopelessness and vanity of human life and endeavor, in the futility of everything; the opposite of Optimism. "We learn from experience that men never learn anything from experience." (George Bernard Shaw)

ᥱ᎐

Futurism—1. an artistic movement originating in Italy around 1910, marked by an attempt to depict vividly the energetic and dynamic quality of contemporary life, especially by the motion and force of modern machinery. Cf. Social Realism. 2. the prediction of or conviction in the merits of future technology, believed to be a necessary or sufficient cure for today's problems. Since futurists rarely consider human cupidity and vice (which will persist, no matter how fancy our toasters get), they have a lot in common with advocates of Dialectical Materialism.

Galenism—the doctrines of Claudius Galenus (130-200 A.D.), a physician and medical writer, relating to his principles and methods of treating diseases. Galenic remedies consisted of preparation of herbs and roots by infusion, decoction, etc., which makes him the patron saint of snake oil vendors.

❧

Gallicanism—a movement originating among the French Roman Catholic clergy that favored restrictions of papal control and the achievement by each nation of individual administrative autonomy. Cf. Ultramontanism.

❧

Gallicism—a French phase or idiom appearing in another language, such as *savior-faire* and *c'est la vie*.

❧

Galvanism—1. electricity arising from chemical action, especially from the decomposition of metals. 2. in medicine, treatment by electricity generated from a Galvanic cell or battery. 3. a process for rustproofing steel by electroplating the surface with zinc. Named for Luiggi Galvani (1737-1798), professor of anatomy at Bologna. As an idiom, to "galvanize" is to stimulate or shock a person into accepting a proposition or commitment.

❧

Galvanotropism—in biology, the disposition exhibited by an Organism (especially plants) to grow toward or away from an electric current. Also, Electrotropism.

❧

Gangsterism—the moral philosophy of mobs, drug addicts, social out-
casts, cowards, and fools who believe that violence is a practical alternative to reason. If people cannot grasp the concept of trade (giving
value for value), "there is no way to determine the justice of anyone's claims, desires, or interests... One's wishes are limited only by
the power of one's gang" (Ayn Rand). Gangsters have nothing to
trade but death. They recognize no power greater than a fist or a
gun or a jail, and when confronted by a person of reason, their first
impulse is to take him hostage.

Gangsterism continues to be a serious problem in Sicily, Moscow,
Hong Kong, Glasgow, and many American cities. However, it's the
quasi-Gangsterism of political parties that's more dangerous, for two
reasons: 1. political gang warfare results in a legal victory, giving state
power to the winning gang; and 2. such victories, by their example,
teach the ignorant and weak to forget reason and human rights and
join gangs. Cf. Democratism.

Gargoylism—a medical term describing a person with grotesque con-
genital deformities, often accompanied by Dwarfism.

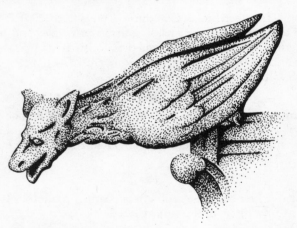

Garibaldianism—the policies of Giuseppe Garibaldi (1807-1882), Italian
patriot, who worked to effect the unity and independence of Italy.

Gaullism—the political movement led by General Charles de Gaulle
(1890-1970) and supporting him as the rightful leader of the French
government in exile during World War II and of the Republic of
France, which he ruled after the war. Also, De Gaullism. "No country
without an atomic bomb could properly consider itself independent." (de Gaulle)

Generationism—see Traducianism.

Genevanism—synonym for Calvinism, from John Calvin's residence in Geneva.

જ

Genteelism—a delicate or more polite word or phrase that substitutes for a cruder term; a Euphemism. For example, "full-figured woman" is a Genteelism for a woman with large breasts.

જ

Gentilism—the state of being not Jewish; in Scripture, a pagan, a worshipper of false gods; Heathenism. Among Mormons, a Gentile is a person neither Jewish nor Mormon. In Judaism, it refers to all non-Jews (and especially to Christians).

જ

Geocentrism—the belief that the earth is the center of the universe and that the Sun and planets revolve around it.

જ

Geomagnetism—the Magnetism of the earth and its magnetic field.

જ

Geomalism—in biology, a tendency toward equal lateral development because of gravity. It explains why you have arms on both sides of your body, for instance.

જ

Geophagism—the practice of eating clay, chalk, or other earth. Every few years, some Yankee reporter stumbles across the handful of people in rural Mississippi who practice Geophagism, writes a big story in the *New York Times* about them, and perpetuates the myth that all Southerners eat dirt.

જ

Geotropism—a power or tendency of plants to grow downward or toward the earth because of gravity.

જ

Germanism—an idiom of the German language; an expression derived from or like the German; a German mode of thought or action; a devotion to Germany and things German. "German: A good fellow maybe, but it is better to hang him." (Russian proverb)

જ

Giantism—the condition of being a person or thing of extraordinary size or importance. In mythology, the Gigantes were a race of manlike beings with enormous strength and stature who warred with the Olympians. In medicine, the condition is probably caused by an excess of growth hormone during fetal development. Also, Gigantism.

જ

Gladiatorism—the act or practice of gladiators, a class of men in ancient Rome who fought in public armed with deadly weapons, usually in pairs. An audience vote determined the fate of the loser (usually death). The modern sports of wrestling, boxing, and movie Criticism by pairs of obnoxious opponents appear to be its legacy.

ঽ৯

Global Do-Goodism—epithet hurled by American conservatives to mock the Peace Corps during the 1960's, especially during the Johnson Administration. Cf. Cultural Imperialism.

෨

Globalism—a recently coined term that evokes the concept of thinking in terms of the entire planet rather than a narrow region. Usually paired with Environmentalism and often in the context of chastising a nation for wasting natural resources or polluting the planet. In politics, Globalism refers to the promotion of world-wide cooperation instead of Parochialism and Nationalism.

෨

Gnosticism—an eclectic system of philosophy and religion that flourished during the first six centuries A.D. Trying to mediate between Christianity and Paganism, Gnostics taught that knowledge, more than philosophy and faith, was the means of salvation. According to their doctrine, all existence—spiritual and material—originated in the deity by successive emanations, called "eons." Christ was said to be a higher eon than vegetables, for instance. The system combined features of Orientalism, Platonism, Dualism, and Christianity and maintained the central theme of man's ability to know something about God, rather than relying totally on revelations or faith. In opposition, there's Agnosticism, which doubts any ability to know God.

෨

Goldwynism—An unintentionally funny remark attributed to Hollywood studio boss Samuel Goldwyn (1882-1974), of Metro-Goldwyn-Mayer (MGM). Some examples: "A verbal contract isn't worth the paper it's printed on." "In two words: Im-possible!" "Anybody who sees a psychiatrist ought to have his head examined." "If Roosevelt were alive, he'd turn in his grave." And our favorite: "I'm sick of all these old clichés—get me some new ones!"

෨

Gongorism—an imitation of the intricate, affected writing style which characterized the work of the Spanish poet Luis de Gongora y Argote (1561-1627).

෨

Gothicism—1. rudeness of manners; Barbarism; darkness. 2. in architecture, the term denotes the styles of pointed towers prevalent in Western Europe from the mid-12th century to the mid-16th. Chief characteristics include the predominance of the pointed arch, the prolongation of vertical lines, the absence of columns and rectangular surfaces, and the substitution of clustered shafts and contrasted surfaces. The style originates from the Goths, an ancient tribe from the Baltic that overran the Roman Empire. Therefore, "gothic" refers to barbarians lacking culture and taste, especially in literature—from which we get the "gothic novel," filled with damsels in distress and malicious hobgoblins.

෨

Gradualism—1. the belief in or policy of advancing toward a goal by gradual, often slow, stages. 2. in philosophy, the theory that conflicting concepts are not insoluble but can be related by other concepts which contain parts of the opposing concepts.

Grangerism—the practice of using illustrations taken from a number of books to illustrate a work; the mutilation of a book or books to get illustrations to create another book. Named after James Granger (1723-1776), the author of *Biographical History of England*, illustrated with this method. The book you're holding, which contains a number of charming drawings cut from books from Dover Publications, is an example of Grangerism. Convenient, eh?

Grecism—1. an idiom of the Greek language. 2. in architecture, a style evoking the architecture of Greece from 500 B.C. to the Roman conquest. See Hellenism.

Greenbackism—the policy of a U.S. political party organized in 1874, advocating the use of inconvertible paper money called "greenbacks" because they were printed in green ink. They were first issued by the Federal Government in 1862 to finance the Civil War. Greenback Party members demanded that the notes constitute the only legal currency, because they had bushels of them and they resented the influence of Eastern bankers who still traded in gold. See also Bimetallism, which sprang up at the same time. If you become curious about U.S. history and the fate of the modern world, this is an excellent topic for further research, since the Greenbacks finally won. To prove it, check your wallet.

Groin Terrorism—bizarre accusation made by Detroit news anchor Bill Bonds, who claimed homosexuals were deliberately trying to spread AIDS through "zipper warfare" and "Groin Terrorism." As deplorable as this is, there is further insanity to consider: Mr. Bonds is still on the air in Detroit, and his show is twice as popular as the competition. Yipes.

Grumpism—term used by Norman Macrae to describe the prescient Realism of "grown-up mature people" (i.e., Grumpies), who predicted that the monetary boom of the 1980's was destined to bust because it was based on numerous flawed economic notions. He was particularly critical of Margaret Thatcher's massive increase of public

spending (for health care, education, and defense) while simultaneously reducing taxation. The only problem with Grumpies is that
no one will listen to them. Unlike socialists, conservatives, liberals,
and moderates, Grumpies have nothing to offer except the hard
fact of life: There is no free lunch.

Grundyism—prudish, extremely conventional behavior. Named for
the character Mrs. Grundy in the play *Speed the Plough* by Thomas
Morton (1764-1838). "The tyranny of Mrs. Grundy is worse than
any other tyranny we suffer under." (Herbert Spencer)

Guerrillaism—the principles and practices of fighting as guerrillas,
harassing the enemy with small, strategic raids and strikes at vital
points instead of wide-scale warfare.

Guild Socialism—an English socialist doctrine of the early 20th century in which industry was to be owned by the state but managed
by councils of workers; derived from the feudal system of craft guilds
which held a legal monopoly on certain trades and controlled the
process of apprenticeship. See Feudalism. "It represents an open em-
bodiment of the basic motive of most statists...: the entrenchment
and protection of mediocrity from abler competitors, the shackling
of the men of superior ability down to the mean average." (Ayn Rand)

Gutturalism—a manner of speaking in which sounds are produced
in the throat as opposed to the front of the mouth, giving a characteristic tone to certain languages like Dutch, German, and Scottish. One of the prime objectives in learning to speak Dutch, for
instance, is to avoid spitting on others when pronouncing their "g."

Gymnosophism—the supposed practices of Indian monks, as described by some confused early Christian writers. The term is Greek for "naked sages." Actually, only the ascetic Jains practiced Nudism, while Buddhists wore those fetching saffron robes. (Tragically, whether they wore anything *under* their robes is lost to history.) Clement of Alexandria (150-215 A.D.) went on and on about these guys, but he got it mostly wrong—part of a long tradition of Western scholars misunderstanding Indian religion. See Hinduism, Buddhism, Jainism.

છે.

Gymnospermism—in botany, the traits of a plant with exposed seeds, like a conifer.

છે.

Gynandromorphism—in entomology, the condition of having one side male and the other side female. In the Linnean system of botany, a class of plants whose stamen and pistil are consolidated into a single body.

છે.

Gynomonoecism—in botany, the traits of a plant with both pistillate and monoclinous flowers.

છે.

Gypsyism—any or all of the characteristics of gypsy life, including wandering, cajolery, thievery, etc. Gypsies, a vagabond race found throughout the world, live as nomadic tinkers, traders, fortune tellers, etc. Ethnologists believe they descended from an obscure Hindu tribe. Their langauge, which they call Romany Chiv, is a Hindu dialect related to Sanskrit but corrupted with the languages of the lands in which they have lived. Thus, in the vocabulary of Anglo-Scottish Gypsies, there are Greek, Slavic, Romanian, Maygar, German, and French ingredients—a rich testament to their migratory ways.

Haeckelism—the theories of Ernst Haeckel (1834-1919), German scientist and philosopher; particularly his theory that the life history of the species is recapitulated in the development of the individual: "ontogeny recapitulates phylogeny." See Hegelianism.

Hahnemannism—of or relating to Samuel C.F. Hahnemann (1755-1843), the German physician who founded homeopathy, the doctrine or theory of curing diseases with minute doses of medicine, which in a healthy person would produce a condition like that of the disease being treated.

Hamiltonianism—the political and economic policies of Alexander Hamilton (1757-1804), George Washington's *aide de camp* during the American Revolution and subsequently a leader of the Federalist Party. Though eager to create a monarchy or aristocracy similar to the British system, Hamilton devoted most of his life to strengthening the new Federal Union established by the Constitution of 1787, written partly at his instigation. See Federalism.

Hamiltonism—a system of mathematical functions used to generate the equations of motion of a dynamic system. Named after Irish mathematician William Hamilton (1805-1865).

Hasidism—see Chasidism.

Heathenism—1. the worship of something tangible (sun, moon, fire, etc.), as in Paganism. 2. the rites, beliefs, or religion of a heathen nation, especially those who rejected Christianity. The term originates from the Old English *haeth*, meaning a wild and desolate country, and can be applied to all manner of idolatry and Barbarism.

૨૦

Heautomorphism—same as Automorphism.

૨૦

Hebraism—1. an idiom or manner of speech in the Hebrew language. 2. characteristics or principles of the Hebrew people. See Semitism.

૨૦

Hectorism—the disposition or practice of one who scolds, torments, or monitors others (a hector). The word is derived from Hector, a Trojan War hero and a bully who treated everyone with insolence.

૨૦

Hedonism—the philosophy of the Cyrenaics and the noted Greek philosopher Aristippus (435-356 B.C.), who taught that pleasure was the only conceivable object in life and therefore the highest good. Somewhat modified by Jeremy Bentham and called Utilitarianism. Roundly condemned by most religions, which view pleasure as sinful. See also Objectivism.

Hegelianism—a system of logic and philosophy introduced by Georg Wilhelm Friedrich Hegel (1770-1831) and quite difficult to summarize, since it begins with the notion that nothing exists and concludes with praise for a "World Historical Individual" whose actions are compelled by idealistic Mechanisms beyond his control and whose duty is to advance the German race. Not coincidentally, Hegel was hired to lecture the Prussian military. Since Hegel's works are mostly gibberish, we would do better to examine his influence on subsequent philosophers:

"An individual, with all his drives and powers, is nothing but the raw material of the World Spirit, which grasps him with an all-consuming historical passion. Thus the abstract Spirit acquires concrete power of actualization. The individual as raw material for the historical efficacy of the World Spirit is primarily power, the motor force of history, whose direction is prescribed by the Spirit. The Hegelian hero is completely guided by the World Spirit, and the World Spirit uses him, cunningly, for its own ends." (Hartmann) We hope that clears things up.

Hegel argued that a proposition ("thesis") must be opposed by a direct contradiction ("antithesis"). Truth comes from the reconciliation by a third proposition derived from the first two ("synthesis"). This basic premise is largely responsible for modern Activism, which proceeds from the notion that you may scream for anything no matter how outrageous, and the result will be a compromise of what exists with what you think ought to be. Thus, environmental activists demand paper without cutting trees; social activists describe "justice" without property rights; and spoiled children want results without effort. Tacit agreement with Hegel has disarmed most of their victims, since we are inculcated to "see both sides" of any dispute and presume that all claims are equally valid, since reality is unknowable.

The basic issue is whether we are capable of perceiving and proving an absolute, immutable truth. As a disciple of Immanuel Kant, Hegel was quick to say "no," thus claiming to possess the absolute truth that there was no such thing as absolute truth.

Among other, less-respectable achievements, the Hegelian philosophy is credited with inspiring Hitler and Marx, who "stood Hegel on his head" by claiming that ideas do not exist and that everything we believe is determined by Historical Materialism.

છ

Heightism—a term used to accuse a person or group who discriminates against short people, especially in employment practices. From the "politically correct" lingo in vogue on U.S. college campuses. If they ever re-make *The Wizard of Oz*, the Munchkins will probably file a class-action suit against the Wicked Witch alleging Heightism. It would be more lucrative than melting her.

છ

Heliotropism—disposition to turn toward light, especially the characteristic of a plant to grow toward the sun or toward light.

છ

Helleborism—the medicinal use of the herb hellebore, practiced by the ancients. The powdered root of the white hellebore was used to destroy insects on plants. Used on humans, it's intended to bring you to your senses. You'll need it if you study enough Isms.

છ

Hellenism—1. an idiom of the Greek language. 2. the tendency toward intellectual and physical perfection and the love of the beautiful—

all traits of the ancient Greeks. The Hellenistic period was the era between the Hellenic and Greco-Roman periods, noted for the decadence of Greek art and literature. See Classicism, Grecism.

Helotism—slavery, serfdom; from the condition of the enslaved Helots in ancient Laconia. In a classic Frank Capra movie, the term was used to condemn Consumerism: "Who are the Helots? Why, they're a lot of heels!"

Hemimetabolism—in zoology, the condition of insects undergoing an incomplete metamorphosis. In other words, the caterpillar doesn't make it to butterfly.

Hemimorphism—the condition of a crystal with an asymmetrical center.

Henotheism—belief in or worship of one god without denying the existence of other gods, a doctrine of religions that attribute supreme power to one of several divinities in turn: the Greeks had Zeus et al., the Vikings had Odin et al., and so on. Read the Bible carefully and you'll notice that the Judeo-Christian tradition is more accurately henotheistic than monotheistic. God describes Himself as a "jealous" god, and in the First Commandment, He does not declare Himself unique, merely supreme: "Thou shalt have no other gods before me."

Herbalism—the knowledge and employment of herbs, especially for medicinal uses. The Chinese are world leaders in this "science," exerting powerful demand for rhinocerous horn, said to be an aphrodisiac.

Hermaphroditism—in biology, the state of partial or complete development of male and female sexual organs in a single individual (a hermaphrodite). Named for Hermaphroditos, in Greek legend the son of Hermes and Aphrodite, who became united with the nymph Salmacis. In one of every 5,000-7,000 babies, there is considerable doubt as to the infant's sex, since the genitalia is either indistinct or abnormal. When these people grow up, they usually choose a gender and undergo surgery. Hermaphroditism is not related to Transsexualism or Transvestitism, which refer primarily to psychological rather than biological conditions. Also, Hermaphrodism.

ༀ

Hermitism—the practice of people who retire from society and live in solitude, mainly for religious meditation and devotion.

ༀ

Heroinism—heroin addiction. A white, crystalline, bitter powder, heroin was originally refined from opium as a pain killer but became popular as a "recreational" drug, to which many are addicted.

ༀ

Heroism—the actions or qualities of a hero: bravery, courage, intrepidity, etc. In classical mythology, a hero was a demi-god born of the union of a god and a human, regarded as mortal but partaking of immortality, and placed among the gods after death. In literature, the hero is a character who must undergo ordeals or adventures of uncertain outcome to win a coveted possession or gain knowledge. Broadly, a role model worthy of admiration and emulation ("hero worship") or a socially approved act of bravery, such as rescuing someone from a burning building. Medals are bestowed for Heroism on the battlefield, though rarely for intellectual independence and integrity, which are the true hallmarks of Heroism. "A hero is no braver than an ordinary man, but he is brave five minutes longer." (Ralph Waldo Emerson)

ༀ

Hetaerism—1. the practice of a courtesan, concubine, or female paramour (in ancient Greece, a *hetaera*). 2. the condition in primitive societies when the women were considered common property; open concubinage. Also, Hetairism.

ༀ

Heteroecism—in botany, a condition characterized by a different state of development occurring in a parasitic Organism (especially fungi) as it changes from one body to another, as in the rust of wheat, oats, and other cultivated grasses.

ༀ

Heterogonism—1. the quality or state of spontaneous generation, or abiogenesis. 2. a condition in which the parent produces offspring differing in structure and habit from itself, but in which after one or more generations the original form reappears.

ༀ

Heteromorphism—in entomology, the quality or state of deviating from the standard or normal form, or existing under different forms at different stages of development.

≈

Heterosexism—according to a printed list of "Manifestations of Oppression" at Smith College, it's "oppression of those of sexual orientations other than heterosexual...; this can take place by not acknowledging their existence." Part of the "politically correct" lingo, Heterosexism is an accusation hurled at someone who allegedly discriminates against homosexuals or bisexuals, especially in employment practices. Often, though, it's used as a "Thought Police" tactic to pillory anyone who expresses personal distaste for homosexual practices.

≈

Hibernianism—1. pertaining to Hibernia (now Ireland), or to the Irish people. 2. an idiom of Irish English, such as "faith and begorra." (Also, Hibernicism, Irishism.)

≈

Hierarchism—dominion or authority organized by a system of rank (a hierarchy); hierarchical principles or power. In religion, a body of people who control the government of a church and the administration of sacred things, or a rank of sacred beings (angels, archangels, saints, etc). In psychology, the theory that humans have a hierarchical order of needs and aspirations (survival, family, education, honor), which proceed from the simplest and least intellectual to the highest and most abstract, and that pursuit of abstract values cannot arise in those still struggling for food and shelter.

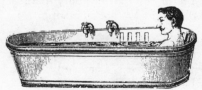

Higher Criticism—critical study of Biblical texts with regard to questions of their character, composition, editing, and collection. Cf. Lower Criticism.

≈

Hindu Fundamentalism—a radical religious movement in India which seeks absolute control of the state and, if successful, would result in severe persecution of Muslims, Sikhs, Tamils, and anyone else who does not worship the Hindu pantheon.

≈

Hinduism—any of various forms of modified Brahmanism with additions of Buddhism and other religious and philosophic ideas, characterized by a belief in reincarnation, in a supreme being of many forms, in the view that opposing theories are aspects of one eternal truth, and in a desire for liberation from earthly evils. Hinduism, the religion of about three-fourths of the population of India, is also practiced on Bali.

No Indian religion ever called itself Hinduism; Westerners coined the term to describe an immense spectrum of belief that covers the Polytheism, Dualism, Monotheism, sacrificial cults, and magical rites performed by the people of the Indus Valley. In fact, "Hindu" is the Persian word for the Indus River and also refers to the land though which it flows. When Darius I of Persia conquered and extended his empire to the banks of the Indus, the Hindus were the people who inhabited the area. "Hinduism is nothing but an orchid cultivated by European scholarship. It is much too beautiful to uproot, but it's a test-tube plant not found in nature." (Heinrich von Stietencron)

≈

Hippie-ism—never actually an Ism, as far as we know, but it was a philosophy and a political movement that deeply affected American history, and we were there to witness it. Of course, there's the old line "If you remember the '60s, you weren't there" —meaning that most hippies were stoned most of the decade, which isn't far from the mark.

The immediate precursor to Hippie-ism was the Beat Generation: jazz-oriented, coffee-drinking poets of the bongo variety, allergic to daylight, employment, religion, and responsibility. Everything was "like, cool, man." In the 1950's, this was revolutionary, since most people were thinking linoleum and liking Ike. But Beatniks were the first to feel the consequences of Hiroshima and the nuclear age and "drop out" of society in protest. Existentialism began to make sense, because the concept of "tomorrow" had been drastically compromised.

The 1963 assassination of Pres. John Kennedy also killed a happy, youthful, hopeful mini-era. The Vietnam war heated up, the South exploded with racial conflict, women demanded status higher than chattel, and the Beatles crossed the pond to explain it all: "All you need is love." Hippie-ism was born.

In hindsight, of course, we looked pretty silly. Love beads, incense and peppermints, bell-bottoms and Flower Power. It came so fast, and it was so unlike our lobotomized elders, that it seemed sane and safe. No more war. Love your brothers and sisters. Tune in, turn on, drop out. Power to the people.

There were three hot-spots: Berkeley, California, which gave Hippie-ism its politics (mostly Marxist re-treads with anarchist racing stripes); London, which submitted the proposition that wildness is a fundamental human right; and a chemistry lab somewhere (the Rockies? M.I.T.?), which supplied millions of doses of LSD—which was not particularly helpful, since it gave us notions of Heroism way out of proportion. We really thought it would be easy to dismantle everything hateful in America: Republicans, the CIA, Dow Chemical, the phone company, etc. Why the phone company was universally despised is a mystery. Maybe because it was so smug: they had just invented the transistor, and the Plastic Smile and touch tone dialing was being introduced all over the country.

Yes, of course, it was the Plastic Smile that united hippies and made us livid. In the midst of Vietnam, Mick Jagger, the Pill, and race riots, the "straights" were deaf to reason and were learning to say "Have a nice day." Cops were smashing our skulls, but shopkeepers and secretaries kept trudging to their jobs like zombies. It was weird, Kafkaesque, horrible. Singer Pat Boone held a special, macabre fascination: he never frowned, he believed in God, and he was intensely creepy. We figured he was a Nazi or a robot.

It was over by 1974. Who can sustain a revolution when the anthems have a disco beat?

The high point of Hippie-ism was the unparalleled celebration at Woodstock, New York in 1969. It was messy, disorganized, unforgettable. Offhand, we can't think of any other time in history when 300,000 young adults lived together in the open and celebrated their vitality. There was no purpose, no agenda, no flags, no flagwavers. (These are just facts; we're not glamorizing Hippie-ism. It was not glamorous.) It was an innocent statement of hope that, for today, for now, for as long as we could get away with it, it was good to be alive. Many left Woodstock to report for active duty. Many left and had to cut their hair for work. But none left without wishing it could be like that every day, forever and for everyone.

Hippies were not great geniuses or innovators. But we numbered in the millions, and we remember with pride being young and free.

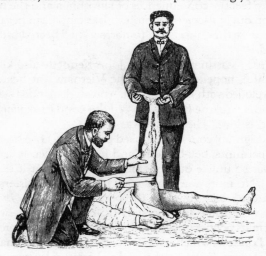

Hippocratism—the doctrine or system of Hippocrates (460-377 B.C.), Greek physician, relating to medical practice. The Hippocratic Oath pledges a physician to prolong life and to "do no harm"—a creed sworn by all young doctors of the time. It is still regarded as a basis for medical ethics, though doctors today are equally concerned with the legal aspects of malpractice and "100% diagnosis," which has discouraged them from specializing in obstetrics and neurosurgery.

ॐ

Hippophagism—the act or practice of eating horseflesh. "Nothing does as much for the insides of a man than the outsides of a horse." (Ronald Reagan)

Hirsutism—excessive hairiness, used most often to describe an unusual condition in women caused by a hormonal imbalance. Women often suffer from unwanted hair growth as a side-effect of cancer treatments involving big doses of testosterone. Also, anorexia often prompts the growth of heavy body hair, as the body attempts to insulate itself in the face of massive loss of fatty tissue. See Virilism.

ॐ

Hispanicism—an idiom or mode of speech peculiar to the Spanish, Portuguese, or Latin American tongue.

ॐ

Hispanism—1. a movement in Latin America promoting Spanish culture. 2. a term or feature characteristic of Spain.

ॐ

Historical Materialism—a major tenet in Marxism which regards material economic forces as the base upon which socio-political institutions and ideas are built. Marx thought ideas (good and evil, true and false) were derived from economic relationships, which in turn were merely aspects of historical progress, from agriculture and handicrafts to large-scale industries and mechanization:

"In the social production which men carry on, they enter into definite relations that are independent of their will; these relations of production correspond to a definite stage of development of their material powers of production. The mode of production in material life determines the general character of the social, political, and spiritual processes of life. It is not the consciousness of men that determines their existence, but, on the contrary, their social existence determines their consciousness." (Karl Marx, *Critique of Political Economy*)

By itself, the theory was fairly harmless, perhaps a clever reiteration of Determinism, which holds that our behavior is governed by forces beyond our control. Hardly a revolutionary idea. But Marx also believed that material progress would lead to the impoverishment of the working class, and thus proclaimed that their only chance for survival was to seize political power and take over the means of production.

For the record, note that Marx was full of beans. Where private enterprise and Capitalism exist, wages and opportunities for "proletarians" shoot skyward, primarily because competition and mechanization keeps lowering the price of stuff. He also goofed in predicting that seizing the means of production would result in the transformation or "withering away" of the state. Where a "Dictatorship of the Proletariat" has been implemented, the masses got exactly what they bargained for: a dictatorship ruled by mobs of easily deceived peasants and workers. (See Communism.)

That all of this sprang from a half-baked theory of history is tragic. Indeed, Marx conquered two-thirds of the world with nothing more than a contradiction: he asserted that history generates explicit economic forces which impel the downtrodden to revolt, a process we cannot alter or oppose; but immediately after the revolution, history will have no further role in opposing or modifying the resulting Communist "utopia." To a certain extent, this last bit proved to be true. After the Communist Revolution in Russia, natural historical change largely ceased, and today the Soviets find themselves with a society mired in the 1920's. Communism is a one-way process of economic suicide.

ॐ

Historicism—1. a theory of history which holds that events are determined or influenced by conditions and inherent processes beyond the control of humans. See Determinism. 2. deep, even excessive, respect for historical institutions. "History is bunk." (Henry Ford)

ॐ

Histrionism—the acts or practice of stage players and the theatrical method; hence, affectation.

≈

Histrionicism—1. the art of staging a drama or dramatic representation. 2. something done for theatrical effect.

≈

Hitlerism—the principles and practices of German dictator Adolf Hitler (1889-1945), as expressed in Germany's Nazi party. See Naziism.

≈

Hobbism—the principles of Thomas Hobbes (1588-1679), a materialistic English philosopher who believed an absolute monarchy or benevolent dictator was the best possible form of government. In "a state of nature" (i.e., without government and living in anarchy), Hobbes thought people incapable of regulating their own morals and religion. Therefore, a coercive government was necessary (and natural) to keep the peace, since it is the only way to control the problems created by inherently selfish, irredeemably aggrandizing humans. See Absolutism. "The condition of man ... is a condition of war of everyone against everyone." (Hobbes)

≈

Holism—1. the idea that things are greater than the sum of their parts. Also, Wholism. 2. a New Age health care doctrine that advocates treating an ailment not only by treating, for example, a virus, but also by considering the total mental and physical health of the patient.

≈

Holometabolism—the condition of having passed through a complete metamorphosis, such as when a caterpillar makes it all the way to butterfly.

છે.

Holy Rollerism—members of a religious sect, a bizarre branch of Methodism, who, when under religious fervor at their meetings, display great emotion, roll on the floor and over one another, babble in gibberish (a.k.a. glossolalia or "speaking in tongues"), and often, in their excitement, remove their clothing.

છે.

Homeomorphism—1. in chemistry, a similarity in the crystal form of unlike compounds. 2. in math, a one-to-one correspondence between the points of two geometric figures that is continuous in both directions.

છે.

Homochromatism—the state of being monochromatic.

છે.

Homoeroticism—sexual arousal by one's own sex. Also, Homoerotism.

છે.

Homoiothermism—the trait of being warm-blooded, having a body temperature mostly constant and mostly independent of the temperature of the environment.

છે.

Homoiousianism—the beliefs of an obscure 4th-century religious sect that believed Jesus was similar to, but not the same as, God.

છે.

Homomorphism—1. in biology, similarity in appearance but not in structure or origin. 2. in zoology, resemblance between the offspring and the adult.

છે.

Homostylism—in botany, the condition of a plant with the same form or length in all flowers.

છે.

Hoodlumism—the violent practices of gangsters, thugs, and destructive youths. For more information, watch *The Wild One* with Marlon Brando.

છે.

Hooliganism—British synonym for Hoodlumism. Commonly practiced at football (soccer) matches, Hooliganism has come to mean destruction for the sake of destruction.

છે.

Hopkinsianism—doctrines of Samuel Hopkins (1721-1803), a Calvinist who emphasized total submission to God's will.

ૈ☙

Hospitalism—the adverse physical and mental conditions caused by a stay in a hospital. Ill-managed hospitals are extremely dangerous environments where patients tend to infect each other. They can also be quite depressing.

ૈ☙

Hottentotism—a characteristic of the Hottentots, an African people related to the Bushmen; specifically, a kind of stammering. The Hottentots are shorter than and considered inferior in intellect to surrounding tribes, and their language is noteworthy for its clicks.

Hoydenism—boisterous, rude traits, especially in a young woman. "One more drink and I'll be under the host." (Dorothy Parker)

ૈ☙

Hucksterism—the traits and practices of crass, aggressive peddlers. An irresistable force of nature, Hucksterism draws idle minds toward aluminum siding salesmen, provided they're offering a free Ginzu knife.

ૈ☙

Huguenotism—the doctrines, beliefs, or practices of the Huguenots, a sect of French Protestantism derived from an influential reformer of the 16th and 17th centuries. The Huguenots were horribly persecuted during the Inquisition: "The Parisian populace were indiscriminately murderous and cruel, killing every Huguenot they knew. The Spanish envoy wrote: 'Not a child has been spared. Blessed be God!'" (Lord Acton)

ૈ☙

Humanism—1. a cultural and intellectual movement of the Renaissance that emphasized secular concerns as a result of the study of the literature, art, and civilization of ancient Greece and Rome. 2. a mode of thought in which human affairs or interests are of chief importance. 3. a system of philosophy centering on human interests; specifically, the 20th-century humanist movement in the United States, organized to counter the growing influence of Mysticism. In England, Humanism is identified with Bertrand Russell (1872-1970) and the Oxbridge "mafia." "The splendour of human life, I feel sure, is greater to those who are not dazzled by the divine radiance." (Russell)

🙚

Humanitarianism—1. philanthropy. 2. the doctrine that Jesus Christ possessed a human nature only. 3. the theory that humans may become perfect without divine aid. 4. a doctrine that our duties are limited to our human relations and surroundings. 5. none of the above.

   The basic impulse that motivates all humanitarians of the philanthropic persuasion is a compulsion to acquire a sense of their own existence through other people. They become missionaries whose mission is defined in terms of influencing someone else, and their only contribution is interference with their victims' lives—whereupon the humanitarian derives a perverse sense of efficacy in proportion to the degree of interference. "If you pick up a starving dog and make him prosperous, he will not bite you. This is the principal difference between a dog and a man." (Mark Twain)

🙚

Humism—the ideas and teachings of David Hume (1711-1776), a Scottish philosopher renowned for his Skepticism. "Beauty in things exists in the mind which contemplates them." (Hume)

🙚

Humorism—an old medical theory that all diseases originate in four basic body fluids called "humors." Humorism is still advanced in parts of Asia, where a cold is often treated by scratching dozens of abrasions across the chest and arms to let out the "cold air."

🙚

Hussitism—the religious theories of John Huss, a Bohemian reformer burned alive in 1415, thus depriving us of knowing exactly what those theories were.

🙚

Hutchinsonianism—the beliefs and opinions of John Hutchinson, an 18th-century English philosopher and naturalist who rejected Newton's theory of gravity and maintained that the Old Testament contained a complete system of natural science as well as religion. According to Hutchinson, if the Bible doesn't mention gravity, then it doesn't exist.

🙚

Hutteritism—practices and beliefs of Hutterites, a North American Anabaptist sect originating in Europe. They practice complete Pacifism, Separatism, and perfect Communalism: all community members are assigned jobs, there are no salaries, and all needs are supplied from the common store. Governed by a patriarchal democracy, Hutterites believe in uniformity to the extent of having a required hairstyle, and they believe that Teetotalism is contrary to Scripture. See Anabaptism.

Hybridism—the state of being of mixed origin, a hybrid. A mongrel, for instance, is a dog produced from two different species. Cross-breeding flowers or fauna creates the same condition.

Hydrargyrism—poisoning by mercury. Also, Mercurialism.

Hydrophytism—the characteristics of a plant growing in water or very wet ground.

Hydrotropism—in biology, growth toward or away from moisture.

Hylism—a theory in metaphysics which regards matter as the principle of evil. This term originates from *hylae*, the Greek word for "wood" or "matter," and is central to most of the fire-and-brimstone dogmas that condemn life on earth as sinful.

Hylomorphism—the philospohical theory that every object has two principles: one unchanging and one deprived of actuality with every major change of the object.

Hylopathism—the belief that matter has perception and that spirit and matter are retroactive. Applies to the New Age doctrine of Gaia, which treats the earth as a single, living Organism and discounts the existence of individual life or consciousness. Could also be associated with *We Are the World*, a hit song of the 1980's.

Hylotheism—the doctrine or belief that matter is God, or that there is no God except matter and the universe.

≥∙

Hylozoism—the doctrine that matter possesses a species of life, or that matter and life are inseparable, and therefore rocks can go to heaven (if they're well-behaved).

≥∙

Hyperadrenalism—a pathological condition caused by excessive secretions from the adrenal gland.

≥∙

Hyperbolism—the use of hyperbole, a rhetorical exaggeration not intended to deceive but to add force to a statement, such as when you say "I could eat a horse" to express hunger (see Hippophagism). "I never forget a face—but in your case I'll make an exception." (Groucho Marx)

≥∙

Hyperchromatism—the state of having unusually intense coloration.

≥∙

Hypercrinism—a pathological condition caused by excessive secretions by a gland, especially an endocrine gland. (Opposite is Hypocrinism.)

≥∙

Hypercriticism—excessively harsh Criticism; an exaggerated exercise of the critical faculties. This book is probably full of it.

≥∙

Hyperdactylism—the presence of extra fingers or toes.

≥∙

Hyperdicrotism—in physiology, an excessive duplication of the beats in the arterial pulse.

≥∙

Hyperendocrinism—the abnormal increase in the secretions from any endocrine gland. (Opposite is Hypoendocrinism.)

≥∙

Hyperglobulism—abnormal number of red corpuscles in the bloodstream. Could refer to the condition of mashed potatoes in bad restaurants, though.

≥∙

Hyperovarianism—the condition of girls who demonstrate precocious sexuality due to abnormally large secretions from their ovaries. Also, Hyperovarism.

≥∙

Hyperparasitism—in biology, the condition of a creature that is a parasite on another parasite. Do fleas get fleas?

る

Hyperparathyroidism—a painful condition caused by excessive activity of the parathyroid gland.

る

Hyperpituitarism—excessive production of anterior pituitary hormones, especially growth hormones resulting in acromegaly and Giantism. (Opposite is Hypopituitarism, which causes Dwarfism.)

Hyper-Realism—see Super-Realism.

る

Hyperthyroidism—a morbid condition resulting from abnormal function of the thyroid gland, where the victim suffers from excessive Metabolism and eats large quantities of food but remains hungry. (Opposite is Hypothyroidism.)

る

Hyperurbanism—a linguistic term used to describe a speech pattern employed by someone trying to imitate a dialect he perceives as superior to his own. Could describe some Americans who affect a British accent to sound "sophisticated."

Hypnotism—an abnormal condition of the mind induced by artificial means, in which a person is unusually open to suggestion and may appear to be controlled entirely by the commands of another; a passive mental condition or induced Somnambulism caused by rhythmic sensory input (as in night driving on an empty highway).

Hypocorism—1. a term of endearment or pet name, like "sugar pie." 2. the use of silly sounding words ("baby talk"), especially by adults, like "koochy-koo."

Hypocritism—the practice of feigning a belief or an attitude for the purpose of public approval, especially one who expresses piety or religious faith when he is destitute of sincere belief. Common among criminals seeking a lenient sentence and politicians trying to squirm out of a scandal.

Hypophalangism—the condition of having fewer than the normal number of bones per finger or toe.

Hypopituitarism—abnormally reduced activity of the pituitary gland, the master endocrine gland responsible for the normal functioning of all other glands. The condition manifests in many ways, including obesity and Dwarfism. Also called Hypohypophysism.

Hypothyroidism—abnormally reduced activity of the thyroid gland, often resulting in goiters.

Hypoptyalism—deficient secretion of the salivary glands.

Hypsistarianism—the doctrines of an Asiatic sect in the 4th century whose beliefs were derived from Christians, Jews, and pagans.

Ibsenism—a characteristic of the dramatic literary style of Henrik Ibsen (1828-1906), a Norwegian dramatist and poet who criticized Conventionalism. "The minority is always right." (from Ibsen's *An Enemy of the People*)

❧

Iconism—the practice of making figures that represent or delineate a person or idol, as in the Greek Church; making an image of Christ or a Christian saint. Cf. Idolism.

❧

Idealism—1. the advocacy of noble goals or principles. Superman, fighting for "truth, justice, and the American Way," was an idealist, for example. 2. in philosophy, a system or theory which claims that reality consists exclusively of ideas and denies the existence of material bodies.

Plato (427-347 B.C.) believed all things have eternal, perfect forms, which he called "ideas." In the Platonic sense, ideas are the patterns from which the Deity made the "material" world, even though what we perceive as physical existence is only an imperfect shadow of the ideal reality. Politically, Plato saw the "philosopher king" as the best possible form of government—a proposition amply discredited by Plato's disastrous attempt to rule Syracuse by an ideal dictatorship.

The Catholic Church absorbed Plato's views via St. Augustine, who taught that life was an illusion and that the only true reality was salvation in the hereafter. This doctrine has dominated Christianity ever since, with the exception of Latin American priests who now practice a "liberation theology" that favors Communism.

The connection is not oblique. Throughout the 20th century, many declared Communism a political or social "ideal" that mankind was too selfish or too foolish to practice. Thus, any strict code of behavior or proposal based on human performance will often be discredited by calling it "too idealistic" —on the implicit premise that mankind is incapable of anything that approaches noble conduct or heroic achievement.

Plato's legacy was amplified by Immanuel Kant, who taught that man is incapable of knowing anything about reality, a doctrine accepted by most Western philosophy today—and squarely opposed to the teachings of Aristotle, who was Plato's pupil and chief critic. See Kantianism.

Identism—the doctrine of Frederich Willhelm Joseph von Schelling (1775-1854), a philosopher of metaphysics who claimed that we can learn nothing from "tautological" statements such as "A is A," because the subject and the object of such statements are identical.

Idiologism—a peculiarity of speech usually arising from an affectation of the brain.

Idiomorphism—the characteristics of something with its own, individual form.

Idiotic Theism—pejorative description of various theories like Monogenism which assert that humans arose from one original set of parents (Adam and Eve) or from god-like ancestors.

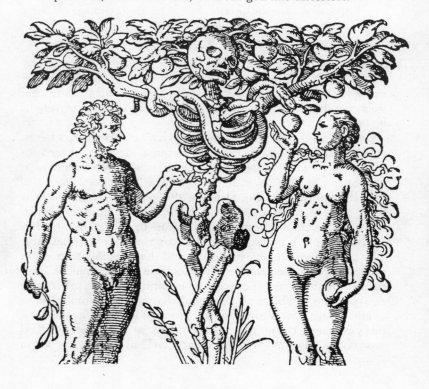

Idiotism—1. the conduct of a foolish person, or of someone incapable of progressing past the mental age of four. 2. the manner of a common person who speaks in a vulgar way or who voices opinions without education or professional knowledge; an idiom from a person who is unwise or silly. "In the first place God made idiots. This was for practice. Then He made school boards." (Mark Twain)

કર

Idolism—the worship of images or representations, usually of a man or an animal; a pagan deity. Historically, idols were usually statues or images carved from wood or stone or formed of metals, especially silver or gold. However, modern pagans are more apt to worship money, people, or Isms, which become objects of veneration when they are symbolized by totems or rituals. "The art of government is the organization of idolatry." (George Bernard Shaw)

કર

Illiberalism—the state of having a narrow mind which resists exposure to universal or contrary opinions; a characteristic unworthy of a free-thinker who profits from considering a range of views and who tolerates those with whom he disagrees.

કર

Illuminism—1. the doctrines of the Illuminati, a secret society founded in 1776 by Adam Weishaupt, a law professor in Bavaria who sought a higher degree of virtue than that reached in ordinary society. The Illuminati were promptly suppressed by the Bavarian government in 1785. 2. pertaining to certain heretics, such as the Alumbrados who appeared in Spain in 1575 and later in France. Their principal doctrine was that, through prayer, they had attained so perfect a state that they did not need ordinances, sacraments, and good works. 3. characteristics of anyone who claims to possess extraordinary knowledge or enlightenment. Specifically, the intellectual leadership based in New York City.

કર

Illusionism—1. in philosophy, the Platonic doctrine that the material world is an illusion. 2. in art, a style of painting that exploits perspective to emphasize three-dimensionality, so that pictorial space seems to be an extension of real space.

કર

Imagism—1. in poetry, a style that employs common speech, free verse, and precise images. Ezra Pound sarcastically dubbed it "Amygism," after influential imagist Amy Lowell. 2. the art of creating mental images or pictures. Like imagination, it is the power of the will working on the materials of memory. Dissatisfied with the order prescribed by nature or suggested by accident, Imagism selects parts of different concepts or objects of memory to form a whole that's more pleasing, more sublime, or more awful than has ever been. Gener-

ally, Imagism is the power of the mind to decompose its conceptions and to recombine elements of them at its pleasure.

Immaterialism—the doctrine of the existence or state of immaterial
substances or spiritual beings. In philosophy, it refers to Idealism,
the belief that no material world exists and that everything is reduc-
ible to ideas and mind.

Immediatism—1. in U.S. history, a policy advocating the immediate
abolition of slavery. 2. the quality or state of being immediate, i.e.
without a medium or without the intervention of another cause
or means, producing effect by direct agency. See Automatism.

Immersionism—the doctrine that advocates full immersion in water
as necessary for Christian Baptism.

Immoral Existentialism—according to the Vatican, this is the doctrine of Simone de Beauvoir (1908-1986), whose works *The Second
Sex* and *Mandarins* were banned by the Vatican in 1956. The ban
actually helped publicize her books, and she was suddenly a famous
heretic who preached "free love" and the emancipation of women.
   This was a clear example of long-entrenched Catholic
Phallocentrism—a bunch of old men in skirts trying to tell women
what they can and cannot read. There is something deeply sinister
about the Church's opposition to feminist literature, equal rights
for women, and choice in the disposition of female anatomy. In the
words of a pro-choice activist, "When we talk about women's rights,
we can get all the rights in the world—the right to vote, the right
to go to school—and none of them means a doggone thing if we
don't own the flesh we stand in, if we can't control what happens
to us, if the whole course of our lives can be changed by somebody

else that can get us pregnant by accident, by deceit, or by force."

The Church has steadfastly opposed birth control, abortion, ordination of women—anything that might permit the "weaker sex" to win its freedom. Having lost all credibility with women in the industrialized Western countries, the dour celibates in Rome have focused their power-lust on the women of Latin America and Asia, hoping that there might be a few centuries left in the game of preying on the ignorant. Damn them to the Hell of their own invention; few have ever equalled their sin on earth. And thank Jefferson— not God—for the separation of church and state in America.

ða

Immoralism—in philosophy and ethics, a doctrine that advocates indifference and/or opposition to standard morality. "Morality consists in suspecting other people of not being legally married." (George Bernard Shaw)

ða

Immortalism—the doctrine of the possibility of unending life, especially to those who make themselves (or parts thereof) frozen prior to death, on the theory that whatever is about to kill them (cancer, say) can be reversed in the future, when they will be defrosted. The science of freezing and defrosting living tissue is called cryonics. See Deathism. "We have an obligation ... to the dynamic inherent in personal life to secure our perpetual existence and growth." (Max Moore) "Millions long for immortality who don't know what to do on a rainy Sunday afternoon." (Susan Ertz)

ða

Imperialism—1. imperial state or authority; the system of government by an emperor. 2. a national policy of expansion or growth by the acquisition or subjugation of foreign territory by military force.

ða

Impersonalism—the practice of having aloof ties with individuals or groups.

ða

Impressionism—a style of painting so named by a group of journalists who saw Monet's much derided *Impression: Sunset in 1874*. Compared to the academic artists of the Salon who thought there was only one way to paint a landscape, the Impressionists (Pissaro, Monet, Renoir, Cezanne, Van Gogh, Gaugin, and Sisely) went to the open country and painted with a short strokes, bright colors, and a fresh vision, noting how light and shade were reflected in the moving waters of the rivers, how some tones and colors seemed to vibrate, and how the outlines of solid objects appeared to lose their solidity under certain atmospheric conditions. Their work expressed the essence of country life with uncompromising honesty in terms of the artist's impressions. Works by the Impressionists are today extraordinarily valuable.

ða

Incendiarism—1. the practices of a person who maliciously sets fires. 2. a person who advocates inflaming volatile situations and who promotes quarrels.

એ

Incivism—lack of Patriotism or interest in national and civic issues. "Patriotism is the last refuge of a scoundrel." (Samuel Johnson)

એ

Incorporealism—belief in an insubstantial existence, not consisting of matter or having a material body. In law, having no existence except as a legal concept; not tangible; not sizeable.

એ

Independentism—the principles of the Independents, a religious body which maintains that every congregation of Christians is a complete church, subject to no superior human authority and competent to govern its ecclesiastical affairs. In England, a Congregationalist.

એ

Indeterminism—in metaphysics, the doctrine that the will is not wholly governed by motives or prior causes but has a certain freedom of action and spontaneity. Opposite of Determinism.

એ

Indifferentism—1. the state of being dispassionate, especially toward differences in religion or philosophy; a kind of Agnosticism. 2. tolerance of acts or beliefs that aren't specifically prohibited in the Bible. Also, Adiaphorism. 3. in metaphysics, the doctrine of absolute identity. 4. in the Roman Catholic church, a heresy which consists of being indifferent to a creed while insisting on morality.

એ

Individualism—1. the state of individual interest or attachment to the interest of individuals over the common interests of society. See Objectivism. 2. the doctrine or theory of government which recognizes the legal independence of the individual in every relation of life, as opposed to Collectivism and Paternalism. 3. in philosophy, the doctrine that only individual things are real and that individuals, not the masses, create actions.

Industrialism—devotion to or employment in industrial pursuits and the principles of industry, characterized by large-scale enterprises, mass production, mechanized manufacturing, or other operations through which marketable commodities are produced.

Ineffectual Anti-Establishmentarianism—a political philosophy held by many young Americans, characterized by having no distinctive political attitudes other than a deep mistrust of the U.S. political system. "Because many of these young people had lived the hard-pressed lives about which New Jersey rocker Bruce Springsteen sang, economist Robert McElvaine called them the 'Springsteen Coalition'." (James MacGregor Burns). More often called "Baby Boomers," of which there are two subsets: Pre-Boss Yuppies and Post-Police Unemployed. You need an in-depth knowledge of Album-Oriented Rock (AOR) to appreciate what we're talking about. Consult your local FM radio station.

Infantilism—1. speech disorder found in very young children. 2. a disorder of adults who exhibit extremely childish features or behavior. Cf. Pee Wee Herman and millionaire athletes who whine about their salaries.

Inflationism—a government policy or practice of promoting growth through expansion of the money supply.

Infralapsarianism—the doctrine of the Infralapsarians, a class of Calvinists who believe God planned the Creation and the Fall, elected the Chosen for redemption, and condemned the rest to Hell. Opposite of Supralapsarianism.

Infusionism—the religious doctrine that the soul is a part of the divine element and pre-existent to the body, into which it is infused with the breath of life. Opposed to Creationism and Traducianism.

ॐ

Ingenious Sophism—a Sophism proceding from morally or politically "correct" premises, which are thus immune to unwanted infection by reason or debate. Examples: Since free public education is a fundamental human right, children should be compelled to attend state-supported schools. Soviet version: Since Socialism is a historical necessity, children should be compelled to attend state-supported schools. Catholic version: Since children are born sinful...

ॐ

Institutionalism—1. social philosophy of Thorstein Veblen (1857-1929), American economist who argued that economic Classicism and Marginalism were identical, that religion shaped awareness of economic relationships, and that technology is the prime agent of social change. Cf. Historical Materialism and Hegelianism. Veblen's chief claim to fame rested on his ability to coin snappy phrases, like "conspicuous consumption." 2. strong belief in the propriety of established social and public institutions, like religion. 3. insane behavior adopted to survive imprisonment in an institution. Common in prisons, post offices, and boarding schools. Watch *One Flew Over the Cuckoo's Nest* for more information.

ॐ

Instrumentalism—in philosophy, a pragmatic doctrine which maintains that thought is instrumental in change and that the value of an idea is measured by its effect on society.

ॐ

Intellectualism—1. the doctrine that all knowledge is derived from the intellect, the faculty of the human mind which receives or comprehends ideas communicated by the senses or by logical thought processes. 2. an excessive devotion to reason and intellectual matters, without considering the significance of emotion.

ॐ

Interactionism—a philosophical theory that the mind and the body interact and may affect each other. Sheesh—how much did someone get paid to come up with this one?

ॐ

Interestism—the state of being interested. It applies to someone who appreciates all philosophies, lifestyles, and nationalities without holding a personal affiliation or being party to their policies or doctrines— a person who loves the world and can accept, in a state of serenity, the freedom to choose for himself how he should live. Travel and discovery broaden the mind and contribute to a person's growth. They permit the privilege to gain understanding and view differences in races and historic inheritances with equanimity and compassion. Interestism is a state of non-judgmental acceptance of the wide variety of interesting ways of being and thinking that exist in the world.

Interiorism—a philosophical doctrine that says truth comes from introspection rather than examination of the world. In other words, contemplate your navel, not the ocean.

Internationalism—1. the concept of cooperation between nations for the common good, sometimes in opposition to the best interests of one nation. 2. the concepts of Internationalists, who uphold and advocate the principles of international law, especially as conceived by admirers of Communism. There have been several such groups in history, the first being the International Workingmen's Association, founded in London in 1864 to advance the interests of the world's working classes. The Second International, founded in Paris in 1889, sought to establish Socialism in international law by reason rather than force. The Third International, founded in Moscow in 1919 by Lenin and Trotsky, followed the principles of Karl Marx, who advocated violent overthrow as the only means of change.

Interventionism—the advocacy of interceding in something, especially a government interfering in the affairs of another government or manipulating an economy through tax policies, subsidies, prohibitions, licensing, public spending, royal charters, and 10,000 other methods of screwing things up. From Tribalism to Mercantilism, the state ran the entire economic show—period. After a brief season of Economic Liberalism in the 19th century, state intervention ran amok with a vastly expanded tax base. See Welfare Statism, Socialism, Keynesianism, and Protectionism. The motive for Interventionism is always the same: attempted Populism.

Intimism—a style of painting by Bonnard and Vuillard involving domestic interiors painted impressionistically.

Intuitionalism—1. in ethics, the concept that morality is inherent. 2. in metaphysics, the doctrine that the perception of truth is derived from intuition, the act by which the mind perceives the truth of things immediately at the moment they are presented, without the intervention of other ideas and without reasoning. Also Intuitionism, Intuitivism.

❧

Invalidism—1. the condition of being weak, sickly, wounded, maimed, or otherwise disabled. 2. in law, the quality of having no force, effect, or efficacy; being void or null.

Iodism—poisoning caused by a reaction to or overdose of iodine.

❧

Iotacism—the conversion of a vowel sound into that of the Greek letter *iota*, represented in English by a long "e." For example, saying NEE-ther instead of NYE-ther for the word "neither."

❧

Irishism—an idiom or custom of the people of Ireland, such as wearing green on St. Patrick's Day. Also, Iricism, Hibernianism. "The Irish are a fair people; they never speak well of one another." (Samuel Johnson)

❧

Irrationalism—1. a thought or action that ignores logic and rationality. 2. a belief that the universe is governed by illogical forces or by forces undetectable by rational thought.

❧

Irredentism—the platform of the Irredentists, an Italian political party formed in 1878 to join regions populated by Italians but ruled by other governments. Today, the term describes any attempt to join a region to a country by virtue of mutual cultural or ethnic ties, an argument used to unite East and West Germany in 1990, for instance.

❧

Islamic Fundamentalism—obedience taken to its logical extreme: a religion composed of self-sacrifice and murder for the glory of God, with prayers five times a day. In the Koran (Sura 7), God asks Adam's descendants (before they were born!), "Am I not your Lord?" By answering "yes," they accepted Islam for all eternity. Therefore, the Muslim reciting the credo is only saying that, although everyone is born in the primeval Islamic religion, only his environment makes him holy. Suras 29-31 speak of the *jihad* (holy war) against all who are "peoples of the book" (i.e., Jews and Christians)—not to spread Islam but to enforce Islamic law. The *jihad* is considered the permanent duty of Muslims so long as any part of the world remains outside the jurisdiction of Islamic law.

૨ð

Islamism—the true faith of obedience to the will of God and total submission; the religion set forth by Mohammed (570-632 A.D.). (See Mohammedenism.) The two principal sects of Islam—the Sunnis and the Shi'ites—are virtually at war and jealously covet the Holy Shrines at Mecca and Medina. A third, much-smaller Islamic sect called the Ismailis are based in Paris and headed by the Aga Khan. Their specialty is horse-racing.

૨ð

Ism—a suffix implying a doctrine, theory, principle, belief, system, or practice. It's interesting (and unsettling) how credible any word becomes when these three little letters are attached. "Von Altendorfism" (sounds so impressive!) could be "the system of compiling hundreds of words that end in 'ism' and making droll remarks about many of them." Try it with your name! Scary, huh?

૨ð

Isochronism—a principle discovered by Galileo (1564-1642) when he was 19 years old. While sitting in the baptistry of the Cathedral at Pisa, he observed the equal time of the pendulum swing and noticed that the time of the swing varied not with the width of the swing but with the length of the pendulum. Something isochronal exhibits motions of equal duration.

૨ð

Isodimorphism—in crystals, Isomorphism between two dimorphous substances. (See Dimorphism.)

૨ð

Isogonism—in biology, the production of like reproductive parts from dissimilar stocks, as in certain hybrids; the quality of having like offspring.

૨ð

Isolationism—in politics, the doctrine or policy of minding one's own business and remaining disengaged from foreign disputes and alliances. There has been a constant struggle between Interventionism and Isolationism in U.S. history. Isolationists prevented U.S. entry into World War II for some time, thereby giving Hitler time to work his infamy. But interventionists got the U.S. into the Vietnam War, with disastrous results. Perhaps it's best to remember Thomas Jefferson: "Peace, commerce, and honest friendship with all nations, entangling alliances with none."

Isomerism—in chemistry, two or more compounds with identical atoms but different arrangements; in physics, the relation of two or more nuclides with the same atomic and mass numbers but different energy levels and half-lives.

Isomorphism—1. in crystallography, a similarity of crystalline form between substances of like composition or atomic proportions (such as arsenic acid and phosphorous acid, each containing five equivalents of oxygen) and between compounds of unlike composition and atomic proportions (such as the metal arsenic and oxide of iron, the rhombohedral angle of the former being 85°, 41', while the latter is 86°,4'. The first of these is sometimes distinguished as an "isonomic" Isomorphism; the second as "heteronomic" Isomorphism.). 2. in biology, creatures with different ancestry but similar form. 3. any close similarity between one structure and another, especially in a pattern seen in the whole which can also be seen in its constituent parts.

Isosterism—1. in chemistry, the quality of compounds having the same number of valence electrons in the same configuration but differing in the kinds and numbers of atoms. 2. in pharmacology, the theory that isosteric compounds have similar effects.

Itacism—the modern pronunciation of the Greek *eta*, preferred by the followers of Johan Reuchlin (1455-1522), a German humanist, to the Etacism of the followers of Desiderius Erasmus (1466-1536), a Dutch theologian and scholar.

Italianism—1. an expression, manner, or idiom of the people of Italy. 2. in printing, the use of italics. Also, Italicism.

Izedism—the religion professed by the Izedis, a sect in Mesopotamia and neighboring regions said to worship the devil.

Jacksonism—the political principles and opinions associated with Andrew Jackson (1767-1845), 7th president of the U.S., especially as it relates to Populism ("Jacksonian democracy"). "One man with courage makes a majority." (Jackson)

ॐ

Jacobinism—unreasonable or violent opposition to the legitimate government; an attempt to overthrow or change government by extremely radical means. Derived from the order of Jacobin friars, in whose monastery a group of radical French Republicans met to plot the overthrow of Louis XIV.

ॐ

Jacobitism—the principles of the partisans of James II, King of England, who abdicated in 1688. The Jacobites hated the legitimate government in place and plotted to overthrow it in the manner of the Jacobites of France, who held democratic principles.

ॐ

Jahvism—see Yahwism.

ॐ

Jainism—the religious principles and system of the Jains, a small, wealthy, and influential Hindu sect that forms an important division of the Indian population and holds to a strictly ascetic life. Jains deny the divine origin and infallibility of the Vedas, revere certain holy mortals, and display extreme tenderness for all animal life. Between the 6th and 4th century B.C., at a time of religious awakening and formation of new religious needs for non-Aryan (i.e.,

non-Brahman) classes, Mahavira the Jina (the Conqueror) founded a monastic tradition which later gave rise to the independent
religion called Jainism. Mahavira came from the Kshatriya class and
hence was a noble like Gautama Siddhartha (Buddha). Cf.
Buddhism.

ک

Jansenism—the doctrine of Cornelius Jansen (1585-1638), a Dutch
theologian and Roman Catholic Bishop of Ypres, who denied free
will and held to irresistible grace and limited atonement. He was
condemned by the church for his heresy that man is incapable of
good.

Japanism—a custom or trait unique to Japan and the Japanese; a preference for things Japanese. Also, Japonism.

ک

Jeffersonianism—the elegant simplicity which characterized the
philosophies of Thomas Jefferson (1743-1826), diplomat, author of
the Declaration of Independence, architect, and 3rd U.S. president.
Jefferson supported limited central government, individual rights,
and freedom of speech and religion, and he believed in the dignity
of agriculture and public education. "Sometimes it is said that man
cannot be trusted with the government of himself. Can he, then,
be trusted with the government of others?" (Jefferson)

ک

Jesuitism—the arts, principles, and practices of the Jesuits, known as the Society of Jesus, a religious order founded by Ignatius Loyola in 1534. The popular conception that the order is organized on a military plan is partly correct: the General at the head serves for life and has almost full administrative authority. The supreme power, however, is in the General Congregation, a body elected by members of the Society who take four vows. There are two general classes of members, laymen and priests, with six grades of training and advancement. After the first period of probation (two years), members assume the vows of poverty, chastity, and obedience; the fourth vow is special obedience to the Roman Pontiff. The power of the Society lies in its submission to legitimate authority, but its enemies claim it is unscrupulous in intrigue and deceptive in purpose, tending to the subversion of legitimate government. Hence, the word "jesuitical" has become synonymous with cunning, deceit, hypocrisy, and prevarication.

ॐ

Jim Crowism—in general, an anti-Negro sentiment expressed specifically by segregation and racial discrimination. Derived from laws ("Jim Crow laws") made after the U.S. Civil War which legalized segregation.

ॐ

Jingoism—the principles and policies of Jingoes, people who clamor for war or a warlike, aggressive policy. Originally applied to those who thought Britain should actively support the Turks in the Turko-Russian war of 1877, from a popular song: "We don't want to fight, but by jingo if we do, we've got the ships, we've got the men, we've got the money too." Jingo comes from the oath "By Jingo!" ("By God!"), introduced by gypsies or soldiers at the time. See also Chauvinism.

ॐ

Jism—slang term for ejaculate.

ॐ

Joe Millerism—the art or practice of making, reciting, or retailing jests, especially poor or stale jokes. Derived from Joe Miller (but you guessed that, right?), an English comic actor whose name was attached to a joke book published in 1739.

ॐ

John Bullism—anything typical of the character of the English people. A humorous appellation, it's named for a character in *Law Is a Bottomless Pit* by John Arbuthnot (1667-1735). "The English have an extraordinary ability for flying into a great calm." (Alexander Woollcott)

ॐ

Johnsonianism—a word, idiom, or habit peculiar to Dr. Samuel Johnson (1709-1784), English author and lexicographer, or a style resembling his. "No place affords a more striking conviction of the vanity of human hopes than a public library." (Johnson)

Journalism—1. the business or profession of publishing, writing for, or editing a journal, especially a newspaper or magazine. 2. the profession of a journalist, one who writes, photographs, or broadcasts news. 3. writing characterized by haste and superficiality rather than deep research (the difference between a magazine article and a scholarly thesis, for example). "Journalism consists largely in saying 'Lord Jones Dead' to people who never knew that Lord Jones was alive." (G.K. Chesterton)

૨ક

Jovinianism—the doctrine of Jovinian, a monk in the 4th century who denied the virginity of Mary and denounced Asceticism.

૨ક

Judaism—the religious doctrines and rites of the Jews, as enjoined in the law of Moses in the Old Testament and in the teachings in the Talmud. The oldest of the world's major faiths, Judaism proceeds on the assumption that God has spoken only once, to Abraham, whom God thereby chose forever. Like all mideast religions, Judaism has a specific, non-negotiable claim: that Jews are God's chosen people. This annoys a lot of people—see Antisemitism and Naziism.

૨ક

Junkerism—the policy of an aristocratic, militaristic party in Prussia comprised mostly of young military lords and masters and to which the German statesman Otto von Bismarck once belonged.

૨ક

Junk Sculpturalism—alleged art made from discarded industrial items and consumer products in the 1950's.

Kabalism—the doctrine of a secret, esoteric science originated by the Chaldeans of the Middle East. The *Book of Kabala*, which outlines the origin of the universe, contains its tenets and is allegedly based on 70,000 years of recorded experience. The most ancient Hebrew document on occult learning, the *Siphra Dzeniduta*, was compiled from it. See Cabalism.

Kaiserism—the policy of rule by an autocrat. Derived from the word *kaiser*, the German version of Caesar.

Kakistocracism—the policies and principles of a state ruled by the worst people. The opposite of a kakistocracy is an aristocracy. Though sorely tempted, we will avoid adding a snide comment.

Kantianism—the doctrines and theories of the German philosopher Immanuel Kant (1724-1804), the explanation of which is probably the most difficult task we attempt in this whole book. Kant sought to revive Platonism and carve out a piece of philosophical turf that would be forever monopolized by religion, despite the advance of science and humanity's ability to understand reality. To accomplish this, he segregated the universe into three aspects: the "phenomenal," which men could observe and measure; the "noumenal," which is an object of purely intellectual intuition, a Platonic thing-in-itself that cannot be observed or measured; and a transcendent reality which only God knows because it encompasses such things as infinity.

In the Kantian view: "The conceptions of the understanding depend on the constitution of our thinking faculties, as the perceptions of the senses depend on the constitution of our intuitive faculties. Both might be different were our mental constitution changed; both probably are different to beings differently constituted. Thus the real becomes identical with the absolute, with the object as it is in itself, out of all relation to a subject; and, as all consciousness is a relation between subject and object, it follows that to attain a knowledge of the real we must go out of consciousness." (Mansel)

But Ayn Rand defers: "The entire apparatus of Kant's system goes through its gyrations while resting on a single point: that man's knowledge is not valid because his consciousness possesses identity. His argument, in essence, ran as follows: man is limited to a consciousness of a specific nature, which perceives by specific means and no others, therefore his consciousness is not valid; man is blind because he has eyes ... and the things he perceives do not exist, because he perceives them."

Without exaggeration, Kant's philosophy has dominated 20th-century Western thought, inspiring Subjectivism, Positivism, Hegelianism, Utilitarianism, etc. In law, it demolished the notion of natural rights and established the crusade to let legislators decide the meaning of "justice." In science, it restricted claims of knowledge to the category of guessing "probabilities" of truth. And in politics, it inspired leaders to abandon principles for Pragmatism, which meant judging the rightness or wrongness of an action by its results, since no one was capable of knowing which was which in advance and there were no moral absolutes. On the subject of morality, Kant gave particularly abstruse advice: his famous "categorical imperative" decreed that the only good thing was a good will, which justified anything so long as you are willing to make it a Golden Rule that applies to everyone with equal obligation.

ôô

Karaism—the teachings and beliefs of the Karaites, a sect of Jews founded in the 8th century who adhere to scriptural (rather than oral) teaching and deny the authority of the Talmud as binding. Also Karaitism.

ôô

Karmathianism—the doctrine of a heretical sect of Mohammedans founded in the 9th century by Karmat, who regarded the Koran as merely allegorical, rejected all revelation, fasting, and prayer, and practiced absolute Communism.

ôô

Katabolism—destructive Metabolism, in which complex substances are broken down into simpler waste bodies by a living Organism. Also Catabolism. Cf. Anabolism.

ôô

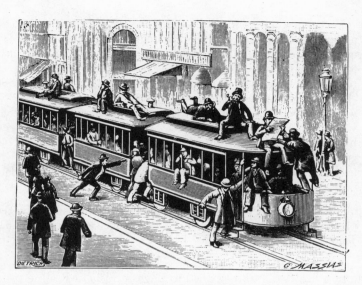

Katamorphism—the process by which simple minerals become complex minerals at or near the earth's surface. Cf. Anamorphism.

ৰ

Keynesianism—the policies and theories of John Maynard Keynes (1883-1946), English economist and writer. To appreciate the Keynesian doctrine, we need to begin with the central idea of Capitalism: that a free market will create optimal employment and allocation of resources. Keynes thought otherwise, and his influence in the modern world can scarcely be exaggerated. Every government on earth today employs Keynesian "fine-tuning," and there is no known cure.

His theory begins with the notion of aggregate demand—i.e., the total produced and consumed by everyone in the society. Keynes showed that profits determined this aggregate, because people won't do something unless they benefit. Next, he observed that there were actually two streams of money in the economy: consumption and savings. Believing investment opportunities become progressively less profitable in more advanced economies, Keynes argued that governments should force interest rates down by printing money and lending it from the central bank at a discount. This would put more money in consumers' hands and encourage them to spend and consume more, thus creating an incentive for investment.

Great theory—with one flaw: it's a recipe for inflation. And when you inflate, very predictable things happen: you wipe out the value of savings and choke off investment. (Keynes later modified his original recipe to include public works spending and public borrowing to increase economic activity artificially. This was enormously popular for a while, until people noticed that government borrowing crowded-out private investment and taxes steadily rose to cope with the massive public debt.)

Keynesianism is a variant of Underconsumptionism: trying to put a penny in the fusebox and short-circuit the financial markets for fast, temporary relief. It is not an economic policy for the day after tomorrow. Tellingly, when asked by Pres. Franklin Roosevelt to explain what would happen in the long run, Keynes laughed and said, "In the long run, Mr. President, we'll all be dead."

A footnote is in order, because it's the truth and it's not irrelevant. John Maynard Keynes was a horrid little pervert who spent half his life as a bureaucrat and the other half writing lurid apologies to the boys he had buggered. This was the sort of "genius" who inspired modern macro-economics and wiped out the gold standard.

Khilistism—the practices of a religious sect in Russia called the People of God and Danielites, who practiced flagellation, celibacy, and Teetotalism.

Kitchen Sinkism—term applied to English Socialist Realism paintings which portrayed working-class environments and themes. Also applied to English playwrights after the success of J. Osborne's *Look Back in Anger* in 1956.

Know-Nothingism—the principles and doctrines of the Know-Nothing (or American) Party, a U.S. political organization from 1853-1856 which sought to exclude foreign-born citizens from participating in government. The Party got its name because its members, after the first secret meeting, declared they knew nothing about it. The term now denotes general Anti-Intellectualism and xenophobia. "When the Know-Nothings get control, (the Constitution) will read 'All men are created equal, except Negroes and foreigners and Catholics.'" (Abraham Lincoln)

Kwazuluism—political aim of the Zulu tribe to establish a new Zulu kingdom in South Africa. Rather unbelievably, it is most vocally advocated by John Aspinall, a white British entrepreneur.

Labadism—the doctrine of Jean de Labadie, who held that God can and does deceive men and that the observance of the Sabbath is a matter of indifference.

❧

Labialism—the tendency to pronounce sounds requiring an articulation of the lips (for instance, the letters b, f, m, p, v); to utter a certain sound by the use of the lips. When Hollywood wants to record an English-language version of a Swedish movie, the first person hired is a "labializer" who specializes in concocting English words that match the mouth movements of the Swedish actors on screen.

❧

Laborism—the principles and practices of the British Labor Party, especially as it relates to supporting Trade Unionism. Also, Labourism.

❧

Laconicism—1. in ancient prosody, a reversed dactyl having four measures and catalectic with a spondee instead of the penultimate anapest. Hah, hah, hah. 2. a concise, pithy mode of expression. According to White House legend, Pres. Calvin Coolidge was notorious for his Laconicism. At a dinner party, a guest once told him she had bet a friend she could get "more than two words" out of him. Coolidge replied, "You lose."

❧

Laconism—the imitation of the Lacedaemonians or Spartans in manners, dress, etc., especially in speaking in short, pithy phrases. The Spartans never wasted their words; they were men of action.

Laicism—secular control of social institutions. Cf. Clericalism, Secularism.

Lamaism—a variety of Buddhism, chiefly in Tibet and Mongolia, so-called from the lamas or priests belonging to it. The highest object of worship is Buddha, regarded as the founder of the religion and the first in rank among their saints. Second highest is the Dalai Lama, currently an old man exiled from Tibet by the Chinese Army. He will soon be replaced by a Mexican boy who was recently declared to be the new oracle. Incidentally, 1991 was the 40th year of Chinese rule in Tibet, a sad anniversary for the placid followers of Lamaism. Hundreds of monks have been killed and scores of temples and monasteries destroyed as the Chinese tighten control.

Lamarckism—in biology, the theory of evolution propounded by Chevalier de Jean Baptiste Pierre Antoine de Monet Lamarck (1744-1829), a French naturalist with a very long name who taught that life has been differentiated from a primitive and simple form and that adaptive responses to environment cause structural changes capable of being inherited. Lamarck disagreed with Charles Darwin, who thought time and "survival of the fittest" produced evolution, whereas Lamarck emphasized environmental causes in the development and success of new species. "Habits form a second nature." (Lamarck)

≈

Lambdacism—a condition that results when the tongue is pressed against the palate and produces a sound similar to the "lli" in "million." This faulty pronunciation is common among children and Asians when trying to say the English "R." It also refers to over-use of the letter "L" in speaking or writing, as in Martial's line: "*Sol et luna luce lucent alba, leni, lactea.*"

≈

Landlordism—the conduct or opinions characteristic of people who own property rented to others. Specifically, the political and ethical doctrine of the superiority of the landed interests. At the time of the American Revolution, it was thought that ownership of land was a necessary qualification for office, and thus voting was restricted to white male property owners under the Constitution. It has since been replaced by universal suffrage, regardless of property, on the principle of "one person, one vote." But landlords still think they're superior, as you know if your rent is due.

≈

Laodiceanism—of or pertaining to Laodicea, an ancient city of Phyrgia Major, or to its inhabitants, who were renowned for being lukewarm and unenthusiastic in their Christianity.

≈

Larrikinism—the quality of a rowdy youth (a "larrikin"), allegedly coined by James Dalton, an Australian police sergeant of Irish birth, when speaking of boisterous, ill-bred, uncouth types, whom he considered as "larking" about.

≈

Lathyrism—the condition of paraplegia induced by ingesting the seeds of the *lathyrus cicera*. Whatever it is, don't eat it.

≈

Latinism—a form of expression characteristic of Latin, the language of the ancient Romans and the bane of modern ninth-graders. Many current languages incorporate Latin, especially Spanish and Portuguese, a lot of English medical and legal terms are pure Latin, and it's still the official tongue of the Roman Catholic Church. Social organizations often adopt a Latin motto—*Lux et Veritas* (Yale Univ.), *Semper Fidelis* (the Marine Corps)—when they want to sound high-falutin'.

Latitudinarianism—undue freedom or laxness of opinion, particularly in theology; one who is moderate in his notions or not restrained by precisely set limits in opinion and who indulges in free-thought. In the Church of England, formerly one who denied or doubted the divine right or origin of Episcopacy, although he admitted its expediency.

Laudianism—the doctrines of William Laud (1573-1645), Archbishop of Canterbury, opponent of Puritanism, and supporter of the Church of England over the Roman Catholic Church. He was executed for treason.

Leftism—the tendency of an individual or party to adopt socialist political policies or other views associated with the Left. See Socialism.

Legalism—1. in theology, the doctrine that good deeds warrant salvation. 2. close conformity to the law, or an expression which is unduly formal and complex; a technicality. "Every law which originated in ignorance and malice, and gratifies the passions from which it sprang, we call the wisdom of our ancestors." (Sydney Smith)

Legitimism—the doctrine or theory of the Legitimists, who in France were adherents of the elder branch of the Bourbon family, descendants of Louis XIV, and in Spain were known as Carlists. They supported legitimate authority, especially the authority of a monarch based on direct descent.

Leninism—the political theories of Vladimir Ilyich Ulyanov, called Nikolai Lenin (1870-1924), Russian revolutionary, especially the methods and tactics he taught and used during and after the Bolshevik Revolution in 1917. The central point: a "dictatorship of the proletariat," springing from the hegemony of the working class. The "New Economic Policy," instituted under Lenin's guidance, was, he taught, a step toward a Socialist Russia. It lasted two years. "It is true that liberty is precious—so precious that it must be rationed." (Lenin)

ˀ❧

Lesbianism—female homosexuality. Named for Lesbos, the ancient name of an island in the Aegean Sea (now called Mytilene), where the followers of Sappho, a Greek poetess, indulged in Eroticism and debauchery. Also, Sapphism, Tribadism.

ˀ❧

Lexiphanicism—the habit of using an inflated, pompous, bombastic, or turgid style of speaking or writing. "Ah, my dear, what symmetrical digits!" (W. C. Fields, admiring Mae West's hand)

ˀ❧

Liberalism—the principles of liberals—especially in religion or in politics—the definition of which is hotly debated. Take your pick: 1. those who advocate greater freedom of thought or action, or 2. those who advocate Welfare Statism. Originally, the term pertained to the Whigs, a British political party. See Whiggism.

Because the question of civil liberty is fundamental to all political theories (especially in the great contest between Capitalism and Communism—one pro, the other con), it's important to consider how words can be twisted to suit a political agenda. When Pres. Franklin Roosevelt declared "a hungry man is not free," he was playing a word game. Freedom, in the political context, refers specifically and exclusively to freedom from government—not freedom from worries, warts, or winter snowstorms. It's equally nonsensical to declare that a man who eats twice a day is not free, compared to someone who eats three times. The issue is not caloric, it's constitutional.

In answer to the New Deal version of Liberalism, we should reflect on the fact that taxpayers are not free and that there's no such thing as a free lunch—somebody always ends up cooking it and paying for it. "I sit on a man's back, choking him and making him carry me, and yet assure myself and others that I am very sorry for him and wish to ease his lot by all possible means—except by getting off his back." (Leo Tolstoy)

ˀ❧

Libertarianism—1. in philosophy, the doctrines of those who believe in free will, as opposed to determinism. 2. in politics, the principles and policies of those who oppose almost all government restriction of private liberty and envision the role of coercive government to consist solely of keeping the peace. Libertarians defy the standard left-right political spectrum, in that they support limited government in both the economic (i.e., taxes) and social (i.e., free speech issues) arenas. Currently, the Libertarian Party is the third-largest political party in the U.S. "That government is best which governs least." (Thomas Jefferson)

Libertinism—exceptional freedom of opinion or practice, especially in sexual matters; debauchery. Practiced by members of a pantheistic sect in 16th-century Holland, who maintained that nothing is sinful except to those who think it sinful and that perfect innocence is to live without doubt. Another group in Geneva, a sect of Christian infidels and voluptuaries, thought similarly, in opposition to Calvinism. Hence, a libertine is a person who indulges his desires without restraint. "Man is the only animal that blushes. Or needs to." (Mark Twain)

Lichenism—the state of intimate union between algae and fungi, producing lichens.

Lipogrammatism—the art or act of creating lipograms, writing that omits all words with a particular letter of the alphabet. In *The Odyssey of Tryphiodorus*, for example, there is no letter "A" in Book I, no "B" in Book II, etc. Apparently, writers do this when they have a lot of free time.

Lipotropism—a condition caused when the body demonstrates an affinity for fats (lipids) and thus excess fat builds up in the liver.

Listerism—a general name for the antiseptic treatment of wounds according to the principles first enunciated by Joseph Lister (1827-1912), English physician. Lister correctly perceived that infection during surgery was a prime cause of morbidity, although his method of preventing gangrene and other complications was somewhat awkward: patients in surgery were sprayed with huge quantities of carbolic acid. There's a lovely anecdote about the invention of rubber gloves: the first pair was molded from a surgical nurse's hands, because the carbolic acid she sprayed on patients was horribly irritating to her skin.

ॐ

Literalism—that which accords with the letter; a mode of interpretation without construction or metaphor. In the fine arts, a disposition to represent exactly without treating in an ideal manner, as in a documentary photograph. In the Bible, strict belief in the Creation Myth, the Deluge, Jonah and the whale, etc.

ॐ

Liturgism—the act of compiling or the compilation of forms of public worships or rituals (liturgies), especially the Christian service of the Eucharist.

ॐ

Localism—1. the state or condition of being local. 2. the customs or speech of a particular locality. 3. the influence of a particular place, especially the narrow-mindedness growing out of affection for a locality. See Provincialism, Sectionalism.

ॐ

Locoism—a disease found mainly among livestock, caused by eating locoweed. Symptoms include odd behavior and paralysis. *Loco* is Spanish for "crazy."

Logarithm—an Ism for someone with a speech impediment.

❧

Logical Positivism—in philosophy, a theory that accepts only statements that have verifiable and measurable consequences and rejects anything hypothetical or metaphysical. Also known as Logical Empiricism. See Empiricism, Positivism.

❧

Lollardism—the principles or tenets of the Lollards, a sect of reformers in Germany who mumbled their prayers and hymns. Another
group in England who followed the ideas of John Wycliffe (1320-1384)
were also known to mumble and whisper their prayers while lying
down. From them we get the expression "lollygag."

❧

Long-Termism—an idea promoted by the British government to
encourage Corporatism without saying so. To get the full picture,
consider the causes and effects of Short-Termism. The cure proposed
by Sir Brian Corby was a panel of stockbrokers, major employers,
and bureaucrats to discuss how big companies in Britain could be
encouraged to put the national interest ahead of profits. "There have
been promises of support from the Stock Exchange, Association
of British Insurers, National Association of Pension Funds, and the
Institutional Fund Managers Association. The Confederation of
British Industry also wants Sir Peter Gregson and Pen Kent.... With
all that lot working together, we may be sure nothing useful will
emerge." (Daily Telegraph)

❧

Lookism—a term used to accuse a person or group of unfairly favoring
someone based on his or her physical traits, especially in employment practices; i.e., discriminating against people considered ugly.
Part of the "politically correct" lingo in vogue on U.S. campuses,
the problem is based on the fact that covers are easier to read than
books. See Ableism.

❧

Loonyism—doctrines of a political party in England that has (unbelievably) risen to fourth place among all parties and recently beat the
Liberal-Democrats in an important by-election. Sadly, the Loony
movement has splintered into two rival factions: the traditional Monster Raving Loony Green Teeth Party (led by Screaming Lord Sutch)
and the Monster Raving Loony Party All-Night Alliance. Loonies
now hold seven council seats in various locales, and it's only a matter of time before they win a seat in Parliament, where they should
feel right at home.

❧

Low Churchism—the principles and doctrines of the branch of the
Anglican Church that opposed excessive Ritualism and rejected

apostolic succession as an essential of a valid ministry. They considered organization as being of minor importance and emphasized Evangelicalism, especially when compared with the "High Church," which catered to the landed gentry and nobles.

ॐ

Lower Criticism—a form of Biblical Criticism attempting to reconstruct the Bible's original texts. Also, Textual Criticism. Cf. Higher Criticism.

Loxodromism—the process of tracing or moving in a loxodromic line, which is the art of oblique sailing by the rhumb, a line which always makes an equal angle with every meridian and is oblique to the equator. Though a primitive mode of navigation, it is superior to dead reckoning.

ॐ

Loyalism—the practice of maintaining loyalty, especially to a government during war or revolution. The Loyalists (or Tories) in America sided with Britain in the War of Independence and were promptly ousted from their property when the Redcoats lost.

ॐ

Lucianism—the theories of Lucian, a 2nd-century Greek religious leader and satirist who denied the resurrection of actual bodies and souls upon the Second Coming of Christ, but held that representatives of both would appear in costume. Lucianists also taught that the souls of animals were not immortal, which will give comfort to Christians with arachnophobia.

ॐ

Luciferianism—the doctrines of a 4th-century sect called Luciferians, who supposedly taught that the soul was a carnal body transmitted to the child by its father. The Vatican has a manuscript of the Kabala with the full version of this esoteric doctrine. The Vatican, however, takes a dim view of lending rare books or publishing heresies, so it's unlikely you'll be able to find out much more.

ॐ

Ludditism—the practice of smashing machines that threaten to replace manual labor and unskilled workers, or any hatred of technology, industry, and modernity. Named for Ned Ludd, a Yorkshire, England resident who went beserk in 1799 and attacked some knitting machines. A decade later, textile workers destroyed more machines, and Ludditism became a political movement (later to be dolled-up in the language of Historical Materialism by Karl Marx). Ludd's French and Belgian comrades threw their wooden shoes into machines, giving us the word "sabotage," from the French *sabot* (shoe).

Fear of unemployment was rife in the 19th century, since no one had ever seen machines before and didn't realize they would make manufactured goods cheaper, thus making it easier for people to buy things. Two centuries later, it's easy to show that mechanization provided more employment, lowered the cost of living, and made it possible for folks like us to live in houses instead of thatch huts.

Today, Ludditism appears in the extremist wings of the environmental movement, whose leaders call for the destruction of cars and power plants so we can all return to the good old days of small family farms, bad teeth, and average lifespans of about 25.

Theresa says: "I thank God for my vacuum cleaner, hair dryer, washing machine, and typewriter. How else could I sit around all day learning about half-witted Yorkshiremen?"

Luminism—19th-century landscape painting on a large, wide canvas, emphasizing the horizon and reducing the size of objects to form vast panoramas with plenty of Realism and atmospheric light. Like the literary Transcendentalism of Emerson and Thoreau, a Luminist landscape tries to overwhelm the spectator with natural beauty.

≥⋒

Lutheranism—the doctrines taught by Martin Luther (1483-1546), German leader of the Protestant Reformation, who founded his own church on the proposition that "true penance consists of self-hate" and that "Christians are to be exhorted to follow Christ through pains, deaths, and hells." Believe it or not, this was considered a liberal alternative to the Catholic Church, which at that time was selling "Get Out of Purgatory Free" cards (a.k.a. indulgences) to the highest bidder.

Lyricism—a composition in the nature of a lyric, which is a poem fitted for song in which the author's emotions are prominent and the words are suitable for the lyre. So much for the traditional definition. Nowadays, it's anything screamed into a microphone, with accompanying cacophony and t-shirt hucksters.

Lysenkoism—the theories of Trofim Denisovich Lysenko (1898-1976), Russian biologist, who claimed heredity is not genetic and acquired traits can be inherited.

Macarism—1. a blessing, used by an austere Christian sect founded by Macarius in the 7th century, which pronounced everybody and everything happy. 2. the tenets of followers of a 4th-century Egyptian monk with the same name who cursed life in the desert.

Macedonianism—the doctrines of the followers of Macedonious. A bishop of Constantinople in the 4th century, he approved of God the Father and the Son but denied the divinity of the Holy Ghost, who supposedly doled out grace and helped people to speak in tongues.

Machiavellianism—the principles or policies of Niccolo Machiavelli (1469-1527), an Italian bureaucrat and political theorist who attempted to gain favor with the reigning prince by addressing a book on the subject of statecraft (*The Prince*) to him. His theory of government was based on practical application of force, cunning, and artifice. Today, the term connotes deviousness, ruthlessness, and amorality. "It is far safer to be feared than loved." (Machiavelli)

Magianism—the philosophy or doctrines of the Magi, a caste of Zoroastrian priests of the Medes and Persians who believed there are two principles, one the cause of good, the other the cause of evil. They were skilled in sorcery and sleight of hand, especially the "art" of producing effects by the aid of superhuman beings or spirits. The word "magic" arises from this source and means "to supply art."

Magic Realism—a style of American painting, halfway between Precisionism and Cubism, with a little Mysticism thrown in for spice. Also, a modern literary style of both North and South America, where unexplained, supernatural things happen that make symbolic and spiritual, if not rational, sense. Consult the works of Toni Morrison and Gabriel Garcia Marquez.

さ

Magnetism—1. the branch of science which describes the properties of magnets and magnetic phenomenon. 2. in psychology, an attribute of people who attract love, affection, or attention, or inspire passion in others. See Charism, Mesmerism.

The term originates from the area known as Magnesia, where the "lodestone" was first identified. These stones, magnetized specimens of iron ore, attracted iron and, when freely suspended, pointed to the earth's magnetic poles. Compasses, videotape, electric motors, telephones, and many other gadgets use Magnetism in their operations.

さ

Mahdiism—the belief and advocacy of the doctrine that a messiah will appear as a great leader of the Islamic faithful. Among Muslims, the Mahdi is the name for a great temporal and spiritual director. Historically, some believed he had appeared, but they were never sure because no leader claimed the title. In Iran, Ayatollah Khomeini (1900-1989) probably had his eye on it, and Mahdiism explains much of his absolute power.

Majorism—an ersatz, bogus Ism created to disguise the fact that British prime minister John Major has no coherent philosophy of government. "Mr. Major is still very much thrashing around in the shadow of Margaret Thatcher, the only British prime minister this century, perhaps ever, to have acquired her own Ism... But here is Mr. Major, only seven months into the job, never won a general election, a slip of a thing, really—and he feels so insecure, he must have an Ism just because *she* had one." (Robert Harris)

さ

Majoritarianism—belief in or practice of majority rule. This pleases most of the people most of the time. See Democratism.

さ

Malapropism—the unintentionally humorous misuse of words due to confusion of spelling or meaning. Named for Mrs. Malaprop, a character in Sheriden's *The Rivals*, who peppered her speech with pretentious words that were always misapplied and mispronounced. Similar to Spoonerism.

Malthusianism—the theories or doctrines of Thomas Malthus (1766-1834), an English economist who believed poverty was inevitable because the increase in human population was always greater than the increase in the means of subsistence. In the absence of war, famine, or plague, he argued, the government should enact measures to limit population. His theory was especially popular among the aristocracy, who had an investment in keeping the peasants poor, and it persists as a modern excuse for Conservatism, on the premise that poverty will exist no matter what we try to do about it.

The defect in Malthusian theory is that it ignores ethnic and sociological factors which distinguish certain societies and classes. For example, the birthrate among white Americans has dropped in proportion to their increasing personal income and education, while the birthrate among lower-income racial minorities has skyrocketed, in disregard of their poverty. Clearly, the birthrate is a matter of economics as well as education, personal choice, and public policies that either encourage or penalize overpopulation, regardless of economic growth.

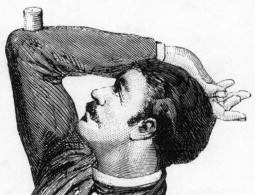

Mammonism—devotion to the pursuit of riches and worldliness, especially with evil intent. Mammon was the ancient god of wealth in Syria, as quoted by Matthew in the Biblical verse, "Ye cannot serve God and Mammon." See Helotism.

Mandaeanism—the system of religion of Mandaeans, once a large group of believers in southern Babylonia or Mesopotamia, now limited to small parts of Iraq and Iran. They believe in Gnosticism mixed with a little Judaism and Parseeism.

Mandarinism—a Mandarinic government or spirit. The Mandarins, or ministers of state in China, were so-named by foreigners, from the Malay and Hindu *mantri* or from the Latin *mandamus*, which means to command. The Chinese equivalent is *kwan*, or public servant. The Mandarins had high status in political and intellectual circles, and they exhibited mannered and elaborate styles of doing business. It's also the name of their language and a duck with beautiful colors. In England, "mandarins" are career civil servants in Whitehall.

Manichaeanism—the ancient Persian doctrine of incessant warfare between good and evil, or light and darkness, espoused by Manichaeus (216-276) in the 3rd century and considered heretical by the Catholic Church. See Dualism.

≈

Manifold Mysticism—similarity between Christianity and Hinduism which offers a la carte Mysticism: "...an intensely emotional kind and a cool, unemotional kind; an ardently erotic and a detached, intellectual kind; cult-oriented and noncult-oriented, nonsenuous Mysticism; naive-imaginative-poetic and reflective-rational-theoretical Mysticism." (Hans Kung)

≈

Mannerism—1. a characteristic trait or style, often carried to excess, especially regarding literature, art, and speech. 2. a style of art from the High Renaissance to the Baroque period in Italy, characterized by a search for novelty and asymmetrical compositions with huge discrepancies in scale and color.

≈

Maoism—the political philosophy of Mao Tse-Tung (1893-1976), revolutionary leader of Communist China whose explicit theory of Marxism is contained in a little red book, available at most libraries or by mail from your nearest Chinese embassy. Mao defeated a corrupt, badly led Nationalist Army in 1949 and then ruthlessly converted China into a workers' and peasants' state—eradicating everyone and everything that even vaguely smacked of Imperialism, Westernism, Nationalism, or Intellectualism.

Like Lenin, Mao was a true believer in Communism. Like Stalin, he tolerated no opposition. "Engage in no battle you are not sure of winning" was a typical Maoist epigram, and we are forced to admit that he achieved enormous victories by careful use of resources and shrewd adherence to this common-sense strategy. Maoism is therefore regarded as a philosophy for winners, even if they begin as barefoot insurgents and face superior "forces of repression."

Unfortunately, this makes Mao the patron saint of Red Terrorism—particularly in places like Cambodia, Laos, Burma, Venezuela, Bolivia, and Peru. It is impossible to estimate how many millions have been tortured and killed in Southeast Asia and South America by Maoist revolutionaries, and it is also impossible to explain what motivates these killers to attack defenseless peasants—unless one remembers the words of Chairman Mao: "Engage in no battle you are not sure of winning."

ટ⯑

Marginalism—a fundamental economic concept that explains why prices, wages, interest rates, and rents tend to be uniform in a free market, despite the fact that there are a vast number of economic players, each of whom has different resources and skills. In 1826, Johann Heinrich von Thunen (describing "diminishing returns") said that labor or capital in an enterprise would be increased to the point at which their increased cost was equal to the increased yield which they produced. The profitable increase in laborers "must be continued to the point at which the extra yield obtained through the last laborer employed equals in value the wage he receives." Likewise, the yield on capital "is determined by the yield of the last particle of capital employed." Therefore, all borrowed capital will be paid for at this uniform rate—the marginal cost.

ટ⯑

Marginal Utilitarianism—the "bottom line" of modern economics; not connected with moral Utilitarianism, but pertaining to the amoral, equal usefulness of all investments, all enterprises, and all units of work.

It's a long story, so we are forced to summarize rather brutally. Classical economists like Adam Smith and David Ricardo stood at the threshold of an economic system never before seen: Capitalism. They did not begin with the surface phenomenon of exchange, but with the abstract concepts of supply, demand, production, competition, and capital. In an effort to explain the workings of "an invisible hand" which determined who produced what, they had to devise a theory of value—i.e., how things were priced. Unfortunately, the theory they chose to elaborate was based on production cost, expressed in terms of sustenance, seed corn, rent, and "toil-and-trouble."

Karl Marx took this notion to its logical and most consistent outcome, attributing all value to labor—which negated the economic function of capital and rents. Marx wiped out the fundamental idea of supply-and-demand, and socialists of every stripe clamored for a "dictatorship of the proletariat," since Marx assumed only workers produced value. Meanwhile, the quest to explain the moral basis of capital stumbled on...

Von Thunen's theory of Marginalism explained rent as the difference in production cost between the producer who was closest to the market and the producer who was farthest away, because transportation costs would be much smaller for the producer who was located nearby and therefore the market would put a premium on the land he occupied. But this was still a cost-of-production theory. Nassau Senior (1790-1864) moved things forward slightly by showing that savings and abstinence (i.e., capital) contributed to value, too. But still, it was difficult to make anyone believe that a 100% capitalist theory of value would play in Peoria. Equating the abstinence of a bloated capitalist with the brute effort of a coalminer was especially hard to swallow.

Enter "utility." Hermann Heinrich Gossen got the ball rolling in 1854 by observing that "the amount of one and the same enjoyment diminishes continuously as we proceed with that enjoyment without interruption, until satiety is reached"—such as the declining enjoyment of successive bites of food. Therefore, Gossen argued, people tend to want a portion of everything and maximum pleasure results from a uniform level of want-satisfaction. This flattened "value" and made everything relative. Labor which creates the means of enjoyment also entails pain, and it follows that we can increase enjoyment by working so long as the enjoyment we get is greater than the pain involved in getting it. With William Stanley Jevons (1835-1882) and Carl Menger (1840-1921), the so-called "Austrian School" took off like a rocket, economists stopped talking about value altogether, and the big issue became marginal productivity. The final degree of utility (pleasure greater than pain) determines who works, how much they're paid, who invests, how much interest you pay the bank, and how much rent you pay your landlord. Everything is explained in terms of equilibrium. Nothing is right or wrong.

And that gave Karl Marx a clear field to run unopposed by capitalist theories. Socialism offered something that everybody could understand—a morality of "social justice," with good guys and bad guys. Cf. Historical Materialism.

❧

Marinism—the use of extravagant metaphors in literature, as characterized by the Marini school of Italian poets in the 17th century,

and the use of extravagant redwood hot tubs, as characterized by
the inhabitants of Marin County, California, in the 20th century.

Market Capitalism—a nonsensical term used by governments to avoid
saying that economic freedom means Capitalism.

Market Socialism—an even more nonsensical term that hopes
nobody is listening too carefully. It proposes to rescue the Soviet
economy by contradicting itself.

Marranism—practices of the Marranos, medieval Spanish and
Portuguese Jews who converted to Christianity under duress and
practiced Judaism in secret. Also Marranoism.

Martialism—bravery or warlike qualities. The term, derived from Mars,
the Roman god of war, refers specifically to war in action, its array,
attendants, costumes, etc. Revived by Time-Life Video in their persistent Hucksterism of old World War II documentaries on late-night
TV. "How good bad music and bad reasons sound when we march
against an enemy." (Friedrich Nietzsche)

Marxism—the teachings of Karl Marx (1818-1883), prominent advocate of modern Socialism whose chief work, *Das Kapital*, is a historical and critical analysis of Capitalism. Maintaining that class struggle is the agent of all historic change, Marx predicted that with industrial progress, the number of capitalists would decrease while the misery, oppression, and exploitation of the working class would increase. Consequently, the middle class would decline, and the aggravated working-class would unite and establish a socialist society.

All of this was precisely wrong. The number of those who accumulated capital has steadily increased in free economies, the middle class has grown dramatically, and Marxist revolutions were instigated exclusively among feudal societies that had little or no experience with either industry or laissez faire economics.

Marx's theories were based upon a "labor theory of value," wherein manual labor was credited with 100% of the value contributed to production. Capital (i.e., savings and financial risk) was mere "exploitation." See Historical Materialism, Dialectical Materialism, and Communism, all of which refer to aspects of the Marxist ideology.

"All I know is, I'm not a Marxist." (Marx)

ઠઅ

Masochism—an abnormal condition in which sexual gratification is obtained from physical or emotional abuse; by extension, pleasure in being abused or dominated or in practicing extreme self-denial. The name comes from Leopold von Sacher-Masoch (1836-1895), an Austrian novelist obsessed with self-inflicted pain linked to sexual pleasure and domination by women. Could also apply to people who attempt to compile books with lots of arcane words and describe them wittily—and to their publishers. Cf. Sadism.

ઠઅ

Materialism—1. an obsession or pre-occupation with things and comfort, as opposed to those who eschew possessions and concentrate on spiritual matters. Many do-gooders whine about how Capitalism causes Materialism, which has led to callousness and shallowness—forgetting, of course, that even the poor would like to have a million bucks so they could buy a new car, fancy house, and other neat stuff. 2. the doctrine of those who maintain the soul is not a spiritual substance distinct from matter, but the result or effect of the organization of matter in the body. Materialists believe that when you die, you're 100% dead and that's the end of your life. In a medieval world monopolized by religions that preached about an immortal soul that either ascended into Heaven or roasted in Hell, Materialism caused a major stir when first introduced as a modern philosophy of science. However, it was hardly "invented" during the Enlightenment; rather, it echoed a similar principle advanced by ancient Greeks as Atomism.

ઠઅ

Maternalism—motherly qualities or characteristics. "An ounce of mother is worth a ton of priest." (Spanish proverb)

૨ે

Mau-Mauism—the terrorist practices of a tribe in Kenya in the 1950's that sought to drive out whites. See Gangsterism.

૨ે

Mazdaism—the religion founded by Zoroaster; from the name of the god Ahura Mazda. See Zoroastrianism.

૨ે

McCarthyism—a general term for the practice of making unfounded and slanderous assertions ("witch hunting"), so-named from the policies and attitudes of Sen. Joseph McCarthy (1909-1957) during a series of Congressional investigations in the early 1950's, in which he accused numerous government officials of treasonous affiliations with the Communist Party. None of his allegations were ever proved, but McCarthy was nonetheless able to ruin many lives. Broadly, the term has come to describe the tactics of anyone who seeks conspiracies, makes harsh, unsubstantiated accusations, or doubts another's Patriotism.

૨ે

Mechanism—1. a behavior used by someone to cope with a situation, as in "defense Mechanism." 2. the parts collectively, or the arrangement of the parts, of a machine, engine, or instrument intended to apply power to useful purpose. From time to time, it has been said that plants, lower animals, and even humans are elaborate machines which have no freedom of thought or moral choice. See Determinism. "What is man ... but a minutely set, ingenious machine for turning, with infinite artfulness, the red wine of Shiraz into urine?" (Isak Dinesen)

≥●

Mechanoporphism—the belief that that the universe can be explained in mechanistic terms.

≥●

Mecism—the abnormal prolongation of a part of the body.

≥●

Medecinism—the political shenanigans of Jacques Medecin, mayor of Nice, France, who fled to South America to avoid fraud charges. His sister Genevieve plans to run for the vacant office, thus continuing a 62-year family hegemony. Among other things, Jacques diverted 10 million francs from municipal subsidies and deposited 5 million in the bank account of a young female acquaintance. He was last seen in Uruguay.

≥●

Medievalism—the spirit, manners, or principles of the Middle Ages, especially in matters of art and religion. "Scratch a collectivist and you will usually find a medievalist." (Nathaniel Branden)

Mediumism—a tenet of orthodox Spiritualism that says circumstances independent of a person's own volition may modify a person's aura, so that strange manifestations (of angels or devils) occur. It is the passive yielding of weak, mortal flesh to the control and suggestions of spirits—a.k.a. possession. Seances and "channeling" have seen a revival in recent years since actress Shirley Maclaine went "out on a limb."

ða

Megalopolitanism—a characteristic of a cluster of several large cities (a megalopolis), such as extensive traffic jams.

ða

Mekhitarianism—the arts and practices of a congregation founded in the late 17th century by an Armenian named Mekhitar da Pietro, to instruct and improve the condition of his countrymen. In 1715, the Venetian Republic granted him the island of San Lazzaro, between the Lido and Venice, where he built his convent. The Mekhitarists are devoted to literary work, especially the translation of European literature into Armenian. You can visit the convent today and see the monks working on their age-old tradition.

ða

Melanism—an abnormal deposit of pigment, especially in the epidermis, hair, and feathers of mammals and birds. Melanin, the pigment in our skin, protects us from the harmful rays of the sun. One thing we've never understood about White Supremacism: If dark skin is supposedly so objectionable, how come whites spend vast sums on cruise vacations and Coppertone to get it? Note, however, that excessive sun-tanning is the main cause of preventable skin cancers.

ða

Meliorism—1. the improvement of social conditions by indirect, practical means—e.g. by making physical surroundings better—as distinguished from po'itical, religious, or moral methods. 2. the doctrine that everything in nature tends to produce a progressive improvement.

ða

Mendelism—the theories of heredity in sexually reproducing Organisms espoused by Gregor Mendel (1822-1884), Austrian monk and naturalist: chiefly, that an offspring is not intermediate in type between its parents, but that the type of one or other parent is predominant. Mendel's work has been applied to the study of the inheritance of disease and has led to an immense body of knowledge as to the predictability of diseases being present in offspring. Currently, research aims at extensive "gene-mapping" that may succeed in proving a correlation of character traits and their genetic transmission.

ða

Mennonitism—the practices and beliefs of the Mennonites, an Anabaptist sect originating in Europe, now mainly found in North America. They oppose Paedobaptism and marriage outside the faith and are noted for their simplicity and plain dress. See Anabaptism, Hutteritism.

❧

Mensabulism—a mystical revelation obtained from a Ouija Board; also called "table turning." "We who well know the value of the phenomenon are perfectly sure that after having charged the table with our magnetic efflux, we have called to life, or created an intelligence analogous to our own, which like ourselves is endowed with a free will, can talk and discuss with us, with a degree of superior lucidity." (*Journal de Magnetisme*, circa 1860)

❧

Menshevism—the policies of Russia's Social Democratic Party, which advocated gradual conversion to Socialism through parliamentary government in cooperation with bourgeois parties (as opposed to Bolshevism). Needless to say, they didn't last long. They were absorbed into the Communist Party.

❧

Mentalism—the belief that objects exist only in the mind of the observer. See Subjectivism, Solipsism.

Mephitism—the trait of having a foul or noxious exhalation or poisonous stench. City dumps and skunks are prime examples. Mephistopheles in *Faust* was so-named to associate the character with mephitis, an awful, destructive smell. Hence, it's the reason we associate the Devil with a bad odor and the ability to destroy.

The hucksters on Madison Avenue would have you believe you'll practice Mephitism if you don't use their New! Improved! deodorant.

ಇ

Mercantilism—an economic theory that guided monarchs and leaders in the 16th century, prior to the invention of Capitalism. The king held the power to grant monopolies of trade and finance, which he did according to whatever increased his treasure (literally, gold and silver).

Mercantilism was based on "fear of goods"—i.e., fear of a trade imbalance that would result in paying out more than received from sale of domestic manufactures. The only surplus mercantilists understood was a profit made in selling, on the theory that "what one gained, the other lost." Therefore, exports were encouraged, as long as imports did not reduce the "profit" made by trading. Quite logically, this degenerated into Bullionism. In more general use, the term connotes Commercialism.

ಇ

Mercurialism—poisoning by mercury. That'll teach you to suck thermometers. Also, Hydrargyrism.

ಇ

Meritocratism—rule by the most deserving, talented, skillful, or successful. Compared to other systems like Aristocratism (rule by elites) and Bureaucratism (rule by paperwork), rule by the most able sounds positively attractive. However, there remains the sticky problem of defining "ability."

In many Western countries, the concept of a Civil Service based on non-partisan, competitive testing of all applicants for government jobs has become something of a cultural icon. Compared to patronage and Cronyism, it seemed irresistable. But civil servants mushroomed in every branch of the Federal system, with massive benefits and cost-of-living adjustments. And once hired, they couldn't be fired. With affirmative action, quotas, and such, Meritocratism yielded to Trade Unionism.

In the private sector, business always approved of giving the spoils to the victor. But in the 1980's, a peculiar victor seemed to claim huge spoils: the market speculator who traded promises, debts, and options. He manufactured nothing, invested nothing, invented nothing. And the tax consultants, lawyers, and bond daddies grew wealthier with each paper transaction, all the while creating nothing but mountains of debt. Reward flowed to the most shameless, the highest rollers, the zaniest lenders.

Thus, both attempts to implement a meritocracy became testaments to stupidity and greed. In government, the well-intentioned Civil Service has grown like a cancer. Private enterprise, no longer adept at making things, plunged into money-changing and Hucksterism. Corporate debt and bank failures have yet to be fully reckoned. Leadership by "experts" has brought us to a kind of fairy-tale denouement, with the Naked Emperor surrounded by stunned peasants.

If Meritocratism takes the blame, so be it. But see Keynesianism, Ableism, New Dealism, etc. "The silence that accepts merit as the most natural thing in the world is the highest applause." (Ralph Waldo Emerson)

৵

Mesmerism—1. Hypnotism, or extraordinary, compelling attraction. 2. the doctrines of Friedrich Mesmer (1733-1815), who claimed that one person can influence the will and nervous system of another by an emanation called Animal Magnetism, which he claimed to possess, or simply by the domination of one's will over that of the other person. Mesmerism has also been defined as "Hypnotism before it wore good clothes, kept a carriage, and asked Incredulity to dinner." (Ambrose Bierce)

Mesodontism—having medium-sized teeth.

৵

Metabolism—1. the chemical changes which take place in an organic body in the process of living and growing. 2. in theology, an early Christian doctrine of some who regarded the Eucharist as embodying both the real and the symbolic presence of God.

৵

Metachronism—an error in chronology made by placing the occurrence of an event after its time—something older women do regularly when asked about their date of birth.

৵

Metagnosticism—in philosophy, the doctrine that a knowledge of the Absolute is within the reach of humans, not through logical processes but through the higher religious consciousness. A major opponent of Agnosticism.

৵

Metagrammatism—same as Annagramatism.

৵

Metamorphism—the condition of having undergone a change in form and structure. Some people believe that, on the day of Christ's Ascension, His body was changed into the Deity. The most common natural example is that of the caterpillar becoming a butterfly. With the invention of liposuction and breast implants, humans are enjoying more options in Metamorphism than ever.

Metempiricism—a system of philosophy based on *a priori* reasoning and Transcendentalism, which means that philosophy lies beyond the limits of experience—and they can prove it! A neat contradiction in terms.

Methodism—methodical action or character, notably in church doctrines practiced by the Methodists, which originated in a religious club founded at Oxford University by John Wesley (1703-1791). The name Methodist was given to him and his companions by students because of the regularity of their lives and the strictness of their religious observances. See Wesleyianism and Holy Rollerism.

Me-Tooism—the practice of agreeing with your opponent and adopting his tactics because he's Politically Correct, because he represents the mainstream view, or because he's winning.

Microcephalism—condition of having an abnormally small head. Characteristic of missionaries who visited certain tribes in New Guinea that practiced ritual head-shrinking.

Microorganism—microscopic plant or animal.

Microseism—faint ground vibration, most likely caused by earthquakes at sea.

Militarism—the system or policy which causes nations to maintain great armies and pay excessive attention to military affairs. Among the ancients, military forces were the principal agents of prosperity, inasmuch as geographical dominion was the measure of a king's or nation's resources and the enslavement of foreigners contributed wealth to an empire.

With the introduction of industry, free trade, and Capitalism, military forces have been almost completely confined to the strategic role of peace-keeping, either by defending national borders or maintaining a "balance of power" that deters international aggression. A standing army no longer adds wealth, it drains it—and today, Militarism is a volatile, "destabilizing" policy which few nations can afford, since increased prosperity depends on international trade.

Two spurious arguments regarding Militarism: The first suggests that capitalist economies depend on armed conquest of Third World markets to "exploit" larger numbers of people, monopolize natural resources, and postpone the inevitable impoverishment of their own workers—all of which is pure Marxism, of course. However, wherever capitalist countries sought trade with Third World countries (outside the context of Colonialism, which was a policy that predated free trade), such relationships were predominantly between private enterprises and Third World governments. Western companies contributed capital, expertise, royalties, and wages in exchange for whatever the locals had to sell—which was usually not much before they were taught modern methods of production. The leaders of these Third World countries typically raked in a bonanza of hard currency, which they promptly salted away in Switzerland.

And that brings us to the second spurious argument: Militarism is only a Western trait. When the subject is the Soviet Union, critics proclaim the obvious necessity for socialist countries to spend two-thirds of their national income on defense. If the Soviets invaded Afghanistan or any of their Eastern European "allies," it was only to liberate their comrades from the horrors of Imperialism. Here, too, the experience of Militarism teaches a harsh lesson: the costs are enormous, the returns paltry. The U.S. withdrew from Vietnam and the Soviets from Afghanistan because Militarism is a pure waste of time and money in the modern world.

❧

Millennialism—the tenets of those who believe in the forthcoming reign of Christ on earth with his saints for a thousand years (the Millennium). In the Bible, Revelations says this time is reserved for Christ; Satan will be bound and restrained from reducing men to sin. Also, Millenarianism.

❧

Millerism—the doctrines and beliefs of the Millerites, disciples of William Miller (1782-1849), an American pre-millennialist who said the end of the world and the coming of Christ's reign on earth would be in 1843. Ooops. See Pre-Millennialism.

❧

Mimiism—after the character Mimi the Deprived Child, who thinks that no one will feed her and that her place at the hearth may be revoked at any moment if she displeases the master of the house. Thus, in practice, a preoccupation with "me," worrying whether Me-Me will get everything Me-Me desires.

❧

Minimalism—an art movement in the 1960's which proposed to make identical, modular units and mathematical formulas into works of beauty. Expression of human feeling is strictly *verboten* to Minimalists (although they are allowed to snicker in private when someone praises their work).

❧

Mischievous Squirearchism—"a government dominated by English public school boys who never forgave Margaret Thatcher for being the only man among them." (*London Evening Standard*)

❧

Misotheism—the hatred of God. "No man hates God without first hating himself." (Fulton J. Sheen)

❧

Mithraism—an ancient mystery religion and the major competitor of Christianity during the 2nd and 3rd century, this Persian cult worshipped Mithras, god of light and truth, and became the religion of much of the Roman army. There's a Mithraist temple in the Yale University art gallery—and Yale's motto is *Lux et Veritas* (Light and Truth). Hmmmm.

❧

Mithridatism—the practice of protecting oneself against a poison by taking periodic, gradually increasing doses of the poison and building an immunity.

❧

Modalism—1. in logic, the doctrine that in the science of reasoning, the employment of modal propositions and modal Syllogisms is of prime importance. 2. in theology, strict conformity to a modal form of worship and the observance of a mode in all rites and ceremonies. It also applies to the Christian doctrine taught by Sabellius that the Son and the Holy Ghost are not persons but mere forms ("modes") of the Father.

વ્ર

Moderatism—the quality of being non-extreme and middle-of-the-road, especially in religious or political opinions. Moderation was a cornerstone of Aristotle's ethics, and in today's atmosphere of anti-intellectual politics, it has become a vital principle among those who wish to please the mainstream. "Whenever you find you are on the side of the majority, it is time to pause and reflect." (Mark Twain)

વ્ર

Modernism—something characterizing current or new usage or style, such as a modern method or idiom. As of this writing, if you accused someone of Ableism or Speciesism, you would be using a Modernism.

વ્ર

Mohammedanism—the religion, doctrines, and precepts of Elijah Mohammed (570-632 A.D.), contained in the Koran; Islam. The Koran teaches five universally binding obligations (the "Pillars of Islam"): daily prayer, fasting during the month of Ramadan, pilgrimage to Mecca, alms-giving, and profession of faith. See Islamism. Also, Muhammedanism. "Silk was invented so that women could go naked in clothes." (Mohammed)

વ્ર

Mohism—the teachings of Mo-Tze, a 5th-century B.C. Chinese philosopher. He advocated the universal love of all mankind and rule by an absolute monarch.

વ્ર

Molinism—the doctrines of the Molinists, somewhat resembling the tenets of the Arminians. Terso de Molina was a Spanish Jesuit in the 16th century. See Arminianism and Jesuitism.

વ્ર

Momism—excessive love of or dependence on your mother. See Alfred Hitchcock's *Psycho*.

વ્ર

Monachism—the state of monks or nuns who choose celibacy, seclusion, and poverty.

વ્ર

Monadism—a philosophical doctrine of Gottfried Wilhelm von Leibnitz (1646-1716), who asserted the existence of monads, indivisible entities which he believed were the ultimate constituent of the universe.

৯

Monarchianism—several doctrines of 2nd- and 3rd-century Christianity emphasizing the unity of God, maintaining that the Father, the Son, and the Holy Ghost are three aspects or manifestations of God. See Trinitarianism.

Monarchism—1. the principles of rule by king or queen, or the love of having kings and queens who enjoy religious or political power by virtue of their birth. 2. the state of government in which the supreme power is either actually or nominally lodged in the hands of a single person. In England, this is Queen Elizabeth II; in the U.S., this is a Kennedy. "Kings are not born; they are made by universal hallucination." (George Bernard Shaw)

৯

Monasticism—pertaining to the monastic system or to a house of religious retirement from ordinary concerns, like an abbey or convent. Among Christians, monasteries were begun in the 4th century, monastic vows in the 6th. The Reformation greatly diminished the number of monasteries, as they were appropriated by sovereigns and transferred to universities. We owe the preservation of nearly all ancient, classical, and early medieval literature to the monasteries. The monastic life is also practiced among the Brahmans, Lamas, and Buddhists, and has been from pre-Christian times.

৯

Monergism—the theological doctrine that humans have no role in the saving of souls and that the Holy Spirit does it all. The opposite of Synergism.

৯

Monetarism—an economic theory, associated notably with Milton Friedman, which holds that Keynesianism and paper money cannot reverse economic fundamentals (supply-and-demand) in terms of money supply. If you print more notes, which are promises to pay at a future date, people will rightly assume that a dollar tomorrow will be worth less than a dollar today.

ॐ

Mongolism—a condition derived from a chromosomal deficiency resulting in a number of defects in the offspring. The preferred term is Down syndrome. It was named Mongolism due to the facial resemblance of victims to those of the Mongolian people. Women who give birth after age 40 run a higher risk of their offspring manifesting defects of this type.

ॐ

Monism—belief in one fundamental reality. This takes three forms: 1. Idealism—only the mind is real; 2. Materialism—only matter is real; 3. the Double-Aspect Identity—mind and body are different aspects of one reality. Cf. Dualism.

ॐ

Monodynamism—the theory that all forms of activity in nature are phenomena of a single force, power, capacity, or talent.

ॐ

Monogenism—the theory that the human race has descended from a single pair or a single ancestral type.

ॐ

Monometallism—the policy of having only one metal (e.g., gold) as a standard in the coinage of a country; the belief in the advantages of a single metallic standard. See Bimetallism.

ॐ

Monophysism—a Coptic Christian heresy that arose as a reaction to Nestorianism. Followers of St. Cyril of Alexandria (827-869), monophysites believed that Jesus had only one nature, His humanity absorbed in His divinity, "as a drop of wine would be in an ocean of water."

ॐ

Monopolism—1. the existence of a firm that enjoys exclusive control of the market in one or more products. 2. real or imagined exclusion of competitors from a market.

To the extent that government licenses are legally enforced monopolies, Monopolism does exist, and it's dangerous to your wallet. However, most people believe government-ordained monopolies are in the public's best interest; without them, we'd be at the mercy of private monopolists. But when no government license or edict distorts the market, freedom of contract and plain self-interest kill any monopolies that do develop. Every attempt to "corner the market" on Wall Street has ended in ruin for those who tried. In a free market, as soon as you demand an uneconomic price for something, you tempt new competitors to go into production. You can count on it: somebody somewhere will find a way to do it faster, better, or cheaper than you. We buy things because they're convenient and priced appropriately—and if they aren't, we do without. Monopolism, every would-be Robber Baron's dream, doesn't work in free societies.

Monopsychism—the doctrine of the existence of only one immortal soul, of which each person is a constituent part.

Monosyllabism—the use of single-syllable words. See Laconicism.

Monotheism—1. the doctrine of the existence of only one God. 2. the belief that Christ has but one will and one energy, both divine.

Monroeism—ambitious foreign policy doctrine of Pres. James Monroe (1758-1831), who proclaimed in 1823 that the New World (North, Central, and South America) was off-limits to European interference. At the time, the U.S. was a third-rate power, so you can imagine how big a bluff this was. But it worked! And ever since, the U.S. has blocked European power in much of the Western Hemisphere (Cuba being the most notable exception).

Monroeism gave way to Adventurism, Atlanticism, and

Pragmatism—the final product of which was Oliver North's selling the Ayatollah Khomeini a case of rocket launchers, lying to Congress about it, and being hailed as a patriot.

ॐ

Montanism—the tenets of the followers of Montanus, a Phrygian bishop of the 2nd century who claimed that the Holy Spirit dwelt in him as an instrument for purifying and guiding men in the Christian life.

ॐ

Moralism—1. the practice of accusing others of violating a code of ethics they may not understand or agree with. 2. a moral maxim, like the Golden Rule. "Go into the street, and give one man a lecture on morality and another a shilling, and see which will respect you most." (Samuel Johnson)

ॐ

Moravianism—the religious system of the Moravians, a sect called the United Brethren, tracing its origin to John Huss (1374-1415), a Bohemian religious reformer. Expelled from Moravia in the beginning of the 18th century, they settled in Saxony in 1722. They were evangelical and preferred to live in separate colonies, called *Heerenhuders*.

ॐ

Mormonism—the beliefs, practices, and government of the Mormons, a Christian sect officially known as The Church of Jesus Christ of Latter-Day Saints. They are followers of Joseph Smith (1805-1844), who claimed to work miracles and to have found an addition to the Bible engraved on golden plates, which he published as *The Book of Mormon* in 1830. After his death, some members of the sect, led by Brigham Young (1801-1877), established themselves in Utah, with the leaders controlling civil and religious affairs. Polygamy was practiced by some Utah Mormons until 1890, when it was formally abandoned due to the prohibition of Congress.

ॐ

Morphinism—addiction to morphine, and the diseased condition caused by this addiction.

ॐ

Mosaicism—the condition in which tissues of genetically different types occur in the same Organism.

ॐ

Mosaism—adherence to the system of laws and doctrines handed down by Moses and contained in the first five books of the Old Testament, known as the Pentateuch.

ॐ

Moslemism—see Mohammedanism.

ॐ

Mosoneism—extreme of hatred of change or of anything new. Sort of ultimate Conservatism.

Mugwumpism—1. in politics, the practice of not supporting your party's candidate; specifically, a Republican who did not support James Blaine in 1884. 2. the condition of a candidate who cannot or will not make up his mind about an issue. 3. acting as a political independent rather than as a party member. From the Algonquin word for "great man."

Multiculturalism—a recent movement, especially in education, to include the art, literature, and history of minority cultures in textbooks and minority participation in all aspects of public life. While Multiculturalism in theory sounds noble, since it seeks inclusion and respect for all, in practice it boils down to condemning anything done or said by "dead, white, European males," no matter how worthy, and elevating anything done or said by someone "oppressed" or "victimized" (often, everyone except white males), no matter how trite or muddle-headed. Also, since the cultures that espouse Capitalism are "oppressors," they can't be part of the "multi-tude," and there's usually a healthy dose of Marxism and Socialism added for good measure. It's currently the gospel for all those who aspire to "political correctness," especially on college campuses.

Multi-Optionalism—According to Miles Kington, "a new kind of novel-writing embracing every possible meaning of a word." Example:
"How would you like it done?" asked the waiter.
"Medium," said John.
The waiter took him to a back room where the medium was waiting.
"I have just contacted the other side," she said.
"Tell them we demand unconditional surrender," said the waiter.

Munchausenism—a tendency to tell exaggerated stories, especially regarding one's allegedly poor health. From Baron Karl Friedrich Hieronymous von Munchausen (1720-1797), a German soldier, adventurer, and teller of tall tales. To learn more, rent a video of the film *The Adventures of Baron von Munchausen.*

ɜ𝄠

Municipalism—the principles or advocacy of local government. The notion was derived from ancient towns subject to Rome but governed by their own laws. From the Latin *municeps*, which means inhabitant of a free town; a free citizen.

Mussolinian Revolutionism— "bogus Populism of those who deceive themselves or want to deceive us into believing that they aim at the good of the people; the abstract Maximalism of those who put on the adjective 'socialist' like a fashionable dress, a lie that pays off." (*London Times*)

ɜ𝄠

Mussulmanism—an archaic term for the faith of Turkish and Persian Moslems.

ɜ𝄠

Mutacism—using the letter "N" abnormally or pertaining to the sound it represents. Also, Mytacism.

ॐ

Mutazilism—the beliefs of an extinct Islamic sect which believed that nothing can be predicated of Allah but eternity and that the eternal nature of the Koran was questionable. They also maintained that man does good or evil of his own free will.

ॐ

Mutism—the conscious or unconscious refusal to respond verbally to a question. See any of Ronald Reagan's press conferences.

ॐ

Mutualism—see Social Mutualism.

ॐ

Myrmecophilism—the situation that exists when a non-ant insect begins living in an ant colony.

ॐ

Mysticism—1. the belief or doctrine that knowledge can come from spiritual illumination that cannot be explained by reason. 2. in theology, a view that proposes direct communication between God and man through the inward perception of the mind. 3. in more general usage, any obscure thought. "There is only one state that fulfills the mystic's longing for infinity, non-causality, non-identity: death." (Ayn Rand)

ॐ

Mytilotoxism—mussel poisoning.

Nagualism—a Mexican Indian mythology first reported in 1812 by Don Pedro Bautista Peno, from missionary sources. The *Nagas* is a great serpent worshipped in *estufas* (initiation caves), impenetrable temples closed to Spaniards. In ancient tradition, the Nagas is regarded as a wise force unto itself.

Nanism—the state of being undersized; Dwarfism. "Better to have loved and lost a short person than never to have loved a tall." (David Chambless)

Napoleonism—same as Bonapartism. "How often we recall, with regret, that Napoleon once shot at a magazine editor and missed him and killed a publisher. But we remember with charity that his intentions were good." (Mark Twain)

Narcissism—1. Egocentricism. 2. in psychiatry, infantile self-love, a normal step in psychosexual development. The word comes from the Greek myth of a beautiful youth, Narcissus, who was enamored of his own image reflected in a pool and was changed into a flower. Also, Narcism. "To love oneself is the beginning of a lifelong romance." (Oscar Wilde)

Narco-Terrorism—the practice of violence and mayhem to protect the business and operations of illegal drug suppliers and to instill fear in the government and populace. Prevalent in Central American countries, where "drug lords" maintain vast cocaine-making plantations. Repeal of extradition treaties is high on the narco-terrorists' agenda, along with better prison conditions for drug lords who turn themselves in. Do you think doing time in a 14-room suite with only three phone lines, one fax machine, and two bodyguards is cruel and unusual punishment? See Terrorism.

&

Narcotism—addiction to or the physical conditions caused by narcotics, medicines that relieve pain and produce sleep but, in high doses, produce stupor, coma, convulsions, and ultimately death. Belladonna, opium derivatives, and hemlock are examples of narcotics.

&

Nancyism—the policies or practices attributed to Nancy Reagan, Ronald Reagan's wife, who is said to have extensively manipulated her husband's second term as President of the United States. "A woman is like a teabag—only in hot water do you realize how strong she is." (Nancy Reagan)

&

Nationalism—1. the state, policy, or principle of being strongly attached to one's country. 2. the policy of a nation's asserting its interests over the common interests of all nations. 3. a trait peculiar to one nation, such as the practice of chewing qat in Yemen.

As a modern concept, the goal of Nationalism is to reunite racial or tribal members under a government of their own choosing, within historic borders. Zionism is an example, but among the new nations in Africa it had an equal impetus as a justification of territorial claims. The most spectacular national reunion recently, of course, is the new Germany.

Historically, nations grew from ethnic or geographic groupings, and these prevailed in law as more practical than religious or theoretical concepts of "nationality." Thus, territory and ethnicity are central aspects of nationhood, especially when expressed in terms of citizenship, internal government, or foreign relations. Nationalism and international feuds were the proximate cause of almost all wars, including World Wars I and II, which were fought largely in the name of national pride.

This is not to deny that nations often incorporate or exploit ideologies or religion to rally their citizens and cement their allegiance. However, the overriding concern of nations and the basic thrust of Nationalism is to preserve or expand the territory by which their statehood is defined. "Men and nations behave wisely once they have exhausted all the other alternatives." (Abba Eban)

&

National Socialism—the formal name for Naziism.

&

Nativism—1. in politics, favoring native-born citizens over national-ized, foreign-born citizens. The term often connotes an anti-intellectual, even racist, opinion about immigrants. 2. in philosophy, the theory that innate ideas exist.

ᘍ

Naturalism—1. a mere state of nature; an uncivilized, wicked, or gross condition. 2. the doctrine of those who deny a supernatural agen-cy in the miracles and revelations recorded in the Bible and other forms of spiritual influence, especially the doctrine that the crea-tion of the universe was due to chance and that all the phenomena of nature are manifestations of that same chance acting inevitably; opposing the doctrine that an omnipotent will or other supernatural cause created the universe and directs its destiny. 3. in the fine arts, a close (although not extreme) adherence to the natural and the real. 4. in literature, a philosophy opposed to Idealism, in that it mirrors what is rather than what should be, and slightly differing from Realism in that it depicts motives and acts unaffected by spiritual desire or hate. The 19th-century writer Emil Zola was considered a Naturalist rather than a Romantic.

Naturism—Nudism with love beads and ceremonies.

ᘍ

Navalism—the policy of maintaining or increasing naval strength. The British Navy, arguably the most influential navy ever assembled, played a crucial role in the development of international trade, es-pecially during the 19th century, when piracy and warfare were sub-stantially eliminated by Britain's command of the high seas. During World War II, the aircraft carrier became a principal means of at-tack in the Pacific, while troop carriers, submarines, and cargo ves-sels were more critical in Europe. The traditional battleship, however, has lost almost all significance in modern warfare, and it's unclear what role naval forces will retain in the future, other than nuclear-powered submarines and a small number of surface vessels to deter piracy and smuggling. "Don't talk to me about naval tradition. It's nothing but rum, sodomy and the lash." (Winston Churchill)

ᘍ

Nazartism—the vows or practices of the Nazarites, a group of Jews who vowed to live lives of extraordinary purity and devotion and to leave their hair uncut after the fashion of Samson.

る

Naziism—the policies and tenets of the former National Socialist Workers Party of Germany and of its adherents and sympathizers in other countries. Core beliefs of the Nazis were that Germany had been economically crippled and "humiliated" by France and Britain, who forced the German people to pay heavy reparations after World War I; that the banking system was ruled by Jews, who profited from Germany's economic woes; that the German race had descended from "pure" Aryan stock, destined to rule the world; that economic and social progress depended on reuniting German-speaking peoples under one government; that Communism was a Jewish-inspired plot to strip Germans of their religion, industries, and nationality; that military strength and absolute obedience to military leaders were essential to German destiny; and that intellectual processes were inferior to Emotionalism, Mysticism, and Nationalism as tools of cognition and social progress.

The Nazi leader, Adolph Hitler (1889-1945), came to power in the early 1930's by a combination of factors, including the weakness of the democratically elected Reichstag and his skillful use of intimidation and power. A devotee of astrology and fanatical religion, Hitler saw himself as the savior of his race and is today most infamous for orchestrating the Holocaust, in which millions of Jews, gypsies, and other "undesirables" were slaughtered. Though we are apt to call any racist or anti-Semite a Nazi, the terms are not really interchangeable. Nazis ruled by an extensive network of spies, including the Hitler Youth, children who spied on their parents and reported even the slightest hint of dissent. More than Racism, a pervasive regimentation of society by its leaders is the hallmark of Naziism. Cf. Stalinism and see Fascism.

Those who think "It can't happen here" should consider the following excerpts from the Nazis' political program, adopted in Munich in 1920: "We ask that the government undertake the obligation above all of providing citizens with adequate opportunity for employment... We demand profit-sharing in big business. We demand a broad extension of care for the aged... the greatest possible consideration of small business in the purchases of the national, state, and municipal governments... an all-around enlargement of our entire system of public education... education at government expense of gifted children of poor parents... the improvement of public health...." You see, evil does not announce itself as evil, threatening to destroy your happiness. Quite the contrary—it humbly defends you, taking nothing for itself, and it prays to God for guidance.

る

Necessitarianism—the doctrine that everything happens according to fixed laws which cannot be changed; also, the doctrine that we have no free will and cannot control our actions, but proceed necessarily and inevitably from motives not of our own making. See Determinism.

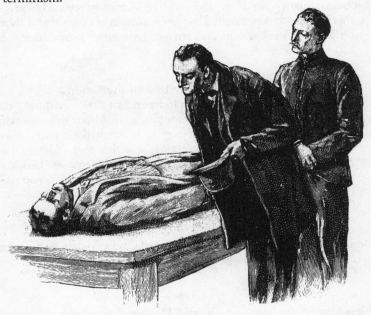

Necrophilism—insane love for dead bodies, in some cases extending so far that it becomes a sexual perversion.

ॐ

Negativism—1. belief in the overwhelming superiority of one's opponents; a philosophy which afflicts minorities and disaffected artists. See Pessimism. 2. in philosophy, any system of negative philosophy, such as Atheism, Existentialism, Nihilism, or Skepticism. 3. in psychology, the tendency in some people to respond to a request by doing nothing or something completely opposite or different from the expected act.

ॐ

Negroism—1. a doctrine advocating equal rights for Negroes. 2. a speech trait characteristic of Negroes. In the U.S., for example, many blacks use the word "be" instead of its conjugations: "I be going to the store," rather than "I am going" or "I will be going."

ॐ

Negrophilism—love for a Negro or the Negro race, especially by a non-Negro.

ॐ

Neo-Catholicism—beliefs of an Anglican who prefers the rites of the Roman Catholic Church. See also Newmanism.

૨●

Neoclassicism—late 18th- and early 19th-century revival of classical motifs and subjects, inspired by the excavation of Pompeii and characterized by Greek motifs and strong, geometric compositions. See Classicism.

૨●

Neocolonialism—the policy whereby a strong nation seeks political or economic dominance over an independent nation without necessarily turning it into a colony. Europeans talk about this a lot when they berate Americans for trying to overrun their culture with McDonald's and *Dallas*. It's certainly true that many foreign destinations for U.S. tourists are, for all practical purposes, U.S. colonies. In most Mexican resorts and Caribbean countries, you never need to exchange dollars for the local currency, and you can watch CNN day and night. Cf. Economic Colonialism.

૨●

Neo-Conservatism—a moderate form of Conservatism and Reaganism. Mostly, it's Welfare Statism in a bad mood, pretending to be Conservatism.

૨●

Neo-Confucianism—a 12th- and 13th-century eclectic philosophy combining Confucianism with elements of Taoism and Buddhism.

૨●

Neo-Darwinism—Darwinism with its later modifications and extensions, especially the theory that acquired behavioral traits cannot be inherited.

૨●

Neo-Expressionism—see Bad Artism.

૨●

Neo-Hellenism—Hellenism brought to a modern standard with the application of ancient Greek ideals to present-day practices or arts, especially as concerning the Italian Renaissance.

૨●

Neo-Impressionism—19th-century style of painting led by Georges Seurat (1859-1891) and his friends. Rather than paint with dabs of color to render the shimmery surface of objects, they sought new ways to depict solid forms, using scientific color theories, aesthetics, and the phenomenon of visual sensation. The most striking feature was the use of a multitude of small dots of color applied with the tip of the brush which, when seen from a distance, blended in the viewer's eye (see Pointillism). Both groups, Impressionist

and Neo-Impressionist, were saying "This is how I, the artist, see it." Later, Van Gogh and Gaugin said "This is how I, the artist, feel it." Meanwhile, academic art maintained the principle of painting how you, the public, wanted it. See Impressionism.

Neo-Isolationism—20th-century Isolationism, or the desire for America to stop being "the world's policeman," since it's expensive and unpopular with the rest of the world, except when they need a cop.

Neo-Lamarckism—the theory that acquired characteristics can be inherited but that natural selection is also a valid consideration in evolution. See Lamarckism.

Neologism—a new word or phrase used in a new way, or any new doctrine. Most of the "politically correct" Isms in this book (Ableism, Ageism, etc.) are Neologisms.

Neo-Lutheranism—the 19th-century revival of orthodox Lutheranism in Germany and Scandanavia.

Neo-Minimalism—"Nicholson Baker more or less invented the minimalist novel by writing *The Mezzanine*, which examined one man's lunch hour in immense detail. You can go one better by writing a novel which describes in great detail what one person does while he's reading a Nicholson Baker novel." (Miles Kington)

Neo-Nomianism—the doctrine that the New Testament is a new law of a gracious and remedial nature which demands our imperfect, though sincere, obedience.

Neo-Plasticism—a theory of art advanced by Piet Mondrian (1872-1944), circa 1912, which held that everything "artistic" had to be entirely abstract. Plus, only right angles in the horizontal or vertical plane were permitted, and there was a limited selection of primary colors. Very artistic indeed.

❧

Neo-Platonism—a philosophical system developed in Alexandria in the 3rd century by Ammonius Saccas and Plotinus. Based on a modified form of Platonism combined with elements of Oriental Mysticism and some Judaic and Christian concepts, it believed in a single source from which all existence emanates and with which an individual soul can be mystically united.

❧

Neo-Pythagoreanism—a revival of Pythagoreanism in 2nd century B.C. Rome and Alexandria, combining it with elements of Platonism and Stoicism.

❧

Neo-Realism—1. 20th-century American philosophy "characterized by a presentationist epistemology and by the assertion of the real status of universals." (Webster's). 2. an art movement, especially in Socialist countries, advocating a realistic presentation. Also, New Realism.

❧

Neo-Romanticism—a nostalgic, fantasy-oriented style of painting developed in the 20th century. Go find a book of Maxfield Parrish paintings.

❧

Neoterism—anything new; an innovation, especially in language. "Compact disc" and "fax" (both verb and noun) are 1980's Neoterisms with enormous influence.

❧

Neo-Traditionalism—a term coined by the market research firm Yankelovich Clancy Shulman in 1991 to describe the death of Yuppyism. "Baby Boomer's are finally starting to grow up. The generation that led the urge-to-splurge frenzy now finds itself up to its graying temples in reponsibilities: children, mortgages, and retirement worries. No wonder deferring gratification has suddenly become fashionable." (*Wall Street Journal*)

❧

Nephalism—non-indulgence of intoxicating liquors or advocacy of sobriety; total abstinence, Teetotalism.

❧

Nephrism—the condition caused by chronic kidney disease.

❧

Nepotism—Favoritism shown to relatives; the practice of appointing relatives to jobs or political offices, disregarding others better qualified. Originally, it was a propensity of popes and other ecclesiastics to heap wealth or honors upon their nephews. "Nepotism: Appointing your grandmother to office for the good of the party." (Ambrose Bierce)

Nestorianism—the doctrines of the patriarch Nestorius and his followers. Born in Constantinople in the 5th century, he was condemned as a heretic for maintaining that the two natures of Christ were not so blended and united as to be undistinguishable. Consequently, while Mary might be called the mother of the Christ, it was wrong to call her the Mother of God. The term also applies to modern Christians of Persia and India who are remnants of the Nestorian sect. Cf. Monophysism.

Neurohypnotism—see Braidism.

Neutralism—the policy of staying non-aligned in foreign affairs, à la Switzerland.

Neutral Monism—the theory that mind and matter actually represent relations and interactions between entities that are themselves neither mind nor matter. Sort of a meta-Dualism. See also Animism.

New Criticism—a theory of literary Criticism which looks closely at the text only, without regard to author intent or historical background. New Criticism regards a work as devoid of meaning beyond that physically contained on the page. This led to Deconstructionism, and college English departments everywhere went to hell in a handcart.

New Dealism—the type of government fashioned by Franklin D. Roosevelt (1882-1945), 32nd U.S. president. Part socialist, part dictator, part patrician, and part comedian, FDR utterly conquered the American people with his warmth, leadership, and personal courage. A polio victim who never complained, this larger-than-life crusader—in an era of larger-than-life crusaders: Hitler, Stalin, Churchill—spent 13 years in the White House virtually as a one-man government that most Americans loved—nay, worshipped.

Everything we take for granted in government today—Social Security, deficit spending, welfare, huge government works projects, etc.—was created by Roosevelt's New Deal. Though his dream was an America with "freedom from fear, freedom from want," the New Deal was a lot of old baloney, largely borrowed from predecessors Teddy Roosevelt and Woodrow Wilson.

After the stock market crash of 1929 and in the middle of the Great Depression, FDR entered as the aristocratic, silver-tongued liberal who promised to fix everything. He even pledged to "reduce the cost of current Federal Government operations by 25%." But during the next 13 years, Federal power and spending grew, and grew, and grew. For the consequences, see Liberalism, Interventionism, Keynesianism, Populism, Welfare Statism, Paternalism, Bureaucratism, Humanitarianism, Internationalism, Socialism, Trade Unionism—all part of the New Deal that was constructed almost at random. "People close to Roosevelt were dismayed by his casual and disorderly intellectual habits... He did not assemble his ideas into a comprehensive and ordered program, with priorities and interconnections. Just as he lived each day for itself, as he liked to tell friends, so he appeared to flirt with each idea as it came along" (James MacGregor Burns).

But a unifying idea *did* exist. The New Deal was a philosophy of government based on a single, unwavering article of faith, a conspiracy theory elevated to dogma: "This great nation will endure as it has endured, will revive and will prosper. So, first of all, let me assert my firm belief that the only thing we have to fear is fear itself... This nation asks for action, and action now!" (Roosevelt)

≈

Newmanism—the views of John Henry Newman (1801-1890), who preached the compatibility of Anglicanism with Roman Catholicism. He later decided that Rome was a better bet than the Church of England, and became Catholic.

≈

New Realism—term given to Socialist art. Also, Neo-Realism.

≈

Newspaperism—the practice of reporting fanciful, scandalous, and disgusting trivia. Just when you think you've heard everything, the *London Evening Standard* offers this: "DOLPHIN SEX CASE / MAN FOR TRIAL / Man Accused of Sexually Molesting Britain's Only Tame Dolphin Sent for Trial at Newcastle Crown Court—Animal

rights activist Alan Cooper was charged with committing obscene acts with bottle-nosed dolphin Freddie in the North Sea last September."

ɛ๑

Nice-Nellyism—1. a Euphemism, especially for sexual terms. 2. excessive modesty, prudishness, especially in a woman.

ɛ๑

Nicotinism—poisoning by nicotine or tobacco, from which the authors of this book are still suffering. We can thank or damn Jean Nicot (1530-1600) for importing to France the tobacco plant, named _nicotiana_ in his honor. Sir Walter Raleigh brought the leaf to England, which provoked King James I to call smoking "a custom loathesome to the eye, hateful to the nose, harmful to the brain, dangerous to the lungs, and in the black stinking fume thereof, nearest resembling the horrible Stygian smoke of the pit which is bottomless." He forgot to mention drug addiction—which is precisely what you have if you smoke cigarettes habitually.

Those who are trying to quit should investigate the amino acid choline as a substitute for the sedative effects of nicotine. The authors recently gave up cigarette smoking in favor of breathing, and if it weren't for choline we would surely have killed each other and several members of the public while going through nicotine withdrawal.

ɛ๑

Niebuhrian Realism—the fiery Moralisms and political pronouncements of Reinhold Niebuhr (1892-1971), evangelistic theologian who deeply influenced American foreign policy before and after World War II. Discounting the benefit of "freed intelligence" (i.e., Liberalism), he taught that all life was an expression of power. Cf. Nietzscheanism. "Man's capacity for justice makes democracy possible, but man's inclination to injustice makes democracy necessary." (Niebuhr)

ɛ๑

Nietzscheanism—the philosophy of Friedrich Wilhelm Nietzsche (1844-1900), German philosopher and poet. He conceived of a man of perfection, the *übermensch*, who exercised his "will to power" over lesser beings and whose ruthlessness was both justifiable and praiseworthy—a concept that surely influenced the German National Socialists (Nazis) in the 1920's. From 1889, he was quite mad, perhaps suffering from tertiary syphillis, and he was nursed until his death in 1900. "Which is it, is man one of God's blunders, or is God one of man's?" (Nietzsche)

~

Nihilism—1. the doctrine that nothing exists or can be known; Skepticism on a grand scale. 2. the theories of certain Russian radicals in the late 19th century, directed at the overthrow of social customs. Later, Nihilism developed into a secret terrorist movement designed to subvert the established order of things, political as well as social—all based on the principle that nobody knew what they were doing, or why. "I never vote for anybody. I always vote against." (W. C. Fields)

Niminy-Piminyism—excessive refinement, affectation, or mincing niceness.

~

Nomadism—the state of being a wanderer who subsists by tending grazing livestock; one who wanders from place to place with no fixed habitation. According to some accounts, pioneers of the film industry were called "movies" because they often fled their rented accommodation on short notice and without paying. The name stuck, and Hollywood is now the movie capital of the world—cash in advance, no pets or children.

~

Nominalism—the principles of the Nominalists, a sect of philosophers in the Middle Ages who argued that universals, or the terms used to note the genera or species of things, are not proper designations of things that exist but are mere names for the resemblances and evidences of things. This sect founded the University of Leipzig.

~

Nomineeism—the principle of conferring offices by official appointment, as opposed to election by the citizens.

≈

Nomism—conduct based on religious law; for example, in Islam, fasting during Ramadan.

≈

Non-Racialism—the advocacy of racial integration of sports in South Africa, to help the country qualify for re-admission to the Olympic Games—and to help it win more medals than it could possibly hope for with all-white teams.

≈

Normanism—an idiom of the Norman (or Northman) language, spoken by the people who left Scandinavia in the 10th century to settle in present-day Normandy in France. They later conquered England in 1066.

≈

Nouveau Realism—term coined by French art critic Pierre Restany in 1960 to describe dissatisfaction with abstract art and the introduction of a new approach: French geniuses would henceforth use existing objects and found material from the urban environment.

≈

Novationism—the principles of the Novationists, one of the sects of Novatus of Carthage, or Novatinius of Rome, who held that those whose faith or obedience had lapsed might not be received again into communion with the Church, and therefore, second marriages were unlawful.

≈

Novembregruppeism—a movement formed in Berlin in 1918 by artists, writers, and architects to take over city planning and march arm-in-arm into a socialist utopia. They sponsored publications, composers, broadcasts, and film productions, merged with Berlin Dadaism, and eventually became Bauhausism.

≈

Nudism—the advocation and practice of living naked, or vacationing periodically that way. Adherents believe Nudism has great physical and psychological benefits.

For some odd reason, Nudism is a common religious, er, thread throughout history. The Dionysian maenads tore their clothes (and each other) apart in orgiastic rites; Indian sects like the Jains and the Ajivikas refused to wear clothes; the Russian Doukhobors held nude marches to protest Materialism; modern-day witches, or Wiccans, perform some ceremonies naked; even American Holy Rollers sometimes doff their duds in religious ecstasy.

Why is Nudism a common element among extreme religious sects? Perhaps it expresses the primal wish to be naked before God like Adam and Eve, to stand pure and free of wordly ties. Or, maybe it's just an excuse to get rowdy. "If God had meant for us to walk around nude, we would have been born without clothes." (Anonymous)

Numism—the study of or interest in coins and medals.

Obiism—the practice of Obi, a system of sorcery once prevalent among the Negro population of the West Indies, where it was brought from Africa by slaves. They owned fetishes in which the power of the Obi was said to reside. See Fetishism. Also, Obeahism.

❧

Objective Idealism—according to Webster's: "a form of Idealism asserting that the act of experiencing has a reality combining and transcending the natures of the object experienced and of the mind of the observer." Cf. Subjective Idealism.

❧

Objective Relativism—the belief that knowledge of the physical world is relative to the observer. See Relativism, Subjectivism.

❧

Objectivism—1. the tendency to deal with external reality rather than thoughts or emotions. 2. the philosophical doctrine of Ayn Rand O'Connor (1905-1982), Russian-born American writer and philosopher who emphasized the objective existence of reality, accepted the validity of evidence manifested by the senses, and restricted the validity of mental processes to those which are demonstrable in logic; also, her steadfast dedication to Individualism and laissez faire Capitalism.

The basic principle which inspired Rand was a revulsion for Russian Mysticism and Bolshevism, which impelled her to research and formulate a rational alternative. Her philosophy, described as a bridge between Aristotelianism and the modern world, was articulated in several novels (most notably, *Atlas Shrugged*) and nonfiction essays—which were almost completely ignored by professional philosophers, primarily because her system entailed a wholesale rejection of Kantianism and Altruism. "Civilization is the process of setting man free from men." (Rand)

≥೩

Obscurantism—the doctrines and methods of a person who hinders and opposes the diffusion of knowledge and enlightenment. "The great mass of people ... will more easily fall victim to a big lie than to a small one." (Adolf Hitler)

≥೩

Obsoletism—something archaic, especially a word or phrase, or maybe just an old garment. See Fogeyism.

≥೩

Obstructionism—the practice of delaying something on purpose, especially regarding legal activities, as when a Senator filibusters to prevent passage of a bill.

≥೩

Occamism—the philosophy of William of Occam, an English Franciscan of the 14th century who is credited with causing the decline of Scholasticism. One of his more memorable contributions was dubbed Occam's Razor—"Entities should not be multiplied unnecessarily"—which meant that there is no reason to debate how many angels can dance on the head of a pin. However, it also calls into question the purpose of even discussing the existence of God, inasmuch as we can avoid the question of who created the earth by simply saying that the earth has always been here. Those who believe in a Creator are thus challenged to say who created the Creator—which leads to an infinite regress of "prior causes," and which Occam thought was a waste of time, anyway.

The whole debate stems from Aristotle's concept of a "first cause" or "unmoved mover," a metaphysical doctrine which St. Thomas Aquinas incorporated into Church dogma in the 12th century and which the Scholastics dutifully amplified by arranging a celestial hierarchy of angels, archangels, saints, and the Trinity of Father, Son, and Holy Ghost. It was this last that proved too much for Occam, and he resolved to simplify the Church's celestial geography by reducing God to a single entity.

≥೩

Occasionalism—name given to the Augustinian-Cartesian theory developed by Nicolas de Malebranche (1638-1715) concerning God's activity in the world. He held that the effect things have on one another is deceiving since, actually, God is the only agent of change and human beings are just instruments for Divine Action. Gottfried Leibnitz modified this slightly by asserting a continuous correspondence in which God worked through humans all the time, not just once in a while.

❧

Occidentalism—the habits and practices of Western peoples. It refers to all countries west of Asia and Turkey; the western quarter where the sun sets. From the Latin *occidere* (to fall).

❧

Occultism—1. the name given to a system of theosophy in the East. Its adherents claim to be able to produce seemingly miraculous effects by purely natural means. 2. the belief in and investigation of mysterious or supernatural things. The half-wits in Sedona, Arizona will bristle, but all the New Age rubbish of crystal healing, channeling, etc. is pure Occultism.

❧

Officialism—1. the condition of being an appointed or elected leader. 2. strict, even excessive, adherence to official routine.

Ogreism—the character or habits of an imaginary monster or hideous giant of fairy tales, who ate humans; more generally, the actions of any brutish, barbarous person. Said to have derived from Orcus, the god of the infernal regions.

❧

Old Maidism—the state of being an unmarried woman who has advanced in years beyond the usual age of marrying; the stereotypical traits of an old maid, such as prudishness and gossiping. If she never marries, she's practicing Spinsterism.

❧

Olympism—the ancient Greek tradition of athletic competitions. Today, it's an international industry dedicated to building elaborate
sports facilities and promoting souvenirs.

ટ&

Onanism—1. masturbation. 2. *coitus interruptus*, male withdrawal from
sexual intercourse so ejaculation occurs outside the vagina. From
the Bible's Onan, who, when instructed to sleep with his dead
brother's wife, "spilled his seed on the ground." God killed him for
it. (See Genesis 38:9.)

ટ&

Oneirocriticism—the interpretation of dreams, either scientifically,
as Sigmund Freud and Carl Jung advocated, or mystically.

ટ&

Ontologism—according to Webster's: "the doctrine that the human
intellect has an immediate cognition of God as its proper object
and the principle of all its cognitions."

ટ&

Opiumism—opium addiction and its physical symptoms.

ટ•

Opportunism—the art or practice of making the most of a favorable occasion, specifically in politics; of turning circumstances to your advantage, even at the sacrifice of principles.

ટ•

Optimism—the disposition to be hopeful and cheerful, with the belief that everything is ordered for the best and that good will triumph over evil. Epitomized by Dr. Pangloss in Voltaire's *Candide* ("All is for the best in this best of all possible worlds.") Cf. Futilitarianism. "The optimist thinks that this is the best of all possible worlds, and the pessimist knows it." (J. Robert Oppenheimer)

ટ•

Orangeism—the beliefs and practices of the Orangemen, a secret society formed in 1795 to promote Protestantism in Northern Ireland.

ટ•

Organicism—1. the doctrine of the localization of disease, which refers it always to a material lesion of an organ. 2. a theory that society as a whole exhibits the same traits and patterns as a biological Organism.

ટ•

Organism—any organized body or living economy, as in an individual animal or plant, or an organized group of people.

ટ•

Orientalism—an Eastern characteristic or expression, such as bowing in greeting; doctrines of Asiatic nations. From the Latin *oriri*, "to arise," since the sun rises in the east.

ટ•

Origenism—the opinions of Origen of Alexandria (185-253 A.D.), who united Neo-Platonism with Christianity, holding that human souls existed before their union with bodies, that they were originally holy but became sinful in the pre-existent state, that all men will probably at last be saved, and that Christ will die again for the salvation of devils.

ટ•

Orleanism—support of the Orleans branch of the French royal family, and its claim to the throne. Quite the lost cause.

ટ•

Orphism—1. the doctrines of the Orphics, a mystical cult associated with the mythological Dionysus (or Bacchus), god of fertility, wine, and drama. 2. a Paris branch of Cubism, circa 1911, originally associated with Marcel Duchamp and Pablo Picasso but later confined to a single artist who drew circles. Not to be outdone by the

French, two American painters took this seriously enough to develop a style called Synchronism.

❧

Oslerism—the theory that a man is useless after age 60. Propounded by Dr. William Osler (1849-1919), a British physician and an unwelcome guest at retirement communities. "A man is as old as the woman he feels." (Groucho Marx)

❧

Ostracism—1. the exclusion from the privileges and comforts of a group or society at large. 2. in antiquity, temporary banishment by the Athenians of a criminal or someone who gave umbrage. It takes this name from the shell on which the vote of acquittal or condemnation was written.

❧

Oughtism—"a disease of the oughtanomic nervous system where the unfortunate victims oughtomatically do what others tell them they ought. Left untreated, Oughtism can result in a total loss of the ability to think." (Steve Bhaermen)

❧

Overoptimism—excessive or groundless Optimism.

❧

Over the Wallism—the condition resulting by escape from one's environmental, genetic, and psychological imprinting and achieving freedom of mind and choice; to escape from the constraints of society and family expectations. A most difficult task to achieve, but the reward is the right to your own mind and the freedom to change it according to your own premises and moral choices; to be uncoercible and immovable in one's ideas of life's purpose and to be unafraid of dissent; to fear no public judgment and to live for no other man. The liberty of action and thought is the private realm of man's mind and requires a commitment to discover the essence and uniqueness of your own individual life. "Great men can't be ruled." (Ayn Rand)

❧

Owenism—the belief in the practices of Robert Owen (1771-1858), an English philanthropist who proposed to reorganize society by introducing a system of socialistic cooperation. It was attempted by his followers twice, in the form of communes, and failed both times. See Socialism.

❧

Owlism—a disposition to roam at night; stupidity.

Pacifism—opposition to violence and Militarism, and the advocacy of peaceful means, like negotiation, arbitration, and passive resistance, to settle disputes and effect change. Pacifists rely on the tactic of non-violent civil disobedience, exemplified by Mohandas Gandhi and Martin Luther King, Jr., wherein opposition consists exclusively of symbolic verbal and passive resistance, even to the extent of being jailed or martyred, without taking up arms in self-defense. Unshakeable faith in the righteousness of one's cause, plus a belief that others can be shamed into justice by the pacifist's self-sacrifice, are the basic principles which drive such behavior.

Recent history has proved Pacifism's power: In India, the passive resistance to British colonial troops, who machine-gunned Gandhi's followers as they prayed and chanted, was so dramatic a statement of honor vs. dishonor that it most certainly hastened the colony's independence. In America, the vicious harassment and assassination of civil rights leaders galvanized Federal legislation and law enforcement and led to the vindication of Martin Luther King Jr.'s campaign for racial equality and social change.

On the other hand, history also teaches that Pacifism is pointless when opposed by a ruthless and superior force which has little regard for human suffering or "fairness." To the extent that pacifists have succeeded in shaping public opinion or resisting armed opponents, the cultural and political sympathies they claim to have "awakened" already supported the idea that bloodshed is the wrong way to overcome dissent or maintain the status quo. Thus, Pacifism works in those societies already committed to peace, while something stronger is needed to defeat a bloodthirsty aggressor.

❧

Paedobaptism—the doctrine of baptising infants only.

☙

Paenism—the practice of singing songs or shouting cheers of triumph.

☙

Paganism—the worship of false gods, or the system of religious opinions maintained by pagans. To Christians, a pagan is anyone who is not a Christian, Jew, or Muslim, although non-Christians are considered ineligible for salvation since they don't accept Jesus Christ as savior. But Paganism is more an issue of worshipping one or more gods in the form of totems, or attributing spiritual dimensions to natural phenomena like sunlight and lightning. Arguably, all religions have a pagan element, to the extent that they worship anything. See Mysticism and Fetishism. "Scratch the Christian and you find the pagan—spoiled." (Israel Zangwill)

Paludism—another name for malaria, a chronic but treatable disease once thought to be the result of breathing swamp gas (read *Daisy Miller*), now known to be contracted from the bite of an infected mosquito. Common in swampy areas and tropical regions of the world. Sufferers have attacks of fever, chills, and sweat, so the American pioneers called it "fever 'n ague."

☙

Pan-Africanism—a political association of African dictatorships, whose purpose is to obtain complete control of their economic destiny and more Western aid. Military coups and civil wars periodically rearrange the spokesmen.

☙

Pan-Americanism—political movement advocating the close cooperation among the countries of North, Central, and South America.

☙

Pan-Arabism—devotion to the idea of cultural or political unity of all Arab peoples. Iraq's dictator Saddam Hussein appealed to this sentiment to gain support for his Anti-Americanism, even though he had roused the world's ire in the first place by invading Kuwait, an Arab nation. But Fanaticism is always quick to disregard any inconvenient truth, and Saddam's propaganda was effective enough that many Arabs, especially Palestinians and Jordanians, revered him as the only Arab leader with the guts to "stand up to the West." Pan-Arabism is often used as a cloak for Anti-Western and Anti-American sentiment and action. See Pan-Islamism.

જી

Panchromatism—having sensitivity to all colors. Color photographic film is an example.

જી

Pancosmism—a tenet of metaphysics or cosmology that holds that the material universe constitutes all there is; opposite of Transcendentalism.

જી

Panculturalism—aesthetics or social philosophy in favor of everything, with a propensity to Egalitarianism.

જી

Panderism—the employment, character, or vices of a person who acts as an agent for other's lusts or vices; a pimp. To pander is to supply prostitutes or to cater to the base instincts or crude beliefs of a constituency, either in politics or commerce. See Populism.

જી

Pan-Germanism—pertaining to the unification of Germany in 1990 and the politics of a united Germany. Also, Pan-Teutonism.

જી

Panhellenism—a plan or scheme for the political union of all Greeks.

જી

Pan-Islamism—doctrines concerning a union or confederacy of all Islamic nations, the aim of most Mohammedans, which would enable them to resume their efforts for the conquest of the world instead of just warring among themselves. See Pan-Arabism.

જી

Panlogism—in philosophy, the doctrine embodying the theory that the universe is the manifestation of the "logos" or pure reason, sometimes attributed to God but also said to exist as an organizing principle of nature.

જી

Panpneumatism—a philosophy combining elements of Pantheism and Panlogism.

જી

Panpsychism—the belief that every object in the universe has either a mind or a soul. See Animism.

ᘒ

Pan-Slavism—a scheme or movement for the amalgamation of all the Slavic races into one confederacy, having a common language, government, and literature. Arguably, the Soviet Union achieved this by military occupation and the imposition of Socialism throughout Eastern Europe after World War II, although a Soviet Empire was probably not what Slavic nationalists had in mind.

ᘒ

Pansophism—a claim to possession of universal knowledge, a characteristic of most cult leaders. See Cultism. Speaking of cults, Dioscor, St. Cyril's successor, had a girlfriend named Pansophia, so you could say he practiced a slightly different kind of Pansophism.

Pantagruelism—1. a deprecatory term for the profession of medicine. 2. the humorous contemplation of life, from the name of one of Francois Rabelais' characters. "It's a funny old world. You're lucky if you get out of it alive." (W.C. Fields)

ᘒ

Pantheism—the doctrine that everything is God, in contradistinction to the doctrines that God is everything or that God is some Thing. Thomas Jefferson (1743-1826) was a noted pantheist.

ᘒ

Panzoism—in biology, a term used by Herbert Spencer (1820-1903), English philosopher, to denote all the elements or factors which constitute vital energy or life.

ᘒ

Papism—doctrines and policies which tend to support the preeminence of the Pope in church government; used as a term of contempt by opponents of the Roman Catholic Church. See Catholicism.

આ

Parabaptism—Baptism which has not been regularly or publicly performed; uncanonical Baptism.

આ

Parachromatism—irregularity in color perception; color blindness.

આ

Parachronism—an error in chronology; the mistake of making the date of an event later than it was in reality.

આ

Parallelism—1. the state of being in tandem in construction or direction. 2. in literature, a similarity of construction or meaning in passages closely connected, especially common in the Old Testament and other Hebrew writings. 3. various systems of philosophy in which two universes or two aspects of experience are said to exist in parallel. See Dualism.

આ

Paralogism—in logic, a reasoning false in point of form; that is, in which a conclusion is drawn from premises which do not logically warrant it; a logical fallacy, of which the reasoner himself may be unconscious.

આ

Paramagnetism—the property of being attracted by a magnet and of assuming a position parallel to that of a magnetic force.

આ

Parasitism—the behavior of an animal or plant which derives its existence and nutrients from another, without offering anything in return, and often to the detriment and death of the host. Formerly, one who frequented the tables of the rich and earned his welcome by flattery.

આ

Parkinsonism—a nerve disorder characterized by trembling hands, muscle rigidity, slow movement and speech, and a mask-like face. Discovered by Dr. James Parkinson (1755-1854), and also called Parkinson's disease and Ballism.

આ

Parliamentarianism—the advocacy of a legislative, or parliamentary, system of government, as in England. See Menshevism, Republicanism.

આ

Parnellism—the doctrine of Charles Stewart Parnell (1846-1891),

Irish National leader, who led a movement in favor of home rule in Ireland.

æ

Parochialism—1. parochial government; management of a parish by a parochial board. 2. a narrow-minded viewpoint. 3. accusation hurled by juvenile artists at anyone who declines to finance their work of "genius."

æ

Parseeism—the religion and habits of the Parsees, or fire worshippers. They are the modern Zoroastrians of the ancient Persian religion whose forefathers were driven from Persia into India by Islamic persecution in the mid-7th century. The modern Parsees are the commercial class in India. See Zoroastrianism.

æ

Partialism—1. bias in favor of something. 2. in theology, the doctrine that the atonement of Christ was made for only part of humanity (!). See Calvinism, in which predestination is considered God's way of saying that all men were created equal, but some are more equal than others.

æ

Partial Journalism—in Britain, the practice of shaping and twisting television programs to discredit Capitalism. It happens when broadcast organizations are funded by taxation and protected from competition by monopoly status.

æ

Particularism—1. devotion to specific or individual interests. 2. in theology, the doctrine of particular election, favoring the election of those who qualify according to highly detailed criteria. 3. the practice of a state promoting its own interests and conserving its own laws, as distinct from the federated whole.

æ

Partyism—devotion to a particular political party. Cf. Mugwumpism.

æ

Passivism—the belief in or practice of being inert and not reacting. "Whatever you want is fine with me, dear."

æ

Pasteurism—the use of an attenuated virus progressively made stronger as an inoculation for the treatment of certain disorders, particularly hydrophobia. Devised and developed by the French biologist Louis Pasteur (1822-1899).

æ

Pastoralism—1. the maintenance of livestock as a principal economic activity, as in Australia, where there are 16 million people and

160 million sheep. 2. pertaining to rural life, such as charming simplicity and a leisurely, carefree pace.

Paternalism—the practice of managing people and groups in a fatherly, intrusive way, especially regarding government policy; excessive government regulation and supervision of individuals, based on the presumption that the masses are incompetent to make decisions about their education, employment, finance, and safety. Paternalism is prominent in modern America and continues to grow, as every detail of individual life becomes subject to regulation and government planning—an attitude so contemptible that it deserves no comment whatsoever. However, for the benefit of those unacquainted with the concept of human rights, the most fundamental freedom is the right to guide your own life, for better or worse, without being perpetually scolded like a child who cannot be trusted to cross the street by himself. Whether it entails mandatory seat belt laws, Social Security, or Federal deposit insurance that "liberates" us from choosing trustworthy bankers over incompetent ones, persistent Paternalism insults every thoughtful adult and reduces self-respect and self-reliance. "The only thing that saves us from the bureaucracy is its inefficiency." (Eugene McCarthy)

Patriarchism—government by the patriarch or head of the family. Typical of Catholicism, Monarchism, and the Mafia.

Patricianism—the doctrine of privileged birth or unequal political conditions. In ancient Rome, patricians were the nobility, descendants of Senators, not the plebs. The term now applies to anyone of aristocratic birth or in the upper classes of society.

Patriotism—love of and devotion to one's country; the passion which influences one to serve his country, either in defending it from invasion or protecting its rights and maintaining its laws and institutions in vigor and purity, often in disregard of other considerations. See Nationalism. "I only regret that I have but one life to lose for my country." (Nathan Hale)

Patripassianism—the doctrine that God the Father shared the sufferings of Jesus Christ. See Theopaschitism.

Paulinism—in Christian history, a term introduced to denote the teachings found in, or deducible from, the writings of St. Paul.

Pauperism—the state of being poor or destitute of the means of support; the condition of indigent people requiring community assistance, or those whom the community refuses to support.

Pecksniffianism—the hypocritical affectation of high moral principles; an unholy marriage of Moralism to Nice-nellyism. Named for Seth Pecksniff, a character in Charles Dickens' *Martin Chuzzlewit*.

Pectoriloquism—in medicine, a phase of disease in which the patient's voice seems to proceed from the point of the chest on which the ear or a stethoscope is placed. People suffering from tuberculosis often manifest this phenomenon, which is due to speech resounding in lung cavities produced by destruction of lung tissue.

Pedagogism—the characteristics, business, or manners of a teacher or schoolmaster who instructs children. Usually, it refers to someone narrow-minded and pedantic. In antiquity, a pedagogue was a slave who attended the children of his master and conducted them to school and places of amusement, often tutoring them as well.

In Germany, the pedagogic attitude blended with strict Paternalism to create a nation of obedient and terrorized victims ripe for Naziism. "The vanity of teaching often tempts a man to forget he is a blockhead." (George Savile, Lord Halifax)

৯৯

Pedanticism—ostentatious display of learning, often exhibited by university professors and those whose job entails explaining a complicated subject to an audience of unwilling listeners; the overrating of any kind of knowledge, particularly in matters of trivial importance. "An expert is one who knows more and more about less and less." (Nicholas Murray Butler)

৯৯

Pedestrianism—1. the exercise or practice of walking. 2. a mundane phrase, behavior, or quality.

৯৯

Pelagianism—the doctrines and teachings of Pelagius (360-420 A.D.), who denied the doctrine of Original Sin.

৯৯

Peonism—the condition of being a peasant or a farm worker in Latin America or the southwest U.S.; a menial worker, especially one who is compelled to work out a debt or is paid in the form of sharing a small portion of the harvest.

৯৯

Perfectionism—1. the doctrine of the Perfectionists, a community founded and propagated by John H. Noyes (1811-1886) in Oneida, New York. Noyes believed in the doctrine of Christian perfection, which teaches that some people attain moral perfection while alive. 2. a philosophy of attaining perfection in all endeavors; the practice of aiming high and always falling short of the mark, thus becoming unable to finish anything. The fact that dozens of new Isms will enter the language soon after this book is printed would drive a perfectionist nuts.

≈

Peripateticism—1. the philosophical system of Aristotle and his followers, so called because he and his students used to debate while walking about (being peripatetic) in the Lyceum at Athens. See Aristotelianism. 2. the trait of wandering or roaming around.

≈

Peronism—the political philosophy and system of Juan Peron (1895-1974), dictator of Argentina, and his followers. Espousing Fascism and violent Nationalism, Peron took power in 1946 with the support of Argentina's working class, who worshipped him and his charismatic wife Evita. Peron and his relatives and toadies embarked on an orgy of greed, violence, and corruption on a scale not seen since the reign of Caligula.

Peron blended elements of Naziism and Fascism and ruled through censorship and violence—and with the help of the former Gestapo agents he hired. When Peron took power, Argentina had a $2 billion surplus of hard currency. When he was finally deposed, the country was virtually bankrupt.

No discussion of Peronism is complete without a look at the woman with the whip, Eva Duarte de Peron, "Evita." Her burning hatred for the oligarchic rulers of the past endeared her to the workers, and women loved her for her tireless support of female suffrage. An illegitimate teenager from the provinces, she came to Buenos Aires to be an actress and climbed to power through a succession of ever more important lovers. Consumed with ambition, she never forgot a friend—or forgave an enemy. Once, after being snubbed by the British monarchy, she nationalized all British holdings in Argentina. She also created the Eva Peron Foundation, a charity that gave money to all comers—and filled the Peron's Swiss bank accounts. Hated by the aristocrats and the military, she was worshipped as a saint by the common people. She once said, "If I ever go down, there won't be anybody else left standing up, either." She died of cancer in 1952, before any attempt could be made to throw her out—which would have certainly caused a civil war.

With Evita dead, Peron was soon tossed from power. He spent most of the rest of his days organizing and running the Union of Secondary School Students, a club created solely to provide him with prepubescent mistresses. He returned to power briefly in 1973, accompanied by Isabel, a new wife and Evita-clone, but he died within a year. Isabel succeeded him, but her corrupt and incompetent rule was quickly overthrown. There are still Peronists in Argentine politics, but without Evita, it's doubtful they can ever take power again.

≈

Personalism—1. an aspect of personality; that which is personal, belonging to people, not things. 2. a philosophical movement which maintains that value and reality are found in people. 3. the cult of personality, whether one's own or an ersatz identity borrowed from TV.

Pessimism—an attitude that gives preponderance to the evils and sorrows of existence; the habit of taking a gloomy and despondent view of things—even when there is legitimate cause for Optimism—on the principle that human vice cannot be overcome by virtue, that evil is stronger than good. The opposite of Optimism. See also Futilitarianism. "My Pessimism goes to the point of suspecting the sincerity of the pessimists." (Jean Rostand)

ॐ

Pestalozzianism—the educational system of Johann Pestalozzi (1746-1827), a Swiss philanthropist, which concerned the sensations and conceptions of children, effecting their education by constantly calling all their powers into exercise and encouraging them to rely on the evidence of their senses. Cf. Tolstoyism.

ॐ

Petrarchism—the style of the Italian poet Francesco Petrarca (Petrarch) (1304-1374), who popularized what is today called the Petrarchan sonnet, a 14-line rhymed verse divided into an octet and a sestet. Compare the Shakespearean sonnet, which has three quatrains followed by a couplet. Then there's the Spenserian sonnet—oh, never mind, you should have learned all this in high school. Other Petrarchisms are the use of elaborate conceits, complex grammar, and conventionalized diction, but it's all rather labored stuff to a modern reader. Also, Petrarchianism. "A good death does honor to a whole life." (Petrarch)

ॐ

Petrinism—the tenets taught by or attributed to St. Peter: mainly, that good works are conducive to salvation, compared with the Paulist doctrine of faith and the Johannean doctrine of love.

✿

Phalansterianism—see Fourierism.

✿

Phallicism—worship of the penis as a symbol of creative power, as in the Maypole dance. Also, Phallism.

✿

Phallocentrism—term used by feminists, especially Simone de Beauvoir, to describe the essence of the oppressive rule by men over women, and in no uncertain terms to describe the organ of that rule. See Immoral Existentialism. "I wonder why men get serious at all. They have this delicate long thing hanging outside their bodies which goes up and down by its own will. If I were a man I would always be laughing at myself." (Yoko Ono)

✿

Pharisaism—the notions, conduct, and doctrines of the Pharisees, an ancient Jewish sect who strictly observed religious rites and the traditions of the elders, and whose pretended holiness led them to separate themselves as a sect, considering themselves more righteous than other Jews. Allegedly, however, they lacked sincere belief, so, in general usage, the term connotes hypocrisy.

✿

Phenomenalism—that system of philosophy which inquires into the causes of observable phenomena and which recognizes only the phenomenal as real. Also called Externalism. See Kantianism for the root problem.

✿

Philanthropinism—a system of education, supposedly based on development of so-called natural principles, introduced in Dessau, Germany in 1774 but discarded in 1793.

✿

Philhellenism—the principles of the Philhellenes, who were friendly to the Greeks in their struggle for independence against the Turks.

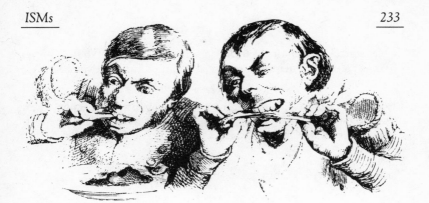

Philistinism—the manners, habits, or mode of thinking of Philistines, residents of Canaan who contested the Israelites for its possession. They were considered uncouth, narrow-minded people, and, considering the times, that's quite an insult. In modern use, a philistine is a commonplace person, lacking refinement and prone to take a stand not from conviction but from the material advantage to be gained from it.

ॐ

Philosophical Radicalism—the 18th-century doctrine of the Rights of Man, as expressed by John Locke (1632-1704) and the American patriots associated with the Declaration of Independence. Their big shift was a denial of the "divine right of kings" and the introduction of personal, individual rights belonging to free and legally equal citizens. "Wherever Law ends, Tyranny begins." (Locke)

ॐ

Philosophism—1. sham philosophy. 2. a pretense of learning and enlightenment; a spurious, deceitful argument.

ॐ

Phoneticism—the quality of being phonetic; representation of spoken sounds by written signs.

ॐ

Phonetism—the science that symbolizes sounds by written characters.

ॐ

Phonism—a sound or sensation of hearing indirectly produced by the effect of something seen, felt, tasted, smelled, or even thinking of it.

ॐ

Phosphorism—chronic phosphorus poisoning. So don't eat glow-in-the-dark paint.

ॐ

Photism—the phenomenom of perceiving as visual sensation stimulation of the other sense organs, as when you hit your head and see "stars," or, to quote Marlon Brando in *A Streetcar Named Desire*, when you "get them colored lights going" during lovemaking.

Photojournalism—photography of news events, especially when photography is the primary focus (no pun intended) of the reportage, as in *National Geographic* magazine.

Photo-Realism—see Super-Realism.

Phrenism—mental activity; mind force; intellectual power.

Physical Realism—see Logical Positivism.

Physicism—the practice of ascribing everything to merely physical or material causes, to the exclusion of the spiritual. See Materialism.

Physiocratism—the economic doctrines of the Physiocrats, followers of Francois Quesnay (1694-1774), a French physician who proposed a political economy with the supremacy of natural order as its basic principle. The Physiocrats believed that all value and profit flowed from agricultural production; merchants and industry were "sterile" employments, incapable of adding wealth to a society. They advocated free trade and the direct taxation of land as the sole source of state revenue, and thus unintentionally helped create a discussion among political economists that resulted in economic Classicism. "Commerce according to the theory of the Physiocrats only transfers already existing wealth from one hand to another." (Roscher)

Pianism—skill at or performance on the piano. Includes everyone from Sergei Rachmaninoff to Jerry Lee Lewis.

Pietism—the fervent religion of the Pietists, a 17th-century religious party in Germany that sought to revive reverence in Protestant churches by stressing personal devoutness and fervor over formality. Hence, in general use, the term is applied in contempt to one who is sanctimonious or makes a display of strong religious feelings. "Piety is the tinfoil of pretense." (Elbert Hubbard)

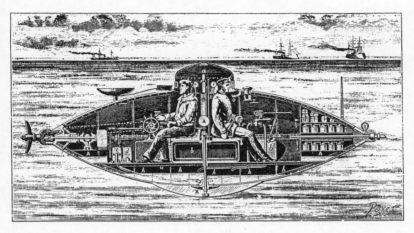

Pilotism—skill in steering, guiding, or charting a course, especially regarding ships and aircraft. "Your true pilot cares nothing about anything on earth but the river, and his pride in his occupation surpasses the pride of kings." (Mark Twain)

ếa

Plagiarism—The act of appropriating the ideas or language of a literary work of another and representing it as your own. "When you take stuff from one writer, it's plagiarism; but when you take it from many writers, it's research." (Wilson Mizner)

ếa

Platonism—the doctrines of Plato (427-347 B.C.), Greek prototype philosopher, and his followers. Plato believed God to be an infinitely wise, just, and powerful spirit who formed the visible universe out of pre-existent amorphous matter, according to perfect patterns or ideas eternally existent in His mind.

Plato viewed philosophy as knowledge of the true nature of things, discoverable in the eternal ideas after which all things were fashioned. In other words, it's knowledge of what is eternal, exists necessarily, and is unchangeable—not temporary, dependent, or malleable knowledge, which we perceive through the senses. Neither is it the product of the understanding, which concerns itself only with the variable and the transitory; nor is it the result of experience and observation. Plato viewed knowledge as being exclusively a product of reason, which, as partaking of the divine nature, has innate ideas resembling the eternal ideas of God. By contemplating these innate ideas, reasoning about them, and comparing them with their copies in the visible universe, reason can gain true knowledge of things.

Platonism was promptly abandoned by his pupil Aristotle, and between these two ancient Greek thinkers the rest of Western philosophy has more or less divided: Idealism and Materialism. "The life which is unexamined is not worth living." (Plato)

ۿ

Playactorism—stage play; histrionics. "(As an actor), you spend all your life trying to do something they put people in asylums for." (Jane Fonda)

ۿ

Playboyism—the policies and practices advocated by Hugh Hefner, an American publisher celebrated for his sybaritic lifestyle, including chasing young women and encouraging them to pose in a provocative manner for the gratification of magazine subscribers. Since the 1950's, Hefner's *Playboy Magazine* has displayed photos of nubile, naked "Playmates," steadfastly opposed government secrecy, religious taboos, shame, and hypocrisy, and encouraged both sexes to admit their repressed desires, to challenge oppressive institutions, and to defend the right to Individualism in the broadest sense. See Hedonism. Footnote: Hefner retired into marriage in 1988. His daughter now publishes *Playboy*.

ۿ

Plebeianism—the conduct of plebeians, the common people (plebs) of ancient Rome, as distinguished from the patricians. Plebs were considered vulgar, low bred, and coarse.

ۿ

Plein-airism—a style of painting developed in mid-19th century France by painters who worked outside (the term means "outdoors"), painting their direct impressions of nature. See Impressionism.

ۿ

Pleochroism—the property of some crystals to exhibit different colors when viewed at various angles.

ۿ

Pleomorphism—in biology, the ability of some Organisms to exist in two or more distinct forms during a life cycle. This does not apply to born-again Christians.

ۿ

Plesiomorphism—the close resemblance in the form of crystallization of certain substances which are unalike in chemical composition.

ۿ

Plotinism—the beliefs and teachings of Plotinus (205-270 A.D.), a Roman philosopher who held that the human soul emanated from God and at death was either reincarnated or reunited with Him.

ۿ

Plumbism—lead poisoning. "Col. Mustard, in the Billiard Room, with the lead pipe." (from the board game Clue)

Pluralism—1. the quality or condition of being more than one. 2. the philosophical theory that many "reals" or "real things" exist and that there is a plurality of ultimate elements, which others refer to as matter, spirit, etc. 3. the political doctrine or practice of encouraging Biracialism, Multiculturalism, and Liberalism, all of which promote cultural diversity. It's the democratic ideal: a society in which multiple religions, races, practices, and prejudices are tolerated and encouraged. John Stuart Mill (1806-1873) created the classic defense of Pluralism by noting that freedom of speech stimulates the production of valuable new ideas, erodes the influence of blind tradition, and poses no threat to reason. "He who knows only his own side of the case, knows little of that." (Mill)

Plutonism—the Plutonic theory, which holds that most, if not all, changes on the earth's surface are due to fire. This ancient theory was developed when the universe was thought to be composed of four elements: fire, water, earth, and air. Plutonists favored fire to the exclusion of the others, perhaps because fire caused such vivid damage.

Pococurantism—negligence; heedlessness; apathy. "Science may have found a cure for most evils; but it has found no remedy for the worst of them all—the apathy of human beings." (Helen Keller)

Poikilothermism—the ability of bacteria, plants, and cold-blooded animals to adapt themselves to the temperature of their environments. We probably need a word for this, but you'd think it could be a tad less complicated.

૨&

Pointillism—see Neo-Impressionism.

૨&

Politicalism—party spirit or zeal; excessive dependence on political processes to achieve minute results. "Being in politics is like being a football coach: You have to be smart enough to understand the game, and dumb enough to think it's important." (Eugene McCarthy)

૨&

Polydaemonism—a form of religion in which a multitude of demons or spirits are thought to govern natural phenomena. This primitive mythology is prevalent among the Indonesians, native Hawaiians, and other indigenous island peoples who attributed catastrophic natural phenomena (volcanos, tidal waves, hurricanes) to evil spirits which had to be appeased by sacrifices and offerings.

૨&

Polygenism—the theory that the members of a species have descended from more than one pair of progenitors. Parents sometimes suspect this condition of their children, especially when the kid resembles the milkman.

Polymastism—the presence of more than two breasts.

૨&

Polyphonism—multiplication of sounds, as in the reverberations of an echo. In music, the condition of having many sounds and voices, as in an orchestra.

૨&

Polysyllogism—in logic, a Syllogism formed by a chain of connected Syllogisms.

૨&

Polysynthesism—the combining of several words into one long one. "It's a little-known fact that the evening news on German TV usually consists of a single word which describes all the earthquakes, plane crashes, and soccer results of the day." (Neenan & Hancock, *Let's Blow thru Europe*)

દ્યે

Polytheism—the doctrine or faith involving a plurality of gods or invisible beings superior to man, each having an agency in the government of the world. Greek and Roman mythology and the modern Hindu religion have many such supernatural characters.

દ્યે

Polythelism—the occurrence of more than one nipple on a breast.

દ્યે

Pop Artism—an art movement begun in London in the 1950's. The basic idea was that mass urban culture—expressed in advertising, comic strips, etc.—was a vernacular shared by all, irrespective of professional skills, and therefore to hell with professional skills. In the U.S., the most successful exponent was Andy Warhol (1930-1987), whose art lay chiefly in manipulating the mass media—if you can call that art. "I am a deeply superficial person." (Warhol)

દ્યે

Populism—1. the philosophy of the Populist Party, a U.S. political party that sought to represent farmers and laborers in the 1890's, advocating increased currency issue, free coinage of gold and silver, public ownership of railroads, and a graduated federal income tax—all of which echoed the demands of the Communist Manifesto, and all of which were later adopted by law. 2. the policy of appealing to the lowest common denominator among an ignorant or easily deceived constituency, usually involving a proposal of public largesse or deficit spending. "The people are to be taken in very small doses." (Ralph Waldo Emerson)

દ્યે

Porism—in math, according to Webster's, "a proposition affirming the possibility of finding such conditions as will render a certain problem indeterminate or incapable of numerical solutions."

દ્યે

Porphyrogenitism—the mode of succession in some royal families, notably the Byzantine, whereby a younger son, if born "in the purple" (after the accession of his parents to the throne) was preferred to an older son, who was born before the parents' accession.

દ્યે

Positivism—a doctrine or system of philosophy inculcated by Auguste Comte (1798-1857), French philosopher and mathematician, and characterized by its respect for positives only, excluding all knowledge except that gained by actual experiment and observation of natural phenomena. Comte asserted that all speculative thinking passes through three stages: the theological, the metaphysical, and the positive. In the first and second, deductions, founded upon either superstition or hypothetical data, are worthless. Only in the positive stage can human knowledge be placed on a sure foundation, he said. Comte was thus convinced that a positive obligation to the welfare of others was the only real morality. See Altruism.

&

Post-Impressionism—pertaining to the artistic styles of Paul Cezanne, Georges Seurat, and Vincent Van Gogh.

&

Postmillennialism—the belief that the second coming of Christ will follow the Millennium. See Millennialism.

&

Postmodernism—the late 20th-century movement in art, literature, and architecture, begun as a reaction to Modernism. One example is New York artist Mary Kelly, who put her son's dirty diapers in her artwork.

&

Poujadism—political policies named for Pierre Poujade and the Poujadistes, a French party that represents the interests of "the little fellow" and small business. In 1953, Poujade organized a strike of shopkeepers to protest taxes, and the party made a substantial showing in the 1956 elections.

&

Poussinism—the French Academy's late 17th-century doctrine that art should satisfy the intellect, and that painting should therefore be judged by design and linear drawing skills.

&

Praetorianism—the practice of controlling society through force or fraud, especially when a minority is holding the reins. Standard operating procedure for Communism, Fascism, Peronism, and Totalitarianism in general.

&

Pragmatism—1. meddlesomeness. 2. in philosophy, the doctrine that truth consists of the verification of a prediction and that the value of any proposition or principle is determined by its observable results. Hence, truth is not absolute but statistical. 3. the policy or practice of valuing opportunities and political action according to near-term results that can be reasonably predicted from known costs and market conditions, in disregard of moral principles or long-term consequences.

&

Pre-Capitalism—theories which attributed any surplus or social progress to Mercantilism. Pre-capitalists argued that only foreign trade made a net addition to a country's wealth. Pre-capitalist production was equally primitive: economies of scale were limited to whatever the merchant himself could afford to put at risk.

❧

Precisianism—the practice of one who is rigidly ceremonial and exact in the observances of rules, forms, or requirements, especially in religion and especially as a trait of Puritans. See Formalism.

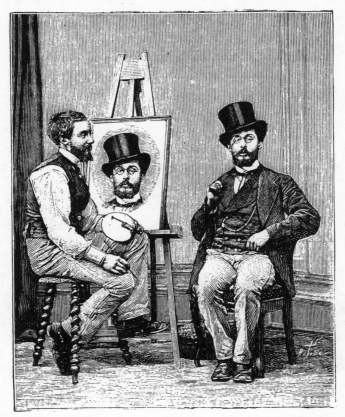

Precisionism—excessive exactness; the quality of being precise and punctilious. In art, see Cubism and Magic Realism.

❧

Predestinarianism—the belief in fate or unchangeable destiny. In theology, the belief that God has unalterably determined whatever comes to pass, including which souls are to be saved. In other words, the unchangeable purpose of an unchangeable God, espoused chiefly in Calvinism. "He that is born to be hanged shall never be drowned." (English proverb)

❧

Pre-Existentism—the doctrine that the soul has an existence prior to that in the human body.

ૐ

Prelatism—the office or dignity of a prelate, who is a clergyman of a superior order, having authority over the lower clergy such as archbishop, bishop, etc.

ૐ

Pre-Millennialism—the doctrine that the reappearance of Christ on earth must precede the Millennium. Opposed to Post-Millennialism and derived from Millennialism.

ૐ

Pre-Raphaelitism—in art, a strict adherence to painting characteristics of the Italian school before Raphael, revived about 1847 by the English Pre-Raphaelite Brotherhood, who often signed their works "PRB." They also wrote poetry, in the romantic and medievalist style of their art, which was attacked by critics as "the fleshly school of poetry."

ૐ

Presbyterianism—the doctrines, principles, discipline, and government of Presbyterians, a Christian denomination which teaches a modified Calvinism and holds that there is no church order superior to that of the Presbyters. They vest church government in associations of ministers and ruling elders, all possessed of equal powers, without any superiority among them either in office or in order.

ૐ

Presentationalism—a style of theatrical performance in which the story is presented directly to the audience, with no attempt at Realism. Bertolt Brecht (1898-1956) advocated a non-dramatic style of theater where the actors presented a story without acting in the conventional sense—the way someone on the street would describe an incident he has seen, speaking other people's words without actually pretending to be someone else.

ૐ

Presentationism—according to Webster's: "the doctrine that in perception, or in all forms of knowledge, there is an immediate awareness of the things perceived. Also Presentative Realism."

ૐ

Priapism—persistent and abnormal erection of the penis, usually without sexual desire and often painful.

ૐ

Priestism—the tenets, policy, characteristics, or power of priests or the priesthood.

ૐ

Priggism—exaggerated propriety, self-righteous Moralism, and fussiness about trivialities. See also Nice-nellyism, Pecksniffianism.

Primitivism—a belief that qualities of primitive or early culture are superior to those of modern civilization. Rousseau talked endlessly about the value of primitive nature and exalted the idea of the "noble savage" uncorrupted by modernity, with all his natural virtues intact. Primitive art (a.k.a. outsider, naïve, or folk art), made by or in the style of untrained artists, generally shows an intense creative energy, although technical purists fault its inaccurate perspective, limited palette, etc. An exalted Primitivism is a close kin to Ludditism.

આ

Primordialism—1. continuance or observance of primitive ceremonies. 2. devotion to conditions thought to have existed in the primordial state.

આ

Priscillianism—the doctrine of a Christian sect named for Priscillian, Spanish Bishop of Avilla, killed for heresy in 385 A.D. in the first instance on record of execution for heresy under a Christian government. The execution met with strong disaproval from Gregory of Tours and other distinguished ecclesiastics. Priscillian's doctrine was substantially that of Manicheanism.

આ

Prism—a solid, transparent polygon which disperses white light into the multi-hued spectrum.

આ

Probabilism—1. doctrine of Skepticism that says nothing is certain, so believe what is probable. 2. in Roman Catholic theology, the doctrine that forbids action or interpretation of law according to one's inclination, unless there is a balance of probability in favor of such. Also, Probabilliorism. See Equiprobabilism, Pragmatism.

≈

Probationism—1. belief in a period of testing or trial after death. 2. belief in the value of probation as an alternative to confinement in prison, especially for young offenders, consisting of supervision by skilled social workers who spend most of their time gathering, processing, and filing paperwork.

≈

Prochronism—chronological error when something is assigned a date earlier that the actual one. See Anachronism.

≈

Procrusteanism—inducing conformity by violent or arbitrary means. From Procrustes, a fabled robber of ancient Attica who forced travelers to lie on a bed, then lopped off their limbs to make them equal to the length of the bed. If they were too short, he stretched them.

This was one of our favorite Isms, since we thought there was absolutely no reason for anyone to remember this grisly practice. But then we saw an essay that referred to a "bed of Procrustes," denouncing laws which compel identical treatment for everybody in every situation, regardless of each person's individuality, and the term suddenly became vivid: Big Brother is a Procrustean.

≈

Professionalism—1. the following of an art, sport, etc., as a profession. 2. the duties or ethics of business-like, honest conduct toward clients, especially in the context of professions that are notoriously unscrupulous or have so few qualifications that practitioners are compelled to boast of their Professionalism.

≈

Prognathism—the condition of having protrusive jaws.

≈

Progressivism—1. early 20th-century political philosophy which maintained that the natural rights concepts contained in the Declaration of Independence were basically bunk and that Darwinian "progress" was more important than checks-and-balances. Progressives advocated political leadership by experts, to promote the grand unfolding of human progress. 2. early 20th-century educational philosophy, championed by John Dewey (1859-1952), which opposed teaching theoretical knowledge. "There is no obvious social motive for the acquirement of mere learning." (Dewey) 3. generic term applied to various schemes of social reform, generally involving a reduction of civil liberty and enlargement of government power. "Progressive taxation," for example, takes more from your pocket when you have more to be taken.

ᐁ

Prohibitionism—the policy or advocacy of forbidding something, especially the manufacture and sale of alcholic beverages. In the U.S., Prohibition, created by the 18th Amendment to the Constitution, lasted from 1920-1933. In effect, the act made almost every adult a criminal. While it is grimly true that alcohol causes enormous suffering, it is also true that most drinkers imbibe intelligently and in moderation, and recent medical studies suggest that moderate drinking is actually healthier than abstinence. Some anthropologists believe alcohol was the catalyst for civilization: the need to grow crops and maintain a brewery to make beer is what prompted early man to change from a hunter-gatherer existence to an agricultural society. To outlaw something humans have been enjoying for millenia is the height of noxious Paternalism. See Volsteadism. "The sway of alcohol over mankind is unquestionably due to its power to stimulate the mystical faculties of human nature." (William James)

Proletarianism—the openly Marxist-Stalinist agenda and tactics of the Militant Tendancy, a Labourite "hard left" faction based in Liverpool and London. The Labour party has repeatedly purged its ranks of Militant supporters, but the battle is far from over. Efforts to recapture Liverpool's city government after being run into the red, both economically and politically, have only partly succeeded.

ᐁ

Propagandism—the practice of promoting an idea, principle, or political entity through the deliberate creation and spread of information favoring the cause in question and often disparaging the opponent. In general, the term connotes the tactic of spreading lies. Propaganda plus terror equals social control in a totalitarian society. "Propaganda is that branch of the art of lying which consists in nearly deceiving your friends without quite deceiving your enemies." (F. M. Cornford)

ᐁ

Prophetism—the act or art of one who claims to speak for God and/or see future events; the state of being prophetic. Also, Pythonism.

ह

Prosaism—the trait of being dull or commonplace.

Proselytism—the making of converts to a religious sect or to any opinion, system, or party, especially by means of force and/or forceful persuasion. In Christianity, Jehovah's Witnesses are notorious proselytes. "In politics as in religion, it is equally absurd to aim at making proselytes by fire and sword. Heresies in either can rarely be cured by persecution." (Alexander Hamilton)

ह

Protagonism—the state of being the lead character in a story or the leader of a political cause. You are always the protagonist. The other guy is the antagonist. Cf. Antagonism.

ह

Protectionism—in political economy, the policy of aiding or guarding home industries by paying bounties on domestic products or by imposing tariffs on imported products. We are accustomed to thinking of Protectionism as a topic of modern legislation, especially regarding products from Europe and Asia, but the impulse to protect domestic manufactures has a long history in politics and was arguably the cause of the American Civil War.

It began with George Washington, who imposed trade tariffs in 1789 that raised the price of American-made and imported goods and had the net effect of taxing planters in the South who manufactured neither and who suffered again when Britain struck back with protectionist tariffs on cotton and tobacco. In 1832, South Carolina convened a special legislative session to declare "null and void" all protectionist taxes, thus setting in motion a chain of events that led to secession when Congress refused to repeal tariffs. And you thought the Civil War was about slavery.

The current brouhaha about GATT points to a new "trade war" in the making, with Europe on one side and America on the other—like a bad flashback to 1789. You'd think in 200 years the benefits of free trade might have made more of an impression on politicians. See Economic Liberalism.

Protestantism—the religion of all non-Catholic Western Christians. Specifically, the principles taught by Martin Luther (1483-1546), a German monk and reformer who more or less instigated the Reformation. Luther's 95 *Theses*, posted on the door of a German cathedral, sparked a major Schism in the Catholic Church and established a wave of non-Catholic sects based on the principle that ordinary Christians were competent to profess their faith without adhering to the dicta of Popes. The chief Protestant tenet is that the Bible is the one rule of faith and practice. Therefore, the decrees of the Pope or other dignitaries of the church are not infallible or obligatory. Justification by faith, individual responsibility, and the right to believe and worship according to one's conscience are cardinal points in the system.

Protest Intellectualism—the belief that intellectuals not only are the conscience of a nation, but also must provide an agenda for change and participate in the activity for that change. "In the 18th century, there was an imposed separation between the world of the intellectuals who were kept quite out of touch with practical politics, and the world of power which tolerated no participation." (Stanley Hoffman) Simone de Beauvoir (1908-1986) became a prominent figure in French Feminism precisely because she was willing to break with tradition and actively take part in protest marches and demonstrations. Similar tactics in the U.S. gave women's liberation a high-profile status during the 1960's under the leadership of Betty Friedan.

Protoorganism—in biology, an Organism that cannot be classified definitely either in the animal or the vegetable kingdom.

Proverbialism—a well-known idea, phrase, or principle, such as something mentioned in a maxim or proverb: "A bird in the hand is worth two in the bush."

Provincialism—1. a peculiar word or manner of speech in a district remote from the metropolis. 2. in general, that which is narrow, local, unpolished, rural, and lacking in Cosmopolitanism. "In New York, you must either be a New Yorker or an invader of modern Troy, concealed in the wooden horse of your conceited Provincialism." (O. Henry)

Prussianism—the spirit, system, and methods associated with the Prussians, especially Militarism and strict discipline.

Psellism—stuttering.

Pseudohermaphroditism—see Virilism.

Pseudo-Mysticism—a substitute for religion which seeks the Absolute in union with the people, the nation, the party, or the leader.

Psilanthropism—the doctrine or belief of the mere human existence of Jesus, i.e. that he was only man and was a humanitarian. Compare with Monophysism and Nestorianism.

Psittacism—mechanical, repetitive speech without much meaning. Listen to any George Bush speech.

Psychism—the doctrine of Francois Quesnay (1694-1774), a French physician and economist who stated that a subtle fluid is the animating principal in men and animals.

Psychologism—1. the emphasis on psychological aspects when developing a religious or philosophical theory. 2. a term from psychology tossed around to impress a layman, also known as "psychobabble."

Psychopannychism—the doctrine or belief that the soul falls asleep at death and does not awake until the resurrection of the body.

Psychotheism—the doctrine that God is pure spirit.

Ptylaism—excessive secretion of saliva; drooling. This term is a good example of an Echoism.

Puerilism—childish behavior in an adult.

Pugilism—the practice of boxing or fighting with the fists; prize-fighting; the manly art of self-defense. The first mention we've found was in connection with a fellow named Jem Belcher (1781-1811), who was remembered for a polka-dot neckerchief he always wore in the ring, until he lost an eye in a bout.

Although boxers still run the risk of ocular impairment, the sport was made slightly safer in 1867 by the Queensbury Rules, which introduced padded gloves at the suggestion of John Douglas, Marquis of Queensbury (1844-1900). The Marquis was also responsible for prosecuting Oscar Wilde in 1895 for "corrupting" his son, Lord Alfred Douglas, a poet known to his friends as "Bosie." The scandal of having an "unmanly" heir was too much for the Father of Modern Boxing to accept without protest. "My toughest fight was with my first wife." (Muhammed Ali)

૨૯

Puppyism—extreme meanness, impertinence, or conceit. Used to describe a fop. (Now, what the heck is a "fop"?)

૨૯

Purism—1. practice or affectation of rigid purity; rigorous Criticism of purity in literary style; specifically, excessive nicety in speech. 2. the doctrine that the New Testament was written in pure Greek. 3. a short-lived art movement that attempted to make Cubism less cubic and more representational.

૨૯

Puritanism—the doctrines and practices of the Puritans, a Protestant sect founded in the 16th century that promoted simplified ritual and strict morality. To avoid persecution, many fled England and landed in America, where nobody liked them much, either. Today, the term is used to describe someone with priggish sensibilities. "Puritanism: The haunting fear that someone, somewhere, may be happy." (H.L. Mencken)

❦

Puseyism—the principles of the Rev. E.B. Pusey (1800-1882) and others at Oxford, England, as exhibited in *The Tracts for the Times*, published about 1883. They proposed to return the discipline and doctrine of the Church of England to a period when there would have been no separation from the Church of Rome. Also, Tractarianism.

❦

Pygmyism—characteristics of Pygmies, a tribe of remarkably short people in Africa, or of anyone unusually small in stature.

❦

Pyrrhonism—the principle of universal doubt or philosophic nescience; the exaggerated form of Skepticism advocated by Pyrrho of Elis (360-270 B.C.)—absolute disbelief in everything except one's own incompetence.

❦

Pythagoreanism—the system of belief attributed to Pythagoras (540-504 B.C.). After traveling about in search of knowledge, he settled in southern Italy and founded a society constituting a philosophical school, a religious brotherhood, and a political association of aristocratic sympathies. The Pythagorean system declined about 300 B.C. but revived two centuries later, and in the Augustan age its views of past earth changes through the operation of fire, water, etc., excited geologists. However, his best-known contributions were in mathematics, especially his "Pythagorean Theorem." Also, Pythagorism.

❦

Pythonism—the art of predicting events or being prophetic. Named for Pythia, a Greek priestess at Delphi who was believed to commune with Apollo and voice his oracles. Also, Prophetism.

Quadrupedism—the trait of having four feet (especially common among mammals). "A closed mouth gathers no feet." (Anonymous)

≥∎

Quakerism—the peculiar manners, tenets, or worship of the Quakers (a.k.a. Society of Friends), a religious sect noted for its Pacifism. The term Quaker was used as a nickname, either referring to the way adherents trembled under the influence of a charismatic speaker or in derision of founder George Fox (1624-1691), who had admonished people "to quake at the word of the Lord." The name is no longer considered derogatory.

≥∎

Quietism—the system of the Quietists, a mystic Christian sect founded in the 17th century by Molinos, a Spanish priest. They maintained that religion consists of the passive contemplation of God and the submission to His will.

≥∎

Quindism—a fifteenth of something.

Quixotism—romantic and absurd notions, schemes, or actions like those of Don Quixote, the hero of Miguel de Cervantes' novel, who was extravagantly romantic and visionary to boot.

Quizzism—1. the act of testing or questioning. 2. the act of eyeing suspiciously or speaking banteringly.

Rabbinism—an expression or belief characteristic of or pertaining to a rabbi, a Jewish teacher or doctor of law who speaks the Hebrew langauge.

&

Rachmanism—the ruthless, rent-gouging attitude of landlord Peter Rachman (1920-1962), who exploited residents of the slum area of Paddington in London, using strong-arm tactics to collect rent. By 1963, press campaigns prompted stringent laws to protect tenants.

&

Racism—1. the belief in fundamental and/or genetic differences between human races—a creed that often leads to the belief that some races are superior to, and should therefore govern, others. 2. an attitude that prompts hatred, prejudice, and discrimination, especially in employment practices, based on race. (Also, Racialism.) The antidote to Racism is Individualism, regarding people not "by the color of their skin, but by the content of their character" (Martin Luther King, Jr.).

Racism is hardly limited to black-white idiocy. Currently, there's a wave of anti-Japanese resentment in Paris: Mme. Edith Cresson, France's prime minister, said the Japanese "sit up all night thinking of new ways to screw us" and "are plotting to take over the world." Of course, we read these quotes in British newspapers, which love to trash the French whenever possible. The Brits accuse the French of hating Japanese and "blacks" (North African immigrants); the French say the Brits despise "Asians" (Britain's Pakistani and Bangladeshi immigrants). Frankly, we're scared to death of both French farmers who vandalize trucks with British goods and British soccer hooligans who vandalize everything. But neither is as menacing as an Alabama State Trooper or Italian gangster—and that's quite enough Racism for now. In a minute, we'll start hating Alan's parents, who have the same surname as a Nazi poet.

And if that influenced your attitude toward us, then you're guilty of Racism, too. Alan's parents are American; names mean nothing in this world. There is no higher (or harder) challenge than that of remaining absolutely impartial toward others, regardless of race, color, or surname. Having lived and worked with whites, blacks, reds, yellows, and browns, we assure you that some people prove themselves worthy of respect and friendship, and some don't. Race is not particularly relevant. All people are capable of dignity and decency; about half make the effort. "We educate one another; and we cannot do this if half of us consider the other half not good enough to talk to." (George Bernard Shaw)

ε‰

Radicalism—the doctrine or principle of making extreme or fundamental changes, especially in government or social conditions, by overturning the status quo. "The worst enemy of the new radicals are the old liberals." (Vladimir Lenin)

ε‰

Radical Monitorism—a proposal in London in 1990 to conduct a weekly census of homeless people to keep their plight in the public eye and embarrass the government.

ε‰

Ramism—the philosophical and dialectical system of Pierre de la Ramee (better known by his Latinized name, Ramus), professor of rhetoric and philosophy at Paris and one of the victims of the massacre of St. Bartholomew in 1572. He opposed Scholasticism and the dialectics of Aristotle.

Ranterism—the practices and tenets of the Ranters, a religious sect which sprang up in 1645 and called themselves "Seekers." Members maintained they were seeking the true church and the true Scriptures, which they felt had been lost. The term also refers reproachfully to the zealous Primitive Methodists who seceded from the more staid Wesleyan Methodists. It comes from "rant," which means to rave in a violent, wild fashion without much thought. See Methodism.

ॐ

Raphaelism—the theory, art, or style displayed in the paintings of Raffaello Sanzio D'Urbino (1483-1520), a celebrated Italian painter.

ॐ

Rastafarianism—the political and religious principles of black Jamaicans who worship Haile Selassie (1891-1975), former emperor of Ethiopia. Marijuana is a sacrament; reggae star Bob Marley is a high priest. Rastafarians are committed to the overthrow of the British government in the West Indies.

Rationalism—1. in philosophy, the doctrine which affirms that reason furnishes certain elements without which experience is not possible. Opposed to Sensualism or Sensism, which says all knowledge is derived from the senses, and to Empiricism, which refers all knowledge to sensation and reflection or experience. 2. in theology, a system of beliefs deduced from reason, as distinct from inspiration, or even opposed to it. This principle, which vindicates

the prerogative of reason to apply itself to the problems of revelation, typically entails the rejection of "supernatural" entities, revelations, miracles, etc. Hence, most theologians disclaim rationalist
tendencies or philosophical commitment to reason, because it would
mean abandoning theology for science and logic. In the laborato-
ries and offices of the business world, however, Rationalism became
de rigueur: "All religion is bunk." (Thomas Edison)

ॐ

Rayonism—1. abstract art depicting bright beams of light crossing at
an angle; distant cousin of Futurism. 2. preoccupation with making
sure you have the steam iron set at the right temperature.

ॐ

Reaganism—the policies, traits, and sayings of Ronald Reagan, actor
and 40th U.S. president. Known as an amiable but often inatten-
tive leader, Reagan was considered a military hard-liner, though he
developed the closest relationship with the Soviets in recent U.S.
history, and a fiscal arch-conservative, though the Federal government doubled in size during his two terms. A classic Reaganism:
"Government is like a baby: an alimentary canal with a big appe-
tite at one end and no sense of responsibility at the other."
    It's so strange to consider that the U.S. was governed for eight
years by a mediocre actor. Yet Reagan's homespun simpleness was
irresistible, as was the catalyst: a 40-year old mess created by Federal bureaucrats who lacked the courage to call a mess a mess. When
Reagan promised to get the government off Americans' backs, the
people ran to the polls and yelled, "Do it! Immediately!"
    Unfortunately, the people weren't prepared to do much else be-
sides lodge a loud protest vote. Tax cuts were great, but don't touch
defense and entitlement spending—don't mess with the mess. Ever
since Roosevelt's New Deal, "pork" (government projects) had become the staple of the republic. Reagan never had a chance.
    Thwarted in his attempt to reduce government, Reagan found
a new enemy: the Soviet Union, which became the "evil empire"—
great title for a B-movie, eh? And like a Hollywood ending, the ruthless Reds got their comeuppance in the final reel: Communism col-
lapsed and the Berlin Wall fell as Reagan rode off into the sunset.
History not only put Reagan in office, it also gave him an Oscar
for Best Bystander. "Sometimes I think America likes Reagan, but
they're a little disappointed they couldn't get Jimmy Stewart." (Ian
Shoales)

ॐ

Realism—1. in metaphysics, the doctrine that there is an immediate
or intuitive cognition of external objects, which exist independently
of our sensations or conceptions (as opposed to Idealism). 2. in
scholastic philosophy, the doctrine which maintains that genus and
species exist independently of our conceptions and expressions, and

that there is an eternal "essence" corresponding to each conception or expression which is the object of our thoughts when we
employ the term. 3. in art, a style which renders subjects in a manner that ordinary blokes can understand and which confines its
artistic efforts to the depiction of real scenes. 4. a method of defining
problems and solutions in terms of actual, rather than imagined,
causes or facts. 5. a 19th-century school of literature which portrayed
humanity as vapid, cruel, and squalid. Flaubert and Tolstoy were
leading lights.

༄

Receptionism—the doctrine that the body and blood of Christ are
received at Christian Communion, but the bread and wine are not
actually transformed. A belief closer to Consubstantialism than to
Transubstantiationism.

Recidivism—the trait of someone who continually repeats old habits,
especially bad ones, as in a criminal who commits a crime after
punishment for an offense.

༄

Reconstructionism—a 20th-century Jewish movement, led by Rabbi Mordecai Kaplan, who believed Judaism is both a religion and
a culture. As such, he said, it must constantly adapt to modern life
so Jews can identify more readily with it.

༄

Redistributionism—the political doctrine or policy of taking money
from one segment (usually, the upper-and middle-income brackets)
of the population and giving it to another segment (usually, the
poor). Example: You have $5.00. I have $1.00. I take your money.
We have done a noble thing.

༄

Redneckism—a trait or idiom of an uneducated class of Americans,
especially white, southern males, who worship pickup trucks and
shotguns, chew tobacco, and often bully racial minorities and in-

tellectuals, especially in conjunction with White Supremacism and Anti-Intellectualism. The term comes from the characteristic sunburned necks of farm laborers. For more information, listen to the songs of Hank Williams Jr., especially "A Country Boy Can Survive."

❧

Redstockingism—policies and traits of a radical feminist group established in 1969, which proclaimed that the conflicts between men and women could be resolved only by collective political action of a Marxist bent. Several factions developed around this central theme, each attempting to re-define Feminism in a more egalitarian, nonhierarchical format.

The Redstocking Manifesto left little doubt who the bad guys were: "Male supremacy is the oldest, most basic form of domination. All other forms of exploitation and oppression (Racism, Capitalism, Imperialism) are extensions of male supremacy..." In general, men were amused—including quite a few "revolutionary brothers" like Stokely Carmichael, leader of the militant Student Nonviolent Coordinating Committee, who quipped, "The only position for women in SNCC is prone."

❧

Redtapism—the system of layering programs or policies with excessive official routine; a bureaucratic practice of adherence to official formalities. See Bureaucratism.

❧

Reductionism—1. in art, the reduction of skill and subject matter to the minimum possible. See Minimalism. 2. oversimplification of a complex issue. 3. the theory that a complex phenomenon can be explained by examining its simplest parts.

❧

Regalism—the doctrine of royal supremacy in ecclesiastical matters.

❧

Regionalism—1. an idiom or literary style peculiar to a particular geographical region, such as a Southernism. 2. in government, the division of a nation into different administrative regions. 3. devotion to one's own region. The extreme and aggressive form of this is Regional Chauvinism, where pride in one's region is so great that it becomes contempt for everywhere else. Ask any Texan.

❧

Relativism—the theory that there is no absolute way to judge anything, because everything is proportionate and conditional to the individual and his or her environment. If a tree falls in the forest and you aren't there, you're not in a position to judge whether it made a sound or not. The tree is, but that's just its own opinion. Essentially, everything is situational. See Subjectivism.

❧

Religionism—1. the practices of religion; piety, conscientiousness, or scrupulousness based on one's religious faith; a system of conduct and laws based on the recognition of, belief in, and reverence for a superhuman, supreme authority; a particular kind of faith and practice entertained and propagated by its devotees. 2. in derogatory usage, excessive religious fervor.

Religious Mysticism—seeking the Absolute in God by means other than reason. Generally okay with Christians, since it agrees with their Anti-Rationalism, even if it's not a specifically Christian God: "If someone wishes to be a mystic by invoking this sort of experience in a believable fashion, his claim should not be denied. The ecumenical spirit is not interested in monopolizing religion." (Hans Kung)

Representationalism—1. in art, the depiction of an object in a recognizable manner, portraying the surface characteristics of an object as they appear to the naked eye. 2. in philosophy, the theory, propounded by John Locke (1632-1704), that when we perceive an object, we also perceive the principal qualities of that object. That is, what we see is what we get.

Republicanism—1. a republican form or system of government, especially a state in which the exercise of power is lodged in representatives chosen by the people, rather than in the people themselves.

2. the principles or practices of the Republican Party in the U.S. "No one has ever attended a Republican mass meeting without a perception of the ludicrous." (Mark Twain)

ɜ⚭

Restorationism—the tenets of the Restorationists, who believed in a temporary future, punishment, and a final restoration of all to the favor and presence of God.

Resurrectionism—the theft of cadavers; grave-robbing. In the early days of Yale University, New Haven residents threatened to burn the school after they caught medical students robbing graves for bodies to study and dissect. Town-gown relations there have been uneasy ever since.

ɜ⚭

Reunionism—the movement to reunify the Anglican and Roman Catholic Churches. See Newmanism.

ɜ⚭

Revanchism—the policy of a state trying to regain areas of its territory lost in war or through a treaty signed under duress. Nazi Germany claimed that its policy of Expansionism and conquest was just Revanchism, trying to reunite the "German peoples." Chinese propagandists currently claim Tibet was never free and should be part of China, and is therefore not being occupied or repressed. Iraq's dictator Saddam Hussein tried the same thing with Kuwait in 1990, with disastrous results. The term is a French word meaning revenge.

ɜ⚭

Reverse Potemkinism— "a post-Soviet Russian tendency to portray the situation as even worse than it is." (*Time Magazine*)

ɜ⚭

Revisionism—the practice of rewriting history books to present your version of what happened, to discredit your opponents, or to hide embarrassing events. For example, Japanese school children don't read that their ancestors were the bad guys in World War II. In the U.S., progressives and multiculturalists are rewriting history to denounce Capitalism as inhumane, Christopher Columbus as rapacious, and all white males as racists. But future historians will probably decide to revise the revisionists. The term for this will be "Post-Revision Anti-Revisionist Re-Revisionism." "History will be kind to me, for I intend to write it." (Winston Churchill)

ॐ

Revivalism—1. the tendency to rejuvenate ideas or trends of the past. 2. the spirit prevailing during a religious revival, when some believe "making a joyful noise" can revive the faith of others.

ॐ

Rheotropism—the property of plants to grow with or against a current of water.

ॐ

Rheumatism—a painful disorder of the joints or the back.

ॐ

Rhotacism—excessive use or faulty pronunciation of the letter "R"; substitution of the letter "R" for another sound, such as "L."

ॐ

Ribbonism—the doctrine of the members of the Ribbon Society, an Irish secret society organized about 1808 to oppose the Orange organization in the north of Ireland. Named for the badge—a simple green ribbon—worn by its members.

ॐ

Rightism—reactionary attitudes, political Conservatism. The familiar right-left political spectrum in the West goes upside-down in the Soviet Union, where rightists are the hard-line Communists and leftists are the crusaders for a free market system.

ॐ

Rigorism—1. the religious dictum which states that in uncertain ethical situations, believers may not choose an action contrary to Catholic doctrine. 2. austerity in opinion or conduct; rigidity in style or living. "Always do right. This will gratify some people and astonish the rest." (Mark Twain)

ॐ

Ritualism—1. the system of prescribed forms of activity in social situations and especially in religious worship; the excessive adherence to ritual. 2. the belief and practices of the Ritualists in the Church of England, who insist on a return to the use of symbolic ornaments in church services. 3. in psychology, Ritualism denotes a profound neurosis which compels sufferers to repeat an activity (such as hand-washing) to alleviate feelings of guilt or inadequacy. If we candidly examined the psychological purpose of religious rituals (such as genuflection), we would be compelled to admit that their primary purpose is to *instill* neurotic feelings of guilt and inadequacy among the faithful.

୨**ଛ**

Roman Catholicism—the tenets, forms, and usages of the Church of Rome, known as the Catholic Church, of which the Pope is the head. Also, Romanism (sometimes derogatory).

Romanticism—the state of being idealistic or fantastic, or a trait of those who are devoted to concepts of Heroism, sentiment, and love; applied especially to the literary method which aims at medieval or romantic forms, rather than classical.

Characteristic of the Romance peoples during the Middle Ages, Romanticism was imbued with the passions and the thrilling adventure of the time. The Romantic school was a name assumed at the beginning of the 19th century by a group of young writers of Germany (Schegels, Novalis, Tieck, etc.) who led a revolt against the stilted form and Prosaicism of the dominant schools of literature, and endeavored to restore the traits which had predominated among other Romance writers. It was also a school of French writers, of whom Victor Hugo was the greatest prose writer and Alphonse Lamartine the greatest poet, which flourished 25 years later than the Germans and with the same purpose. Also used to describe the Lake Poets of England (Southey, Coleridge, and Wordsworth), whose poems were a remonstrance against the conventional form and matter of Addison, Pope, and their contemporaries. An art movement of the same name encouraged 19th-century painters to indulge in Emotionalism. "Is not this the true romantic feeling— not to desire to escape life, but to prevent life from escaping you?" (Thomas Wolfe)

୨**ଛ**

Rosicrucianism—the practices of the Rosicrucians, a fraternity which primarily devotes itself to the study of the secrets of nature and claims knowledge of the occult. First mentioned in 1230, they have been

known by several names, such as Brothers of the Rosy Cross, Rosy
Cross Knights, and Rosy Cross Philosophers, and there are four
Rosicrucian movements in America. The international order, known
as AMORC (Ancient Mystic Order Rosae Crucis), uses a golden
cross with a red cross in its center as its symbol. It sponsors charitable work and promotes the fine arts and sciences.

෴

Rousseauism—the ideas, theories, and principles of Jean-Jacques Rousseau (1712-1778), French philosopher, author, social reformer, and
one of the leaders of the Enlightenment. Rousseau celebrated primitive man and the state of nature, believing it to be far less corrupt
and cruel than life in the 18th century. His favorite book was *Robinson
Crusoe*. See Primitivism. "Nature never deceives us; it is always we
who deceive ourselves." (Rousseau)

෴

Routinism—the trait of sticking to a regular or habitual course or an
unvarying formula. "Routine is a condition of survival." (Flannery
O'Connor)

Rowdyism—the conduct of person, usually a young man, who is disorderly, riotous, and turbulent and who engages in noisy quarrels
for the sake of causing trouble. Cf. Hoydenism.

෴

Royalism—loyalty or attachment to the principles or pageantry of royalty, or to a royal government. "If you find you are to be presented to the Queen, do not rush up to her. She will eventually be brought around to you, like a dessert trolley at a good restaurant." (advice in the *Los Angeles Times*)

ॐ

Ruffianism—the act or conduct of a boisterous, brutal person ready for any lawless act, whether murder, robbery, or Rowdyism. At one time, Ruffian was the name given to the devil.

ॐ

Rubenism—an artistic doctrine advocated by some members of the 17th- and 18th-century French Academy. They reasoned that since painting is primarily concerned with the imitation of nature, and since color is the chief means of effecting this imitation, then color is equal to or superior to line. Cf. Poussinism. It has nothing to do with Peter Paul Rubens, a Flemish artist who loved painting naked fat women.

ॐ

Rugged Individualism—the trait of one who cuts his own path in the world without assistance or sympathy; a characteristic of the mythology of America, especially of the Old West pioneers and immigrants who built their lives without charitable aid or government welfare and redistribution schemes. Though he denied inventing it, the phrase is credited to Pres. Herbert Hoover (1874-1964), who said it described "men and women of honesty whose stamina and character and fearless assertion of rights led them to make their own way in life." Advocates of Victimism take note.

ॐ

Ruralism—the condition of being rustic and of the country, as opposed to the city; an idiom or trait of rural areas and people, such as unsophistication or a slower pace of life. "I have no relish for the country; it is a kind of healthy grave." (Sydney Smith)

ॐ

Russellism—the religious doctrine of Charles Fay Russell (1852-1916), founder of the Russellites, better known as Jehovah's Witnesses. Russell maintained the Second Coming of Christ had occurred, though no one knows His whereabouts. The sect opposes a lot of common medical care like vaccines and blood transfusions and recognizes only one authority, Jehovah—an attitude that has resulted in numerous legal clashes. They do not recognize birthdays, Christmas, and most holidays because they have no Biblical basis.

Most Americans have had some contact with Russellites, who are notorious for going door-to-door, asking if you'd like to discuss world issues, if you consider yourself a moral person, and if you think there's an eternal life—stuff you really want to discuss in your bathrobe.

Russophilism—the sentiments or principles of a person who supports Russia or her policies.

Russophobism—the traits of someone who fears Russia, her power, or her policies. "In America, you can always find a party. In Russia, the party always finds you." (Yakov Smirnoff)

Sabbatarianism—the tenets of people who regard the seventh day of the week as holy, in accordance with the Fourth Commandment. Christians in the early church held this opinion, as the Seventh-Day Adventists and Baptists do now.

❧

Sabbatism—1. in general usage, rest. 2. intermission of labor on the seventh day of the week, thought to be the day on which God rested from the work of creation. The Sabbath is still observed by Christians and some Jews. However, some Christian churches observe Saturday, the seventh day of the week, and some prefer Sunday, the first day, in commemoration of the resurrection of Christ on that day. The heathen nations in northern Europe dedicated this day to the sun, and hence their Christian descendants continue to call the day "Sunday."

❧

Sabianism—in ancient Persia and Chaldea, a form of religion which recognizes the oneness of God but taught the worship of the intelligence supposed to exist in the heavenly bodies. From this abstract worship, many people came to worship the heavenly bodies themselves, an idolatry propagated by those who migrated to Europe and continued among their descendants until they embraced Christianity.

❧

Sacerdotalism—the character or spirit of the priesthood; a tendency to attribute lofty and sacred character to the priesthood. It derives from the word *sacerdotalis*, which means priest, and can be used disparagingly.

ॐ

Sacramentalism—the doctrine of the efficacy of the sacraments as a means of grace. A "sacrament" is actually a military oath that every Roman soldier pledged to his commander, and from this it has come to mean a ceremony involving an obligation. In theology, a sacrament is a visible sign of spiritual grace. More particularly, it's a solemn religious ceremony practiced by Christians, in which their special relation to Christ is said to be created or their obligations to Him are renewed and ratified.

The Roman Catholic and Greek churches hold that there are seven sacraments: Baptism, Confirmation, the Eucharist, Penance, Extreme Unction, Holy Orders, and Matrimony. Protestants generally acknowledge only two: Baptism and the Lord's Supper. The former is called a sacrament because by it persons are separated from the world, brought into Christ's church, and laid under obligations to obey His precepts. The latter is also a sacrament, for by commemorating the death and dying love of Christ, Christians avow their special relation to Him and renew their obligation to be faithful.

Sacramentarianism—the principles or practices of the Sacramentarians, German reformers in the 16th century who opposed the Lutheran doctrine of the Eucharist.

~

Sadduceeism—the tenets of the Sadducees, an ancient and aristocratic Jewish sect who denied the Resurrection, life after death, and the existence of angels.

~

Sadism—a sexual perversion in which one obtains sexual gratification through cruelty and the torture of another. In general use, the term connotes any pleasure derived from deliberate cruelty and the infliction of pain. So named after the Marquis de Sade (1740-1814), notorious for his brutal and perverse writings. Whether de Sade ever actually practiced murder and sexual torture is uncertain, but his novels and plays, in which the most disgusting viciousness is celebrated, landed the Marquis in prison often, and he barely escaped the guillotine. Cf. Masochism.

~

Sadomasochism—a personality disorder where both sadistic and masochistic desires are present. An easy perversion to indulge, since you can just stay home, flog yourself, and play disco music loud enough to bother the neighbors.

~

Saint Simonianism—the doctrine or principles of the followers of the Count de St. Simon (1760-1825), who maintained that shared property and division of the fruits of common labor among his followers was the remedy for social evils. This was another pre-Marxism variation of Socialism.

~

Saivism—devotion to the worship of Shiva (or Siva), the third god of the Hindu triad, representing the principle of destruction. His emblem, the lingam or phallus, is symbolic of the creation which follows destruction. Usually depicted as an ascetic absorbed in yoga, Shiva abides for millennia in total self-sufficiency, and if you dare disturb his meditation you risk being burned by an angry glance. When not occupied by meditation or frying people, Shiva demands recognition and submission from the faithful. Since destruction is liberation of the soul from the chains of existence, "salvation" means death. And you wonder why India has problems. Also, Shivaism.

~

Salicylism—the toxic effects of an overdose of salicylic acid or its salts. In other words, too much aspirin.

~

Salvationism—the tenets of the Salvation Army, an organization known for evangelical work, especially among the urban poor, founded by William Booth (1829-1912). The workers, both male and female, have military titles, wear a uniform, and sing a pretty good song now and then. They also ring handbells incessantly at Christmastime.

Samaritanism—the beliefs and characteristics of the Samaritans, members of a sect from Samaria, the principal city of the ten tribes of Israel. A "good Samaritan" is a model of charity and benevolence, as shown in the parable reported in the New Testament (Luke 10:30-37). In the modern world, "good Samaritan laws" govern doctors and public officials who render assistance at the scene of an accident, with or without the consent of the injured.

૨**એ**

Sans-Culottism—the practices of the Sans-Culottes, who were extreme republicans in the French Revolution of 1789. Literally "without knee breeches," the name was coined by aristocrats to deride the poor members of this popular party at the beginning of the Revolution. But, after the Sans-Culottes had guillotined most of the aristocrats, this lower-class, violent mob took the name as a title of honor. And they probably called the aristocrats Sans-Headottes.

૨**એ**

Sapphism—sexual passion of a woman for other women, so called in allusion to the amorous verses of Sappho (620-565 B. C.), the Greek poetess. Also Lesbianism, Tribadism. "Sweet mother, I cannot ply the loom, vanquished by desire for a youth through the work of soft Aphrodite." (Sappho, *Fragment 114*)

૨**એ**

Sardonicism—the practice of those who are scornfully mocking and derisive. The authors of this book have been so accused. They plead *nolo contendere*.

૨**એ**

Satanism—an evil and malicious disposition, especially after that of Satan, the great adversary of man, Prince of Darkness, chief of the fallen angels; the irrational beliefs and practices of those who worship Satan. Satanists often become murderers, in pursuit of blood sacrifices that celebrate evil and, they believe, please the Devil.

૨**એ**

Saturnism—lead poisoning; Plumbism. In old chemistry and alchemy, Saturn was the name for lead.

Savagism—the state of rude, fierce, uncivilized men in their native habitats. The French philosopher Jean-Jacques Rousseau (1712-1778) extolled the virtues of "the noble savage," whom he saw as free from modern notions of property and propriety. See Primitivism.

※

Saxonism—an idiom of the Saxon language. The Saxons (or "sword men") were a Germanic people who invaded and conquered England in the 5th and 6th centuries. Their descendants are known as Anglo-Saxons, the English race. The Saxon language is English composed of Saxon and English but without Latin, which was introduced during the Roman conquest of Britain several centuries later.

※

Scapegoatism—the ancient Jewish practice of laying all the sins of the community on a goat and then driving it into the desert (see Leviticus 16). In a more general sense, it's the practice of finding one poor schmuck to blame when everything goes wrong.

❧

Scaphism—a barbarous punishment inflicted on criminals by the Persians: Convicts were confined in a hollow tree in which five holes were made, one for the head, and one for each arm and leg. Exposed flesh was smeared with honey to invite wasps, and the criminal was left to die. Considering the modern attitude of Iran toward hostage-taking, human rights, and fanatical enforcement of Islamic laws, we are unable to say that Scaphism is a purely ancient practice.

❧

Schematism—the form or disposition of something. My, that Marilyn Monroe certainly had a nice Schematism.

❧

Schism—a split or disunion between two opposed parties, especially regarding religious or political policies. From 1378-1417, the Roman Catholic Church suffered the Great Schism over papal succession, during which several men claimed they were Pope. In 1954, Marilyn Monroe had a Schism with Joe DiMaggio.

❧

Scholasticism—the methods or subtleties of the system of philosophy taught by the Scholastics (or Schoolmen) of the Middle Ages. Since this era of philosophy was monopolized by the Church and the teachings of St. Thomas Aquinas (1225-1274), scholars did little but debate dogma in minute detail. (See Thomism.) In more general use, the word connotes narrow-mindedness and Dogmatism.

❧

Schopenhauerism—the theories of German philosopher Arthur Schopenhauer (1788-1860), a deeply pessimistic Kantian. Somewhat like the Buddha, he advised the complete elimination of desire to solve the problems arising from the will to live. Not a fun guy. Go read Hedonism and you'll feel much better. "There is no more mistaken path to happiness than worldliness, revelry, high life." (Schopenhauer)

❧

Scientific Realism—a philosophical theory that regarded the scientist as independent of the world he was investigating. Immanuel Kant modified this by saying no chasm could exist between the observer and the observed. See Kantianism.

❧

Scientism—1. the stereotypical traits and assumptions of scientists; often used disparagingly, especially to describe pseudoscientific lan-

guage. 2. the belief that attributes and methods of the natural sciences are appropriate for the social sciences and other scholarly disciplines as well.

۶ه

Scientologism—doctrines of Scientology, a religious movement found-ed by L. Ron Hubbard (1911-1986), American science fiction writer who believed humans are "Thetans," spirits banished to earth 75 million years ago by a cruel galactic ruler named Xenu. Adherents believe in reincarnation and in parting fools from their money as quickly as possible, especially if the fools are Hollywood bird-brains who can give the group free publicity. To call them a religious cult is too charitable by half. For more, see the May 6, 1991 issue of *Time Magazine.*

۶ه

Scillism—poisoning by squill, the bulb of a sea onion used to induce vomiting.

۶ه

Sciolism—superficial knowledge, or a smattering of any subject com-bined with hollow pretense to the possession of more.

۶ه

Scottism—an idiom or word peculiar to the Scots: "kin" means rela-tives, "aye" means yes, etc.

۶ه

Scoundrelism—baseness and turpitude in a person; a rascal without honor or virtue. "When A annoys or injures B on the pretense of saving or improving X, A is a scoundrel." (H.L. Mencken)

۶ه

Screwballism—a behavior that proceeds from the fundamental con-viction that life is wonderful, albeit chaotic and rife with absurdity. We are deeply indebted to famous screwballs like Charlie Chaplin, the Marx Brothers, and Lucille Ball for their gaiety and irreverent

slapstick, without which Western culture would be entirely too logical, modest, and melodramatic. However, do not go into business
with screwballs under any circumstances.

Scripturalism—the quality of being scriptural or written. Commonly attributed to the Scriptures (the Old and New Testaments), but
it can apply to sacred writings of any religion or people.

෨

Secessionism—the doctrine or principles of withdrawing from a treaty
or alliance; specifically, in U.S. history, the formal declaration of
a state renouncing allegiance to the Federal Union and joining the
Confederate States of America, an act attempted by 11 southern
states in 1860.

States that seceded from the Union viewed it as their right, inasmuch as certain provisions of the Constitution (especially regarding
slavery) had been compromised by the admission of new states, and
certain policies of the northern-dominated Congress (especially oner-
ous trade tariffs) violated the basic compromise on which the Federal system was established in 1789.

But the Federal government under Pres. Abraham Lincoln, and
later rulings of the Supreme Court, declared that secession was un-
constitutional. Upon its ratification, they said, the Constitution en-

tailed a "perpetual union" that could not be revoked by an individual
state. Ultimately, the issue of secession was settled by force—the Civil
War. Today, it's presumed that states cannot leave the Union because "might makes right," and no state could successfully resist Federal law backed by Federal troops.

Contrary to those who say Northern capitalists felt no sympathy
for the largely agrarian South, consider this from Fernando Wood,
Mayor of New York City in 1861: "With our aggrieved brethren of
the Slave States, we have friendly relations and a common sympathy... Why should not New York City ... become also equally independent? As a free city, with but nominal duty on imports, her
local Government could be supported without taxation upon her
people. Thus we could live free from taxes, and have cheap goods
nearly duty free. In this (New York) would have the whole and united
support of the Southern States, as well as all the other states."

As we write this, Canada, the Soviet Union, and many Eastern
European countries are battling Secessionism from their states, largely
as a result of ethnic tensions.

ॐ

Sectarianism—the quality of being strongly bigoted and devoted to
the tenets and interests of a particular sect or religious denomination.

ॐ

Sectionalism—narrow-minded interest in and affection for an area
of a country, and prejudice against citizens of another part of a common country.

ॐ

Secular Humanism—an ethical system that promotes humanist values
like tolerance, compassion, and dignity, without relying on religious
doctrine. It is also the label Christian fundamentalists slap on any
teaching or philosophy that does not conform to their narrow views,
especially school subjects taught in a manner not conforming to
their faith, such as a biology class that fails to discuss Creationism.
These people also believe that *The Diary of Anne Frank* is porno-
graphic and *The Wizard of Oz* is Satanic. As secular humanists know,
intellectual freedom is incompatible with religious Fanaticism.

ॐ

Secularism—1. supreme or exclusive attention to the affairs of this
life, as opposed to the interest in an after-life. An ethical system
founded on natural morality, Secularism seeks the development of
the physical, moral, and intellectual nature of man to the highest
possible point as the immediate duty of life. It advocates the practical sufficiency of natural morality apart from Theism, promotes human improvement by material means, and argues against religious
influence in public policy and schools.

2. in India, the non-sectarian policy of the Congress Party, which
has ruled the "world's largest democracy" since independence in

1947. There are several paradoxes (read: myths) here. First, in a democracy the majority should be in the driver's seat. Not so in India, where, if the Hindu majority takes over, there will be civil war. Second, the Congress Party is not a party, as such—it is a family dynasty that tolerates no "secularization" of power, unless your name is Gandhi. And finally, the Sikhs, Tamils, and neighboring Moslems have been sworn enemies of the Hindus for centuries.

Secularism has little to do with the actual business of ruling India. In reality, political power rests with the educated Brahman caste (and to the Nehru-Gandhi clan in particular) because of their historic leadership and the wide belief that Brahmans are supernatural beings. (Indira Gandhi, who ruled India for two decades, was said to be the reincarnation of the goddess Durga.) After the recent assassination of Rajiv Gandhi, the paradox continued with the instant electon of his widow—a Roman Catholic, Italian housewife!—to lead a nation of 800 million semi-literate, religious fanatics. Fortunately, the lady refused, thus putting Secularism in India to its first real test in over 40 years.

Seism—an earthquake.

૨௨

Seismism—the phenomena associated with earthquakes, such as a shaking of the ground, disruption of magnetic fields, etc.

૨௨

Self-Criticism—self-examination accompanied by Criticism, sometimes objective but often harsh and masochistic. During China's Cultural Revolution, it was one of Mao's tools of repression: those accused of counterrevolutionary acts or thoughts had to parade in dunce caps and write long Criticisms and denunciations of themselves. The fad for public confession of sins is still big among TV talk-shows and erring evangelists. "There is luxury in self-reproach. When we blame ourselves, we feel no one else has a right to blame us." (Oscar Wilde)

૨௨

Self-Determinism—1. the philosophical theory that what you are now is determined by what you were before, and you have the power to change yourself. 2. in political theory, it is the right of a people to choose their own form of government and leaders without interference from other nations, especially a colonial or imperial power.

Selfism—exclusive devotion to self; absolute selfishness. See Egoism and Objectivism. "A self-made man, who worships his creator." (John Bright, on Benjamin Disraeli)

Semi-Pelagianism—the doctrine of John Cassanius, a French monk who, in 430 A.D., modified the doctrines of Pelagius (360-420 A.D.) by denying human merit and maintaining the necessity of the Holy Spirit's influences, while rejecting the doctrine of unconditional salvation, the inability of man to do good, irresistable Grace, and the certain perseverance of saints. See Pelagianism.

Semitism—the practice of what is unique to Semitic peoples, especially Jews; an idiom or expression, relating to Shem or his reputed descendants; the Hebrew race or any of those kindred to it, such as the Arabians, the ancient Phoenicians, and the Assyrians.

Sensationalism—1. in philosophy, the doctrine or theory that all our ideas are derived solely through sensations. (Also, Sensationism, Sensualism.) 2. in politics and Journalism, the policy of devoting attention to or amplifying the importance of acts of violence, perceived heresies, and controversial personalities.

Sensualism—1. in metaphysics, the theory which bases all our mental acts and intellectual powers upon sensation; a state of subjection to feelings and appetites, especially those that are erotic or carnal. 2. in ethics, the theory that the gratification of the senses is the highest good.

Sentimentalism—display of tender feelings or exquisite sensibility toward some person or thing, especially of antiquity. In extreme cases, it connotes a weepy Emotionalism. In the old language of art, it was the leading idea which governed the general conception of a work of art or which makes itself visible to the eye and mind of the spectator through the work of an artist. "Sentimentality is the emotional promiscuity of those who have no sentiment." (Norman Mailer)

Separatism—disposition to withdraw from a church or other association, especially a political alliance; traits of a deserter, seceder, or schismatic. Current hot spots are Czechoslovakia, Yugoslavia, and most of the Soviet "Republics," where Socialism has devolved into hysterical, primitive Nationalism.

Serfism—the condition or state of those in the Middle Ages who were incapable of holding property but were attached to the land, transferred with it, and liable to feudal services of the lowest description; being a forced laborer attached to an estate, as formerly in England and Russia; in general usage, the trait of being a slave or any lowly servant. See Feudalism.

Serpentinianism—the practices of an ancient sect of serpent worshippers. See Nagualism.

Sesquipedalianism—a fondness for using long words. For example: "Nothing ... is more overrated than the epidermal felicity of two featherless bipeds in desperate congress." (Quentin Crisp). Also, Sesquipedalism.

Sexdigitism—the state of having six fingers or toes.

Sexism—attitudes or conditions that promote stereotyping of social roles based on gender; discrimination based on sex, especially to the disadvantage of women in employment. Arguably, Sexism arises from sexuality, which divided mankind into two classes, the pursuers and the pursued, and invested them with contrary sexual interests and values. "Men and women, women and men. It will never work." (Erica Jong)

Shakerism—the beliefs and practices of the Shakers, a religious denomination with its principal settlement now in New Lebanon, New York. Shakers believe God has revealed Himself four times, the last revelation being to Ann Lee, their founder, in 1770. They practice continence, Communism, and nonparticipation in political government, and call themselves the United Society of Believers in Christ's Second Appearing. They received the appellation "Shakers" from a shaking movement they make in a ritual dance.

Shaktiism—a sect of Hinduism devoted to the cult in which a goddess (Shakti, wife of Shiva) plays the central role; a monotheistic religion emphasizing the motive force of the feminine principle and hence the importance of the Mother Goddess. The word *shakti* means power, and the goddess is revered as a loving, life-giving Mother, though she can become a furious, chastising Mother. In view of this ambivalence, she is sometimes depicted giving birth to her creatures and then swallowing them up. Humanity is therefore completely in her hands and dependent on her mercy. Good religion for the humble. Also, Saktism.

Shamanism—the religious practices of people who believe good and evil spirits pervade the world and can be summoned through priests ("shamans") acting as mediums. Common among the Finnish, Ostiaks, and Samoyeds of the north, it's also known within the South American Indian community and the Philippines.

Shavianism—a viewpoint, statement, or stylistic touch characteristic of George Bernard Shaw (1856-1950), Irish dramatist and freethinker;

the study of Shaw and his writings. "It took me twenty years of studied self-restraint, aided by the natural decay of my faculties, to make myself dull enough to be accepted as a serious person by the British public." (Shaw)

ॐ

Sheilaism—a form of Individualism experienced by the meek and mild, similar to Taoism. First reported in a 1984 interview with Sheila Larson, a young American nurse: "I believe in God," she said. "I'm not a religious fanatic. I can't remember the last time I went to church. My faith has carried me a long way. It's Sheilaism. Just my own little voice... It's just to try to love yourself and be gentle with yourself." Bless you, Sheila. There's nothing wrong with being little.

ॐ

Shintoism—one of the two great religions of Japan. At its origin, it was a form of nature worship—the natural forces regarded as gods, with the sun being supreme. The soul of the sun god, when on earth, founded the reigning house in Japan, and hence the emperor is worshipped as divine. Today, the essence of the religion is ancestral worship and sacrifices to departed heroes.

"Japan's top manufacturer of women's underwear, Wacoal, provides spacious premises for its deity, a shrine next to the firm's headquarters in Kyoto. Here, solemn observances are held twice a year. Last month, the chairman led his board members through the *torii* arch of the shrine for prayers. With a Shinto priest officiating, they requested the continuing support of the underwear deity. 'We must never neglect these ceremonies, which assure the prosperity of the company,' says a senior Wacoal executive." (*Daily Telegraph*)

ॐ

Short-Termism—1. management emphasis on short-term results to please financial partners, to the detriment of long-range strategy or growth. 2. in London, a term denoting disdain for industrial investment and periodic exploitation of industry for short-term profits, a practice dating to the early 19th century. In 1911, Lord Revelstoke of Barings, approached about a business venture for making use of coal products, said, "I have a horror of all industrial companies, and I should not think of placing my hard-earned gains into such a venture." City bankers traditionally made their money from loans to foreign governments, although this practice was recently curtailed by massive losses in Argentina, Brazil, Poland, etc.

ॐ

Sigmatism—a lisp, or Thigmatithm.

ॐ

Sikhism—sorry, we can't exactly figure this one out. *Sikh* means disciple, and it refers to a militaristic sect in the Punjab formed by Guru Nanak (1469-1538) to link elements of Islamism and Vishnuism

(maybe). Sikhs worship at a jewel-encrusted Golden Temple, carry
ceremonial swords, never cut their hair or wear motorcycle helmets,
and are driving all non-Sikhs out of their homeland. The Indian
government is unable to cope with them—Indira Gandhi was assassinated by her Sikh bodyguards.

Sinapism—a mustard plaster. From the word *sinapis*, meaning mustard.

 za

Sinarquism—doctrines and practices of a Mexican reactionary, fascist movement of the late 1930's. Derived from *sinarquismo* ("without
anarchy"), the movement generally paralleled Naziism and faded
after World War II. It was led by a German, Helmut Oscar Schreit-
er, and a Mexican, José Angel Urquiza.

za

Sinecurism—the state of having a job with pay but no work (the opposite of being an Ism compiler), or an ecclesiastical benefice without cure of souls.

Sinicism—a uniqueness or characteristic of the Chinese people.

Situationism—the psychological theory that any behavior is simply a response to the immediate situation. For example, that boy is hopping on one foot and cursing because he just dropped a book of Isms on his foot.

Skepticism—1. the doctrines and opinions of a doubter. Named for the Pyrrhonists, ancient philosophers who doubted everything and denied the certainty of any knowledge about the phenomena of nature. 2. in theology, doubting the truth of revelation or denying the divine origin of a religion, or the existence, perfection, or truth of God. "A wise Skepticism is the first attribute of a good critic." (James Russell Lowell)

Slavism—a characteristic of the Slavs or Slavic languages. Also, Slavicism.

Slurvianism—slurred speech.

Snobbism—the state or actions of someone who exhibits servility toward people he considers of a higher status, or insolence to those of lower status. Especially, a person who affects a higher rank, station, or culture than the facts warrant and who acts with condescension toward those he considers inferior. "Snobs talk as if they had begotten their own ancestors." (Herbert Agar)

Social Darwinism—1. the application of Charles Darwin's theories of evolution and natural selection to society, especially regarding the alleged genetic inferiority of the lower classes. Championed by William Graham Sumner (1840-1910) and British philosopher Herbert Spencer (1820-1903), who is generally credited with fusing Darwinian theories with biology and sociology in his book *Principles of Biology*. "The poverty of the incapable, the distresses that come upon the imprudent, the starvation of the idle ... are the decrees of a large, farseeing benevolence." (Spencer)

2. the belief that progress emerges from competition and the struggle for survival; the philosophy of laissez faire Capitalism, advocated by many, including writer Ayn Rand and economist F.A. von Hayek. Our resistance to allowing "the Devil to take the hindmost" in a fully competitive society flows from the ideal of Liberalism, which views the individual as a creature to be protected and nurtured against private or public tyranny. In the 1930's, New Dealism and Keynesianism manipulated the money supply and the influence of big government. Later, Presidents Kennedy and Johnson declared war on poverty. Today, the wreckage is all around us—crumbling cities, massive debt, industrial stagnation—but few are willing to admit that von Hayek's 1944 prediction that Interventionism would put us on "the road to serfdom" was correct. But, if we are working only to pay the debts of our parents, how are we different from serfs?

Viewing the debate from the 1990's is daunting. Spencer lived in an era of unprecedented economic growth and "rags-to-riches" mobility. In the U.S., men like Andrew Carnegie started with nothing and rose to great wealth and fame by following rather simple rules: honesty, hard work, and savings. Today, all that gets you is a new Toyota—while someone else makes a killing on junk bond scams or crack cocaine. In the 19th century, government was small, local, and easily bribed. Today, it is gigantic, centralized, and virtually unbribable, and it employs directly or indirectly one-third of the U.S. workforce.

Among those who like laissez faire Capitalism, the question often arises: Is there any hope, or are we forever doomed to paternalistic, intrusive regulation and slow social and economic suffocation? We think there is reason for hope. With a little luck, the collapse of Communism and the Soviet Union, where the "road to serfdom" was pursued at a gallop, will shut up the Marxists and reawaken the world to the blessings of economic liberty and limited government.

ЭA

Socialism—a theory of social reform, the main feature of which is to secure, through common ownership, a reconstructed society with a more equal division of property and the fruits of labor. The means of production, capital, etc. are controlled by society as a whole, rather than by individuals.

Socialism is an ancient idea, practiced by nomadic tribes, early Christians, medieval villages, etc. From time to time, the theory is advanced by various claims in favor of its utility, fairness, or historical necessity—most recently and prominently by Karl Marx, who enunciated the doctrine of "scientific Socialism" based on Historical Materialism. But common ownership and equal division of wealth always produce the same outcome, regardless of religious or political leadership: economic disaster, brought about by rewarding those who do not produce and penalizing those who do. See Communism. "As with the Christian religion, the worst advertisement for Socialism is its adherents." (George Orwell)

Socialist Realism—a school of art officially sanctioned by the Soviet Union in 1934, which produced wall murals depicting valiant and crudely illustrated laborers raising their fists and tools as a symbol of class consciousness. The purpose was to produce art that everybody could understand and to inspire solidarity. Joseph Stalin wanted to develop "engineers of souls" who, through poster art, would convince starving, terrified peasants that it was heroic to work for the state.

❧

Social Mutualism—political philosophy of Pierre Joseph Proudhon (1809-1865), father of classical Syndicalism and Anarchism. Proudhon was a colleague of Karl Marx, but they parted company when Marx ridiculed Proudhon's first treatise on anarchy. Proudhon believed that "property is theft" and that everything could be put right if land ownership were equally divided into tiny parcels and if banks were forbidden to charge interest on loans.

❧

Social Realism—1950's American art movement which confined itself to painting scenes of working-class life to depict victims of Capitalism. See Kitchen Sinkism.

❧

Socinianism—the tenets of the Socinians, who observed the teachings and doctrines of Faustus Socinus (1539-1604) and his uncle Laelius (1525-1562), who denied the doctrine of the Trinity, the deity of Christ, the personality of the devil, the depravity of man, vicarious atonement, and the eternity of future punishment. Their theory was that Christ was a man divinely commissioned, who had no existence before He was miraculously and sinlessly conceived by Mary; that human sin was Adam's sin, and that human salvation was the imitation and adoption of Christ's virtue; that the Bible was to be interpreted by human reason and that its metaphors were not to be taken seriously.

≥♠

Socratism—the doctrines and philosophy of Socrates (469-399 B.C.), the Greek sage whose teaching method employed interrogatories. Instead of laying down a proposition by virtue of its mass appeal or traditional authority, the Socratic method led the pupil to acknowledge it himself through a series of questions put to him. Rather than establish a doctrine, Socrates sought to awaken a more comprehensive pursuit of knowledge, and he gets credit for two first principles of science: the inductive method and the definition of ideas. In gratitude for being forced to examine their lives and cherished ideals, the Athenians condemned Socrates to drink hemlock—which is not much different from the modern reaction to anyone who asks too many questions about today's sacred cows. "There is only one good, knowledge, and one evil, ignorance." (Socrates)

Solarism—according to Webster's: "the interpretation of myths by reference to the sun, especially such interpretation carried to an extreme."

≥♠

Solecism—an impropriety of speech or language, or a breach of etiquette. Modern grammarians often apply the term to any word or expression which violates established grammar. In broader definition, it's any unfitness, absurdity, or violation of the rules of society.

≥♠

Solidism—the obsolete medical theory that changes in the solids of the body, such as expansion or contraction, are the cause of all disease.

&

Solifidianism—the belief that faith alone is sufficient for salvation.

&

Solipsism—the metaphysical concept that oneself is the only reality. Cf. Berkelianism.

&

Somatism—1. in psychiatry, the theory that mental illnesses have physical causes. 2. in philosophy, the belief in physical and corporeal beings only. See Materialism.

&

Somnambulism—a peculiar distortion of mental functions during sleep, wherein a person acts automatically. The organs of sense remain torpid; intellectual powers are blunted. Sleep-walking is the most palpable form, but the somnambulist often goes about his daily routine as well.

Somniloquism—the act of talking in your sleep.

&

Somnolism—the state of being in, or the doctrine of, magnetic sleep. In Roman mythology, Somnus was the god of sleep, described as a brother of Death and son of Night. His Greek counterpart was Hypnos. In works of art, Sleep and Death are represented as two youths sleeping or holding inverted torches in their hands.

&

Sophism—a clever or fallacious argument not supported by sound reasoning, or in which the inference is not justly deduced from the premises. The Sophists, a class of men who taught eloquence, philosophy, and politics in ancient Greece, used subtle and specious reasoning and were generally hated. See Ingenious Sophism.
"These are the days when skies resume
   The old—old—sophistries of June—
   A blue and gold mistake." (Emily Dickinson)

&

Southcottianism—the doctrine of Joanna Southcott (1750-1814), a religious zealot who claimed she was the woman mentioned in the Book of Revelation. Her death did not alienate her disciples, and the sect continued to exist for many years.

๛

Southernism—an idiom, attitude, or accent peculiar to the American South. Examples include "y'all," "damn Yankee," and "Wanna go to a lynchin' , Bubba?"

๛

Sovietism—1. belief in the doctrines of the Soviet Union as an exponent of Communism. 2. the theory of organizing states by councils representing workers, farmers, party officials, etc. 3. a characteristic of Soviet ideology. See Democratic Centralism.

๛

Spartacism—a revolution of slaves, so named for Spartacus of Thrace (d. 71 B.C.), a gladiator who led an uprising against Crassus and the Roman legions called the Third Slave War. (Sorry—no data on the first two.) Crassus was so enraged that he ordered every slave who survived the final battle to be crucified, and crosses with dying men lined the Appian Way for miles. The movie directed by Stanley Kubrick, with Kirk Douglas as Spartacus and Jean Simmons as his fave slave, is a complete education in storytelling. ★★★★!

In Germany during World War I, a group of extreme socialists adopted the name "Spartacists" as a statement that they were wage-slaves-in-mutiny. The group was headed by Rosa Luxemburg and Karl Liebknecht, who attempted an armed rebellion in 1919 and were killed (though not crucified). Some say their example led to modern German Communism.

๛

Specialism—the devotion to a particular branch of a profession or subject, such as science or art; the distinctive work or study of a specialist.

Speciesism—a term used to accuse those who favor one animal species (especially humans) over another (say, worms). Used mainly by environmental and animal rights extremists who see humans as equivalent—no better, no worse—to all life. The funny thing is, these folks argue that superior moral, human tenets like tolerance, liberty, individual dignity, etc. are shared by, say, worms. These people are either incredibly naïve or incredibly arrogant. "A rat is a pig is a dog is a boy." (Ingrid Newkirk)

ॐ

Spencerianism—the philosophy of Herbert Spencer (1820-1903), who attempted to synthesize the various sciences. So now you can go to college and take courses like Biochemistry and Psychobiology. Spencer is also credited with the creation of Social Darwinism and coining the phrase "the survival of the fittest." "The ultimate result of shielding men from the effects of folly is to fill the world with fools." (Spencer)

ॐ

Spinozism—a form of Pantheism taught by Benedict (Baruch) de Spinoza (1632-1677), an Amsterdam Jew who maintained that God is not only the maker but also the original matter of the universe, so that creation was only a development of God. Spinoza's ethical system was a carefully constructed proof which discarded pleasure, wealth, etc. in favor of the constant improvement of one's moral character as the highest and most satisfying aim of life. This "heresy" resulted in Spinoza being evicted from the Jewish ghetto.

ॐ

Spinsterism—see Old Maidism.

ॐ

Spirantism—in phonetics, a fricative, a sound formed by the passing of air between the lips; for example, blowing a "razzberry."

ॐ

Spiritual Atomism—a concept first articulated by Pierre Teilhard de Chardin (1881-1955), a Jesuit priest and geologist. In his search for meta-Christianity, he concluded that "man is poised on the equator of a universe which looks very different from its respective poles." Since there are about 1,000,000,000,000,000 cells in a human body and 25,000,000 atoms in a single grain of virus, humans represent an abyss of synthesis, and, he said, via humans the cosmos is struggling toward a higher stage of complexity-consciousness, to the final evolution of the Omega point. The more complex the Organism, the more consciousness is present.

ॐ

Spiritualism—1. in philosophy, a term embracing systems that are not materialistic—i.e., which hold that mind is not a function of, but something distinct from, matter. Thus, the term covers all systems recognizing the existence of mind or spirit, as well as those which, like the Idealism of Berkeley and the Egoism of Fichte, regard the external world as a succession of notions impressed on the mind by the Deity, or as the product of the mind itself. 2. a system of professed communication with spirits or the supernatural world, chiefly through people with special susceptibility ("mediums"). Spiritualism as a popular form of Mysticism was prominent in Victorian England and 19th-century America. Lately, it has been revived as "channeling" by New Age charlatans. Also, Spiritism.

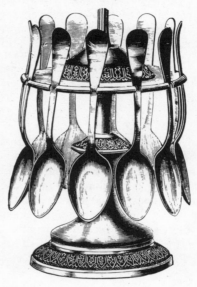

Spoonerism—transposition of phonemes with a comic outcome, as in "Beeping Sluety" (Sleeping Beauty). Named after William Spooner (1844-1930), Warden of New College, Oxford, who once chastised a student by saying: "You have tasted two worms and can leave Oxford by the next town drain." (Translation: "You have wasted two terms and can leave Oxford by the next down train.") He also once offered a toast "to the queer old dean" (i.e., "the dear old Queen").

✌

Squatterism—the practice of living on unclaimed land or in an abandoned house or apartment without legal title to the place. A loophole in British law allows unauthorized invasion of residential property during the owner's temporary absence, whereupon the invaders are deemed to be lawful residents and cannot be evicted unless they burn the house down (which they frequently do). No doubt the worst victims are families who leave for vacation and return to find their house filled with skinheads and drug addicts.

We were slightly luckier: our own house was equipped with a burglar alarm and a big dog, although this did not prevent squatters from invading the house next door and bombarding us with punk music and construction noise every night for three months. When the weather got cold, they built a fire in a boarded-up hearth and ignited the flat above us, and our elderly neighbor barely escaped with her life at 3:00 a.m. Still, the Westminster Council ruled that the "squatters rights" were more important than ours, hers, or the property owner's. We patiently waited another month—and the same thing happened, only this time the "squat" was gutted.

Those who don't live next door to squatters often proclaim their sympathy for homeless people and defend an ancient tradition from feudal times, when peasants could not be evicted from the castle if they had entered when the gates were open. Consequently, British squatters currently possess the Cambodian Embassy, 1,500 private dwellings, and countless flats—paying no taxes and no rent, doing no work, and living off Social Security. Amsterdam and Berlin have similar problems, and it's said that new arrivals in these cities can buy a list of apartments ripe for invasion. The current price to hire a gang of thugs to evict squatters is around $5,000.

ঽ

Stakhanovism—the belief in working as hard as possible and constantly striving to improve efficiency, in the manner proposed by Alexei Stakhanov, Soviet coal miner, in 1935. Praised by Stalin, Stakhanov's heroic effort was widely publicized and became a means through which the Communist system could reward and encourage individual initiative.

ঽ

Stalinism—the political theories and practices of Josef Stalin (1879-1953), Soviet dictator infamous for ruthless purges, show trials, and forced collectivization of Russian agriculture. During his reign, Stalin's theories were called an outgrowth of Leninism and a practical application of Marxism. He advocated that the Soviet Union should become invulnerable as a world power and that her efforts must be directed toward building up her government, industries, and military. In practice, that meant enslaving Eastern Europe, conscripting millions into industrial armies, and killing all who voiced opposition. Britain's Lady Astor, known for her bluntness, once asked Stalin, "How long are you going to go on killing people?" "As long as it's necessary," he replied. He found it necessary to kill about 4.5 million. "A single death is a tragedy, a million deaths is a statistic." (Stalin)

ঽ

Standardism—1. government regulations which enforce minimum standards of fitness and decency—and thereby encourage the incompetent and impede progress. Rather than assist consumers, Standardism defeats natural competition for quality and reputation and inflates prices. Believe it or not, it's actually possible to raise, for example, turkeys, feed them table scraps, dispatch one when you wish, dress it, and serve it for dinner—without any government inspection whatever! But don't even think about getting ambitious and trying to replicate the process on a larger and more scientific scale, because you'll be filling out forms and greeting Safety Inspectors by the truckload.

2. agreement among manufacturers to adopt a common technology or method. A modern paradigm is the compact disc (CD), developed by Philips N.V. and licensed to all the major electronics manufacturers in the early 1980's.

ॐ

Statism—the principle or policy of giving the state extensive control of economic, political, and social life, at the expense of privacy and individual liberty. "The ideological root of Statism (or Collectivism) is the tribal premise of primordial savages who, unable to conceive of individual rights, believed that the tribe is a supreme, omnipotent ruler.... Statism—in fact and in principle—is nothing more than gang rule." (Ayn Rand)

ॐ

Stercoranism—the beliefs of the Stercoranists, ecclesiastics in the 5th and 6th centuries who said that since the sacraments in the Eucharist undergo digestion, God, if truly present, becomes feces. It was a statement of their contempt to forward this opinion.

Stoicism—1. the traits of one who does not display emotion and lives an impassive, calm, austere life. 2. the opinions and maxims of the Stoics, disciples of the Greek philosopher Zeno (335-263 B. C.), who

believed people should repress emotion and passion and submit calm-
ly to the vagaries of life. The name of this philosophy was derived
from *stoikos*, a painted porch where Zeno taught. The character of
Mr. Spock on *Star Trek* resembles a Stoic. "The goal of life is living
in agreement with nature." (Zeno)

👁

Structuralism—1. in psychology, the study of consciousness by introspection. 2. a school of Marxism propounded by French Communist Louis Althusser (1918-1990), which held that Marxism was
"a process without a subject." It is enlightening to consider Althusser's
personal life: "His academic career came to a bizarre end one night
[in 1980] when, in a fit of psychotic rage, he strangled his wife to
death. Judged unfit for trial by reason of insanity, Althusser spent
his final decade mostly in asylums." (*Newsweek*)

👁

Student Revolutionism—a broad U.S. protest movement inspired
by the 1962 "Port Huron Statement," which vowed to "replace power
rooted in possession, privilege, or circumstance by power and uniqueness rooted in love, reflectiveness, reason, and creativity." One of
the outcomes was the hippie movement, which celebrated the peace-
and-love part. The other outcome was class war, both in the literal
classroom and, later, in the Marxist struggle against the "military-
industrial complex." Unlike the traditional left-wing, which saw factory bosses as the greedy ruling class, the student lefties were more
frightened of government.

The catalyst was the Vietnam War. Mobilized and sheltered by
a vast network of anti-war activists, nearly 250,000 boys refused to
register for the draft. Spectacular demonstrations of hundreds of
thousands surrounded the Pentagon and the White House. The
1968 Democratic Convention ended in chaos, as Chicago police
rampaged through crowds of student protesters, live on national
TV. But the Democratic Party wasn't ready for a unilateral withdrawal from Vietnam. They ran Hubert Humphrey against Richard
Nixon for President, and the students saw a monolithic, all-male,
all-white "establishment" ranged against them. "Working with the
system" had failed, just as the militants had predicted. It was time
for Plan B: open warfare.

1969 was the watershed year for campus bombings, student strikes,
youth riots, etc. The authorities struck back, killing four protesters
at Kent State, two in Chicago, two in Mississippi, one in Milwau-
kee. Thousands, then tens of thousands, were beaten and thrown
in jail. Nixon ordered the bombing of Cambodia, refusing to yield
to the students' main demand to end the war. Though Communists
and pacifists vied for their loyalty, most students expressed contempt
for any government. They were anti-war anarchists, mainly from
the comfortable middle class, raised on Wonder Bread and the Ten
Commandments, especially "Thou shalt not kill."

With the end of the Vietnam War came the end of Student Revolutionism in America, partly because the movement had achieved a substantial victory, and partly because anyone who's lived in a commune for more than a year realizes that Communism is for the birds. The hippie movement had its limits, especially if your horizons were wider than a bowl of brown rice and a nose full of tear gas.

੨੦

Stundism—the doctrines of a religious body of Russians, somewhat resembling Methodism, originated in 1860 by emigrants from Germany. It emphasizes brotherly love and the necessity of manual labor.

੨੦

Subjective Idealism—type of Idealism that says everything you experience is merely ideas either created or distorted by your mind. Cf. Objective Idealism.

੨੦

Subjectivism—1. the doctrine that all knowledge is relative and personal, or that it varies according to one's situation; that we cannot prove that what seems true to us also seems true to others; that all claims of knowledge are derived from subjective states or impressions. 2. the belief that concepts of good and right can be determined only by personal feeling. 3. an economic theory which holds that value is in part determined by the varying needs and sacrifices of individuals. It first made an appearance in Adam Smith's

Wealth of Nations and was later used as a Criticism of Capitalism, leading to Marginal Utilitarianism.

❧

Subordinationism—in Christian theology, the doctrine that in the Trinity, God the Father has priority over the Son, who has priority over the Holy Ghost, both in order (the orthodox doctrine) and in essence (an Aryan belief).

❧

Substantialism—the doctrine that, behind the phenomena of consciousness and of nature, there are real substances, whether mental or corporeal. Not too distant from Platonism.

❧

Suburbanism—1. a trait of people who live in villages outside major cities, such as commuting a considerable distance to work. 2. the practice of establishing a home outside a major city to enjoy quieter, safer, cheaper living while remaining near the advantages of a city. Suburbanism has dramatically changed American society since World War II, beginning with the Levittown experiment in mass-produced housing for young married couples, and accelerating into wholesale evacuation of cities by the middle class seeking a more wholesome place to live and raise children.

Prior to World War II, the trend was in the opposite direction: people flooded into cities, abandoning the hardships of rural life for education and employment. The switch to suburban living came first as a response to veterans who returned from the war and wanted thousands of new, small homes. Plentiful gasoline, a growing modern highway system, and an expansion of consumer credit fueled the development of outlying neighborhoods and shopping centers. All this led to the abandonment of inner cities, which rapidly filled with poor, uneducated migrants from the South and immigrants from Mexico, Asia, and elsewhere—which increased Suburbanism even more.

The trend is probably irreversible now that Gangsterism has taken hold in inner-city ghettos. Indeed, with the increasing popularity of "tele-commuting," home offices, satellite television, etc., the latest trend is the movement to "ex-urbia," small communities past the suburbs of people escaping suburbia's growing congestion. In New York City, a sort of elevated suburb exists in the high-rise buildings, while the streets belong to the underclass. "Suburbia is where the developer bulldozes out the trees, then names the streets after them." (Bill Vaughn)

❧

Suffragism—the belief that all competent adults, especially women, should have the right to vote. In the U.S., Suffragettes, led by Susan B. Anthony, Elizabeth Cady Stanton, and others, were women who campaigned for enfranchisement, which they received by

Constitutional amendment in 1920. Also, Suffragetism. "We hold these truths to be self-evident, that all men and women are created equal." (Stanton)

જ્

Sufism—the beliefs of the Sufis, an Islamic sect practicing Mysticism and Asceticism. Also, Sufiism.

જ્

Suicidism—the act of self-destruction by a person sound in mind and capable of measuring his moral responsibility; by extension, destruction of one's social, political, or business life by one's own act. "There are many who dare not kill themselves for fear of what the neighbors will say." (Cyril Connolly)

Supernaturalism—in theology, the doctrine of a divine and supernatural agency in the production of the miracles and revelations recorded in the Bible, and in the grace which renews and sanctifies humanity. As a general term pertaining to Mysticism, it connotes belief in that which is above or beyond the established course or laws of nature. "Supernaturalism is the Mysticism of the materialist." (W.R. Inge)

જ્

Super-Realism—in painting, exact reproduction of a photograph; in sculpture, exact reproduction of a human form by casting it in plaster. Also known as Hyper-Realism.

જ્

Supralapsarianism—the doctrine of the Supralapsarians, a class of Calvinists who held that God decreed the fall of man and the consequent introduction of sin into the world, and that the election of some to everlasting life, with the rejection of others, was formed beyond or before these decrees and was in no way consequent or dependent upon man's fall in the Garden of Eden. Cf. Infralapsarianism.

જ્

Suprematism—style of Russian art developed in the early 20th century which uses geometric figures in an abstract composition, such as Malevich's large black square on a white background. Clever stuff.

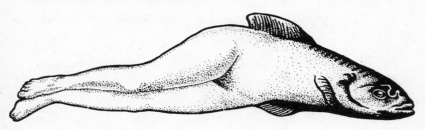

Surrealism—an art movement which began when Dadaism fell apart in 1924 and was described as Automatism. The term applies to some literature of the period as well, but it became closely identified with the paintings of Salvador Dali, H. Arp, and M. Ernst. A surrealist magazine flourished for 12 issues and then went the way of all nutty art magazines. Surrealism is more loosely used to describe fantastic, weird, and horrific images born of dreams and imagination—especially when the artist claims no conscious control over his creations. Devotees said their task was to create a new reality, untainted by reason or morality. No doubt, they succeeded admirably.

&

Survivalism—advocacy or practice of storing food and weapons and barricading yourself and your kin in bomb shelters or isolated areas, in anticipation of a nuclear war or the Apocalypse. Survivalists periodically go berserk and shoot a dozen or so innocent people before commiting suicide.

&

Sutteeism—the practice of self-immolation among Hindu widows on the funeral pyre of their husbands. One of the reasons it was encouraged was that when a widow committed *suttee*, all of her inheritance went to the priesthood. Considered meritorious by the Hindus, it was abolished in British India by law in 1829.

&

Swedenborgianism—the doctrines of a religious sect headed by Emanuel Swedenborg (1688-1772), Swedish scientist and theologian who professed to be the founder of the Church of the New Jerusalem, alluding to the city mentioned in Revelation. He claimed his followers had special insight into spiritual things, believed the regenerate man is in direct communication with angels and heaven, and held that there have been various judgments ending dispensations of divine revelation—the last in 1757, when Swedenborg was told to teach the doctrines of the New Church, as promised in the Apocalypse. As this church is to be eternal, there will be no other general judgments, but each individual will be judged after death.

Swedenborg's first vision of Christ came when he was eating his dinner rapidly. Christ, standing in the corner of the dining room, said, "Eat slower."

There are numerous societies of Swedenborgians in America. Go figure.

Sybaritism—the practices of the Sybarites, who came from Sybaris, Italy and were known for their love of luxury and pleasure-seeking. Therefore, anyone who is devoted to pleasure and voluptuousness is called a sybarite. See Playboyism, Sensualism.

Sycophantism—the act of a sycophant, originally an informer against those who stole figs or exported them contrary to Greek law. In modern usage, it's the behavior of a flatterer, especially someone who praises the wealthy or famous. The sycophant is obsequious and parasitic and tells tales for the purpose of gaining favor. See Parasitism.

Syllabism—writing with syllabic characters. Japanese phonetic characters are syllabic, with a single character standing for a sound (one meaning "wa," another "shi," etc.). In English, it often takes several characters, or letters, to indicate a single syllabic sound. Dictionaries practice Syllabism when they define words: sil′ ə biz′ əm.

Syllogism—1. a logical formula consisting of a major premise, a minor premise, and a conclusion which follows by necessity. 2. an argument expressed in strict logical form, so its conclusiveness is manifest from the structure of the expression alone.

Aristotle determined that there were a limited number of valid Syllogisms which could be deduced from the basic axiom of non-contradiction. The system of logic he devised is known as "classical," as opposed to modern logic and set theory, which discourage use of linguistic terms. The basic strength of Aristotle's system was that it gave users a way to grasp the logic of attributes predicated of a class, or of some but not all of the members of a class. Example:

Major premise: All ruminants are quadrupeds.

Minor premise: All deer are ruminants.

Conclusion: All deer are quadrupeds.

A Syllogism is valid when the conclusion necessarily follows from the premises. If the conclusion does not follow, the error consists in violating one of the 14 valid permutations discovered by Aristotle and constitutes a fallacy if the error deceives the reasoner himself. If it is advanced with the intention of deceiving others, it constitutes a Sophism.

One of the great tragedies of the modern world is that Western philosophy turned its back on the Syllogism, abandoning classical logic as a means of demonstrating just principles of personal and social life. The chief villain, responsible for killing reason as a tool of moral and political thought, was Immanuel Kant, who declared logic useless or defective for those purposes. See Kantianism.

ہو

Symbolism—1. the process of attributing an inner meaning unrelated to the actual powers or constitution of certain things or rituals. Thus, the cross symbolizes both the Catholic Church and the atonement of Christ; the $ sign can symbolize greed. 2. in art, the style exhibited by Odilon Redon, G. Morreau, and Puvis De Chavannes, based on the idea that religious Mysticism should be combined symbolically with Eroticism.

ہو

Symmetalism—the use of two or more metals in assigned proportions as a monetary standard (e.g., so many silver units equaling one gold unit). See Bimetallism.

ہو

Synchronism—concurrence of two or more events simultaneously; the arrangement of history according to dates, contemporary persons, or things being brought together in time. In art, the representation in the same picture of events happening at different times, or the same event at different moments of its progress. Also, a style of painting developed in 1912, similar to Orphism, which stressed color.

ہو

Syncretism—the union of two parties against a third, or the attempted union of principles or parties at variance, especially in religious doctrine. A syncretist attempts to blend incongruous tenets of different schools or churches into a system; especially, the followers of Calixtus, a professor of theology at Helmstadt in the 17th century who tried to frame a religious system uniting the sects of Christianity.

ہو

Syndicalism—an economic movement started in France and now widespread, aiming at the federation of workers in all trades to force labor demands through sympathetic strikes; the Trade Unionism principles which underlie this movement.

ࢬ

Synergism—1. in theology, the doctrine of a faction in the Lutheran church in the late 16th century which denied that God was the sole agent in the conversion of sinners and affirmed that man cooperated with divine grace in salvation. Opposite of Monergism. 2. in chemistry, the product of two or more agents which act upon each other and increase their effectiveness.

ࢬ

Syntheticism—the principles of putting two or more things together, as in compound medicines. In logic, a combination of opposing premises thought to imply an outcome derived from their contradiction. "Synthetic truth" describes the source of empirical conclusions, as opposed to the "analytic truth" of Syllogisms. In psychology, Synthecism is the joining of data, actually or in thought, to form a complex theory of behavior.

ࢬ

Synthetic Cubism—a late phase of Cubism introducing increased color and texture.

ࢬ

Synthetism—a theory of painting advanced by Paul Gauguin and E. Bernard, who believed artists should synthesize impressions and paint from memory rather than from what is in front of them. Their work consisted of flat areas of color surrounded by flat lines. They were probably remembering Iowa.

ࢬ

Syntypicism—the state or quality of being of the same type.

ࢬ

Systematism—rigid adherence to an order or method. Many gamblers, for example, devise a "system" to play games of chance like roulette. The house still wins.

Tall-Blondism—the theory that people with long legs, blond hair, and willowy appearance are smarter, luckier, and happier than short, chubby brunettes and redheads. Satisfyingly contradicted by the theory that blonds are dumb.

અ

Talmudism—charactersitics of or the study of the Talmud, the 63-volume collection of Jewish laws and traditions compiled in the 5th and 6th centuries. Since the Talmud is so detailed, the term can connote nit-picking and excessive arguing over arcane matter.

અ

Tantalism—an act of teasing or tormenting by exciting desire but continually frustrating expectations by keeping that desired object out of reach. It's the art and profession of the strip-tease dancer, for example. Named for the mythical King Tantalus, who was condemned to stand up to his chin in water—which constantly eluded his lips when he tried to quench the thirst that tormented him. Over his head grew all kind of fruit, but when he reached up, the wind scattered them.

અ

Tantrism—a religion based on Hindu Symbolism and the use of the *mandala*. Practitioners reflect on the transiency of everything physical and see the body as the abode of all higher knowledge. Tantric yoga speaks of five *shakras* or wheels in the human body which become the loci of certain deities and principles. Rituals and sacred formulas are believed to open a short-cut to Nirvana.

અ

Taoism—one of the principal forms of Chinese religion, based on the teachings of Lao-tzu (604-531 B. C.), who outlined a natural philosophy that showed the way to peace, harmony, and serenity. One of his gentle visions was to "love the ten thousand things."

Tarantism—a nervous disease, endemic to the area of Taranto, Italy in the 15th-17th centuries, characterized by an uncontrollable desire to dance and supposedly caused by the tarantula's bite. Descendants of the victims of Tarantism protested the hit song "Boogie Fever" in the 1970's because, they said, it was insensitive to their forebears. Just kidding.

Tautologism—1. the use of tautology, the repetition of the same idea in different words, such as "widow woman" or "hot water heater." 2. in logic, the use of a proposition phrased so that all possibilities are true: "The candidate will either win or lose."

Taylorism—1. the theory of "scientific management" introduced by Frederick Taylor (1856-1915), who conducted time and motion studies and encouraged manufacturers to standardize operations to speed assembly lines. Brilliantly satirized by Charlie Chaplin in *Modern Times*. After a strike at the Watertown Arsenal near Boston in 1911, Taylorism was banned by the Federal government. However, it continued to dominate assembly line management in the private sector until the Japanese demonstrated that "quality circles" and worker involvement were equally important.

2. the modification of Calvinism by American theologian Nathaniel William Taylor (1786-1858), who said that man has a free

will, and therefore, there is a distinction between depravity (the tendency to sin) and sin (a voluntary, evil action). A.k.a. New Haven theology.

Teetotalism—the principles and practices of those who abstain from all intoxicants. The term has nothing to do with tea. Rather, it originates from duplication of the initial letter of "total" —*t*-total— for emphasis. Also, Nephalism.

છ

Teleologism—in philosophy, the belief that all things in nature are designed, have a purpose, and are moving toward goals which fulfill that purpose. The famous "teleological argument" states that, since the universe displays order, there must be an orderer, or God.

છ

Tellurism—a modification of the hypothesis of Animal Magnetism, introduced by a Dr. Kieser, who attributed the phenomena to a telluric (earthly, terrestrial) spirit or influence.

છ

Tenebrism—a painting style of the late 16th century, using chiaroscuro to make forms appear to be moving in and out of shadow. From *tenebrae*, Latin for darkness.

છ

Terminism—1. in theology, the doctrine of the Terminists, who held that God has fixed a certain term for one's probation, during which you may accept grace in the time allotted. But there are no extensions, even if the dog did eat your homework. 2. in philosophy, extreme Nominalism, in which universals have no existence whatever. 3. in modern America, the fear that killer robots from the future are going to wreak havoc and speak English with an unintelligible Austrian accent.

&

Territorialism—1. in church government, a system subjecting the church to state authority; especially, a theory or doctrine entertained by Jews before the creation of Israel in 1948, looking forward to the settlement of their race in some country where they would be autonomous or self-governing. See Zionism. 2. a principle advancing the superiority of property owners.

&

Terrorism—the state of being terrified; actions or policies calculated to instill terror; the practice of using violence and intimidation to coerce people to a political outcome. War often entails an element of Terrorism, to the extent that civilian population centers are attacked to weaken the will of an adversary or to humiliate its leadership. As a modern weapon of insurrection or destabilization, Terrorism has been applied with alarming frequency against a range of targets, including Olympic athletes, civilian airplanes, cruise ships, department stores, and discotheques—all of which have symbolic, rather than military, value to the terrorist.

Despite an international impetus to eradicate it, measures to prevent Terrorism are seldom successful, because the modern world supplies terrorists with an almost infinite range of targets and means of attack. After a decade of increasingly urgent concern, the only coherent policy to emerge is that of brutal retaliation against homelands or sponsors of terrorist organizations. Prime instigators of modern Terrorism are the Irish Republican Army, the Palestine Liberation Organization, and a dozen Libyan- and Iranian-backed factions operating in the Middle East—though these groups would argue that their homelands have been "terrorized" by governments who deny fundamental rights to the factions represented by these revolutionaries. In Central and South America, Terrorism has been a tool employed by socialists and dictators alike, often trading atrocity for atrocity.

Resorting to Terrorism denotes a terminal stage of political defeat, insofar as the terrorist perceives no hope of winning by popular support or persuasion. The act of punishing innocent civilians for the real or imagined crimes of their leaders—thus provoking greater hostility and retaliation—is sublimely contrasted by the non-violent tactics of Pacifism, which few tyrants can withstand and which always inspire wide sympathy for the oppressed at each attempt to squelch the dissent. Thus, Corazon Aquino deposed the Marcos regime in the Philippines, not as a terrorist but as heir to the peaceful, thoughtful campaign of her husband, who was forced into exile and then assassinated. See also Eco-Terrorism, Narco-Terrorism.

&

Tetratheism—in Christian theology, the doctrine of the Godhead, in which there are four distinct offices or functions: the Father, the Son, the Holy Ghost, and a Divine Essence. We are still researching which "essence" they thought was divine. A staff poll favored vanilla.

ॐ

Teutonicism—a Teutonic idiom or characteristic; a Germanism. The Teutons were a tribe belonging to the Aryan or Indo-European family, which has been divided into three sections: Moesogothic, the language used by Ulphilas in his translation of the Scriptures made in the 4th century; German, subdivided into Low German (including English) and High German (including modern German); and Scandinavian, with modern Danish and Swedish.

ॐ

Textual Criticism—see Lower Criticism.

ॐ

Textualism—strict adherence to and interpretation of a text, especially the Bible. See Biblicism, Literalism, Fundamentalism.

ॐ

Thatcherism—the political philosophy attributed to Margaret Thatcher, prime minister of Great Britain from 1979-1990. As a homemaker and mother of twins, Thatcher was elected to Parliament in 1959. Slowly rising to prominence, she publicly emphasized traditional (some say "Victorian") values of thrift, industry, and family life and changed the political character of Britain during her 11-year tenure by re-introducing Capitalism and entrepreneurial incentives.

Called "The Iron Lady," Thatcher was responsible for instigating disarmament deals between Ronald Reagan and Mikhail Gorbachev, the successful prosecution of the Falklands War, and the wholesale restructuring of Britain's lopsided Welfare Statism. In a 1988 speech, she summarized her decade of leadership with characteristic pride: "The democratic model of a free enterprise society has proved itself superior. Freedom is on the offensive—a peaceful offensive—the world over, for the first time in my lifetime."

"If I were married to her, I'd be sure to have dinner ready when she got home." (George Shultz)

Theaism—excessive tea drinking; common in Britain.

ॐ

Theanthropism—1. the state of simultaneously being God and man, as in the Christian belief about Jesus Christ. See Nestorianism. 2. a conception of deity with essentially the same qualities as mankind, but on a grander scale; giving human attributes to gods, as in classical mythology.

Theatricalism—the art of dramatic representation; exaggerated Mannerisms. Among the Greeks and Romans, theaters were the chief public edifices, larger than the most spacious temples. Some could hold 40,000 spectators, hence the need for dramatic flourish and Exhibitionism. Also, Theatricism.

Thebaism—the habitual misuse of opium, or its consequences—an archaic form of drug abuse, now that refined opium products like heroin are widely available. Opium dens were dark rooms with bunks in which addicts smoked themselves into a stupor that persisted for days. "Religion ... is the opium of the people." (Karl Marx)

Theism—belief in the existence of God, especially as the creator of the world and supreme judge of humanity; belief in a living relationship between God and man (as opposed to Deism). As a generic term for all forms of Supernaturalism involving a deity, Theism includes Monotheism and is consistent with some forms of Pantheism and Polytheism. Cf. Atheism. "(God) seems to have an inordinate fondness for beetles." (J.B.S. Haldane)

Theocentrism—any system of thought centered around God.

Theogonism—the branch of heathen mythology which addresses the generation and genealogy of the gods.

૨&

Theomorphism—having the form, image, or likeness of God, as opposed to Anthropomorphism.

૨&

Theopaschitism—the doctrine taught by the Theopaschites, who believed God suffered in Christ's crucifixion. See Patripassianism.

૨&

Theophilanthropism—the doctrines of the Philanthropists, a society formed in Paris during the French Revolution to establish a new religion to replace Catholicism, which had been abolished. The system they advocated was pure Deism, and they espoused love of both God and humanity.

૨&

Theosophism—the doctrine of Theosophy and the Theosophical Society, which concerns itself with wisdom concerning God and insight into the divine. Specifically, it's a religious system based on 1. the notion that knowledge of divine things is gained by ecstasy, direct intuition, or special individual relations; 2. supposed intercourse with God and superior spirits; and 3. consequent attainment of superhuman knowledge by physical processes like the theurgy of ardent Platonists, or by the chemical processes described by German fire philosophers. From *theosophia*, which means divine wisdom, and includes *theogenis*, genealogy of the gods. Therefore, Theosophy is the wisdom of not one God, but of all gods.

The modern Theosophical Society was formed in 1875 by Madame Blavatsky (1831-1891), a Russian noblewoman and world traveler. Its international headquarters is now in Adyar, Madras, India. Blavatsky, a truly remarkable Victorian with enormous intellect and learning, gathered massive information on Eastern Mysticism and Buddhist mysteries.

૨&

Theriantropism—the condition of being, physically, part human and part animal—or all professional wrestler.

૨&

Thomism—the doctrines of St. Thomas Aquinas (1225-1274), theologian and philosopher, who attempted to reconcile the metaphysics and logic of Aristotle with Christianity. Aquinas held that faith and reason were the source of knowledge, taught unconditional predestination, defended the "transubstantiation" of the bread and wine into the body and blood of Christ at the moment of their blessing by a priest, and denied the Immaculate Conception. His doctrines are still highly esteemed in Catholicism and by theologians in general. "Reason in man is rather like God in the world." (Aquinas)

૨&

Thomsonianism—a system of botanical medicine named for its found-er, Dr. Samuel Thomson of Massachusetts, who stated that, since minerals are from the earth, they tend to draw people to their graves, whereas herbs, which grow upward, tend to keep people away from their graves. His work prompted Simon and Garfunkel to re-write their song "Sulfur, Iron, Magnesium, and Quartz."

≈

Thuggeeism—the system of plunder and assassination of the Thug-gees, a fraternity of robbers and assassins formerly prevalent in central and northern India. They roamed in bands, lured people to seclud-ed spots, and robbed and murdered them. They preferred strangu-lation and shed blood only when forced by circumstances. The word "thug" comes from this gang, so the term connotes a ruffian or cut-throat.

Toadyism—the behavior of a sycophant, an obsequious flatterer.

≈

Tokenism—the practice of allowing one person or a small number of people into a group to give it the appearance of conforming to a standard of openness deemed moral. In the U.S., this especially applies to hiring one or two blacks at a company and placing them in positions of prominence, in a hypocritical attempt to make the firm look "progressive."

≈

Tolstoyism—the doctrines of Lev Nikolaevich Tolstoy (1828-1910), Russian author, educator, and critic of the aristocracy, which he chronicled in *War and Peace* and *Anna Karenina*. Among other teachings, Tolstoy maintained children know intuitively what they wish to learn, and he brought peasant youngsters to his schoolroom and let them tell him what they wanted to study. He trusted their natural curiosity, and so they tended to learn more.

≈

Tontinism—a system of annuity devised by an Italian, Lorenzo Tonti, in 1653. First adopted by governments to borrow money, it was later applied to life insurance. Under a tontine policy, the subscriber receives no dividends or returns for a certain number of years (the "tontine period"). At the expiration date, the entire fund, with its accumulations, is divided among those still alive who have kept their policies in force. "Buy an annuity cheap, and make your life interesting to yourself and everybody else that watches the speculation." (Charles Dickens, in *Martin Chuzzlewit*)

ॐ

Too Big To Failism—a political doctrine devised recently in the U.S. in the wake of the Savings and Loan mess, wherein the the FDIC (the government bank insurance agency) decreed that certain banks are "too big to fail" and will thus get unlimited funds to protect themselves from a plethora of bad loans. It's a kinder, gentler economics, which claims that bankruptcy can equal prosperity, provided it's a big enough bankruptcy, and that the Republic can withstand any fiscal burden, provided no one looks beyond the day after tomorrow. See Alchemism and Keynesianism.

ॐ

Toryism—the principles and practices of the Tory Party in Britain. The name was originally given to one of the numerous mosstroopers who, during the civil wars of the 16th century, plundered people in the bogs of Ireland. The name went to a political party in England about 1679—originally as a reproach to all who were supposed abettors of the "Popish Plot," and then generally to those who refused to exclude a Catholic prince, James II, from the throne. The nickname, like its contemporaneous opposite Whig, became less strict in its application, until at last it signified an adherent of the party that resisted change and supported the authority of the king, church, and aristocracy. In the U.S., Tories supported Britain in the American Revolution.

Today, the term has been supplanted by "Conservatives," who may be considered modern Tories, except that British Conservatives generally defend Capitalism and economic liberty, while their opponents admire Socialism. See Thatcherism.

ॐ

Totalitarianism—the doctrines or behavior of a government that is controlled exclusively by one political party or faction, which functions according to a centralized scheme and refuses to recognize, and therefore suppresses, all other political parties or debate. Modern examples include Nazi Germany and Castro's Cuba.

ॐ

Totemism—a system, prevalent among the Indians of North America, describing tribes or families by an animal or natural symbol.

Totems are also used in many ceremonies, especially to mark the
stages of religious or social advancement.

ᘒ

Tourism—the act of traveling and sight-seeing for pleasure; the business of providing accomodations and services for travelers. On a
personal level, Tourism is the practice of going places and discovering
that you can't afford to go places as often as you'd like, that money
changers were thrown out of the Temple for good reason, and that
McDonald's is far more successful than you had imagined. "The
British tourist is always happy abroad so long as the natives are wait-
ers." (Robert Morley)

ᘒ

Townsendism—a pension plan, proposed in 1934 by Dr. Francis Townsend (1867-1960), whereby all workers would retire at age 60 and
receive $200 a month from the U.S. government. Since the pen-
sioner would have to spend this sum within 30 days of receipt, a
lot of money would be circulating, and commodities would be bought
in vast amounts. According to Dr. Townsend, this would increase
production, thereby benefiting industry and labor and acting as
a guarantee against unemployment. A similar concept was pushed
by Presidents Franklin Roosevelt and Lyndon Johnson and many
members of Congress, who claimed we could "spend our way into
prosperity." Hah. See Under-Consumptionism.

ᘒ

Traditionalism—1. adherence to age-old beliefs and modes of behavior. 2. a system of religious belief relying on revelation for its support and received by traditional instruction; a faith based on ecclesiastical authority and the traditions of the church, rather than on reason or individual investigation of the Scriptures.

ᘒ

Traducianism—1. the doctrine that the souls of children as well as their bodies are begotten by reproduction from the substance of their parents, as opposed to Creationism and Infusionism. 2. the doctrine that Original Sin is transmitted from parent to child. It's just one more thing our kids can blame us for.

ᘒ

Trans-Atlantic Mystificationism—a deliberate effort on our part to confuse readers on both sides of the Atlantic by including both British and American Isms. Probably a complete waste of time. "Yesterday, I rang my bank in America to say I was wiring a certain amount in sterling. 'What is sterling?' asked the clerk. I suppose I could have mustered some explanation—it's a rapidly fading dependent of the German mark—but I didn't think it was worth the effort." (Mark Steyn)

Having learned what a sterling is, Americans will be curious to know how to ring a bank. Simple: You pull your motor over to the pavement, put a few coppers in the public box, and when the clark answers, just say you have a bit of a kafuffle and would they please put you straight, to avoid a major cock-up.

Say that anywhere in England and your banker will understand every word. Say it in Wyoming and you risk losing your teeth.

ᘒ

Transcendentalism—1. the state or quality of going beyond the evidence of one's senses. In Kantianism and Platonism, it's transcending Empiricism and ascertaining the fundamental principles of human knowledge via Idealism. Transcendentalism was also the religious/philosophical school of Emerson and Thoreau. 2. a fabulously successful fraud perpetrated by Maharishi Mahesh Yogi, who first gained fame in the 1960's as a spiritual advisor to the Beatles. His pupils try to levitate while meditating in the lotus position. The Maharishi's brochure has a cute photo of a girl in deep meditation, floating in mid-air—five inches above a trampoline.

ᘒ

Transformism—the theory that species evolve through gradual modification over many generations. Part of Darwinism.

Trans-Himalayan Esotericism—a secret doctrine concerning the origin of man, preserved by "adepts" in Tibet. Esoteric versions of this ancient doctrine can be found in various Hindu texts, from which the Bible, Koran, and Torah allegedly hijacked big chunks of their own creation myths. See Esoteric Buddhism.

さ

Transsexualism—the condition of a person who has an overwhelming desire to become a member of the opposite sex, or has indeed become another gender through hormone therapy and surgical procedures to change external genitalia. Transsexuals feel compelled to change sex because the truth of who they feel they are—emotionally, psychologically, and spiritually—is contrary to the physical sex they were given at conception.

さ

Transubstantiationism—the belief in the Christian doctrine that, upon consecration, the items of the Eucharist (bread and wine) change entirely into the body and blood of Jesus Christ, and only their external forms remain the same. One of the major points of contention, dating from the Reformation, between Roman Catholicism and Protestantism. Cf. Consubstantialism.

Transvestitism—the practice of a person (usually male) who dresses in the clothing of the opposite sex for psycho-sexual reasons. Also, Tranvestism.

さ

Tribadism—sexual desire of one woman for another. Many women value the female powers as superior to the male's and regard their own sex as intrinsically more desirable. But women traditionally have found little opportunity to develop female relationships, since biology and society lead them to compete for the best male to perpetuate their genes. However, biology is not destiny, and the spiritual and psychological aspects of sexuality often do not follow pure instinct. See Sapphism, Lesbianism.

કે

Tribalism—the state, conditions, feelings, or character of a social group in which individuality is either not admitted or given no legitimacy. Each member of the tribe is viewed as a subordinate unit dependent on the interests, beliefs, and "life" of the whole tribe.

કે

Trichroism—the quality of presenting different colors in three different directions when viewed by transmitted light—a property of certain crystals.

કે

Trichromatism—1. three-color printing, wherein all colors are made from three hues of ink: magneta, yellow, and cyan (plus black). Color comic books and color photos in newspapers show the process clearly. 2. normal vision, in contrast with Daltonism.

Trigger Mechanism—a physical or psychological process caused by a specific stimulus that sets off a reaction, often severe. For example, a strobe light set between 10-25 flashes per second will trigger an epileptic seizure in 80% of the population. Yet another reason to avoid discos.

કે

Trigoneitism—the ability to have three broods in one year.

કે

Triliteralism—the presence of three-letter roots in a language, as in Hebrew and other Semitic languages.

કે

Trinitarianism—a belief in the Christian Trinity (God, Jesus, Holy Spirit), especially as the doctrine of the Trinitarians, a monastic order founded in 1198 to redeem captive Christians from Turks and other infidels. Also called Transpersonalists, Mathurins, and Redemptionists.

કે

Tractarianism—the system of religious opinion and practice promulgated within the Church of England in a series of papers entitled *Tracts for the Times*, published at Oxford from 1833-1841. The leaders of the movement sought a middle course between Romanism and what they considered a rationalistic or latitudinarian Protestantism. As the tracts appeared, it became apparent that they were hostile to Protestantism and favorable to Catholicism. Many who favored this Anglo-Catholic movement joined the Church of Rome, while others remained to represent the High Church of the Church of England. See High Churchism.

Trade Unionism—the principles or practices of a group of workers in a related craft who combine for mutual support and protection, especially for collective bargaining for wages, hours of labor, benefits, etc. Trade Unionism was inspired largely by the theories of Marxism and Socialism, which presume that Capitalism results in the progressive impoverishment of the working class, and thus workers must unite to oppose the moneyed class, especially in the form of labor strikes, work slow-downs, industrial sabotage, etc.

While the concept of collective bargaining is noble and at times necessary to prevent exploitation, most unions have deteriorated into Gangsterism, and their influence in U.S. industry is steadily declining. People are realizing that too often unions promote inefficiency and mob rule, coddling the inept and creating bureaucracy, thus raising costs and, in the long run, decreasing employment opportunities. To wit: "Alan Bulmer, 31, got into trouble with his fellow workers when he finished a week's assignment three hours ahead of time. Instead of sitting down for three hours, he started on a new stint of work. More than 2,000 miners held a meeting last Saturday to object to his working too hard. They demanded that he be demoted for three months and his pay cut." (from a British press report)

Tritheism—the belief that the Christian Trinity is comprised of three distinct beings or Gods.

Trivialism—something insignificant, a trifle. From *trivialis* ("of the crossroads"), hence commonplace and of little importance. Some may consign this book to the category of trivia, but, since we hope to make a pile of money and retire on our royalties, we beg to differ.

Tropism—the orientation or growth of an Organism in response to a stimulus. For example, many plants grow toward the sun, which is why you must turn the plants in your window or they'll grow at an odd angle.

Trotskyism—the principles of Leon Trotsky (1879-1940), a Bolshevik leader exiled from the Soviet Union after he openly opposed the Communist Party and allegedly plotted against the government. Like all Communists, Trotsky advocated international revolution, but he thought it should be accomplished by education rather than force, and he denied the possibility of building Socialism in the Soviet Union. No wonder he was declared an enemy of the state.

Truism—a self-evident, obvious truth that often becomes a cliché, such as "The apple doesn't fall far from the tree" and "You can lead a horse to water but you can't make him drink."

Turkism—the religion, social customs, or political practices of the Turks.

Tutorism—the state of someone who has the duty of guardianship, tutelage, and instruction; to teach, usually outside the normal institutions of education. In an early case, the U.S. Supreme Court ruled that Cherokee Indians were permanently in "tutelage" and therefore ineligible to voice their grievances or sue to enforce contracts with state governments.

Tympanism—in pathology, the condition of suffering from distension by gas.

Tyronism—the state of being a novice (or tyro), one who is in the rudiments of any branch of study or a person imperfectly acquainted with a subject.

Ubiquitarianism—the belief in the bodily presence of Christ everywhere, especially in the Eucharist.

❧

Ugly Realism—an art movement in Berlin in the late 1970's devoted to highly realistic grotesques and satires that spat upon and ridiculed humanity. Real sweet folks.

❧

Ultraism—the principles of people who advocate extreme measures, usually in political, religious, or social matters. See Extremism.

❧

Ultraconservatism—in the U.S., the political principles of the extreme right-wing. The term is usually hurled at anyone who believes in the death penalty for murder, a free enterprise economy, and heterosexual marriage prior to childbirth.

❧

Ultramontanism—the doctrines of Ultramontists, a party of the Church of Rome which places absolute authority in matters of faith and discipline with the Pope, in opposition to the views of those who favored national churches and making the Pope subordinate to an ecumenical council. Cf. Gallicanism.

❧

Ultranationalism—see Nationalism, and multiply by 100. An important element of Fascism.

Uncle Tomism—a pattern of black-white interaction where whites are patronizing and blacks are subservient. The title character of *Uncle Tom's Cabin* by Harriet Beecher Stowe (1811-1896) was an old slave who was servile and deferential to his kindly master. The term is now an accusation thrown at blacks who are seen as obsequious to whites and traitorous to their race, and is now often used against any successful black, under the assumption that he or she must have "sold out" to the white power structure. This really has nothing to do with race, only the age-old pattern of unsuccessful people trying to excuse their failure by attacking anyone who succeeds—at which point their own failure becomes something "pure," to be proud of.

※

Underconsumptionism—a fallacy in economic theory which asserts that "no power of consumption on the part of the labouring classes can ever alone furnish an encouragement to the employment of capital" (Malthus). Therefore, taxation and government spending are required to make people produce things.

※

Uniformitarianism—the theory of geologists who maintain that all ecologic changes and phenomena are due to agencies working uniformly and uninterruptedly, as opposed to Catastrophism, which refers such changes to great, occasional convulsions. Uniformitarians say that the influence of the agencies now working continued during all the eons of geologic time and is sufficient to account for all the phenomena in the structure of the earth.

※

Unilateralism—1. doctrine of taking action without consulting with or asking permission from your opponents. 2. a single-issue political theory in Britain, arising from the 1960's peace movement and still a force in foreign policy debates, which proposes to end the threat of nuclear war by unilaterally disarming the West. The theory, vehemently espoused by the Campaign for Nuclear Disarmament, was that the Soviets would disarm and quit threatening us if we disarmed and quit threatening them. Why *we* had to disarm first was never clearly explained. The latest version maintains that, since the Cold War is over, we can safely disarm anyway. British conservatives are still suspicious.

Unionism—1. the principles of uniting or combining; specifically, the system of uniting workers in the same industry or trade (see Trade Unionism). 2. adherence to and advocacy of a particular union, especially support of the Union side during the U.S. Civil War; or, in British politics, the tenets of those who opposed Home Rule and the disruption of the legislative union between England and Ireland.

Unitarianism—1. a system advocating centralization, especially in government. 2. the doctrines of Unitarians, whose beliefs vary from pure Deism to an acceptance of the Bible and the divinity of Christ, with many intermediate beliefs touching various doctrines made fundamental by other churches. They emphasize the oneness of God, tolerance for all religious belief, and virtuous character. Unitarianism in the U.S. developed under Dr. William Channing (1780-1842) in the early 1800's.

Universalism—the doctrine of one who believes all people will be saved, in opposition to the concept of eternal punishment; specifically, a sect founded about 1750 which believes in the ultimate salvation of all and which directs its Criticism against an eternal hell—and in some cases against any suffering after death.

Unnaturalism—the state or character of being not in conformity to nature or not agreeable to the real character of persons or things.

Untruism—something obviously false; the opposite of Truism.

Urbanism—the character and lifestyle of people who live in large cities; a fatal attraction to bright lights and big cities. Taking New York as an example, we urge you to avoid Urbanism at all costs. "Our present city populations are so savage that they drive even the most public-spirited country people to put up barbed wire all over the place. They are no more to be trusted with trees and animals than a baby can be trusted with a butterfly." (George Bernard Shaw)

Ursinism—something pertaining to or characteristic of bears; laziness and fuzziness, especially among humans who resemble bears.

ða

Utilitarianism—1. the doctrine that the greatest happiness of the greatest number should be the goal of all social and political institutions. 2. the doctrine that virtue is founded on utility, or that utility is the sole standard of morality. That is, actions are right because they are useful, and they are right in proportion to their promotion of happiness, and vice versa. In the 19th century, utilitarians, led by Jeremy Bentham (1748-1832), articulated this philosophy in opposition to doctrines of those who claimed to know the will of God. See Benthamism, Pragmatism.

Utopianism—chimerical schemes in theory or practice which purport to offer ideal happiness and the perfection of mankind, usually through Socialism.

Utopian Socialism—political theory which states that if only people would give their money, means of production, and stuff to the state voluntarily, there'd be no unemployment or poverty. As you know if you've read this far, some people will fall for anything.

Utraquism—doctrine of 15th-century Hussites who thought lay Christians should receive the wine as well as the bread in the Eucharist.

Vagabondism—the condition or habits of someone who strolls from place to place without fixed habitation or visible means of livelihood, like a hobo or wanderer. In general usage, the term connotes laziness, shiftlessness, and vagrancy.

Vaishnavism—the worship of the Hindu god Vishnu, who forms the Trimurti (Trinity) with the other two great gods, Brahma and Siva. Vishnu is the Preserver, considered by his worshippers the supreme god of the Hindu pantheon.

Valentinianism—the beliefs of a sect of heretics in the 2nd century, named for Valentinius, their founder. A branch of the Gnostics, they regarded Christ as a kind of phantom. See Gnosticism.

Valetudarianism—the state of feeble health in a person of sickly constitution seeking to recover. It also refers to the traits of someone overly concerned with his health. "My doctor gave me two weeks to live. I hope they're in August." (Ronnie Shakes)

Vampirism—figuratively, the practice of extortion or preying on others in a ruthless manner; literally, a belief in blood-sucking corpses or ghosts, which has existed for millenia, especially in the Slavic and Greek cultures and among the Wallachians and Serbs.

The explanation for Vampirism given by Esotericism is that there is a phenomenom known as "half-death," whereby the astral soul disengages itself gradually and, when the last link is broken at death, separates from its earthly body. Some souls depart with unfinished business in the material realm, so they hang around and do their mischief, with blood being their source of nourishment. The solution, courtesy of Hollywood, is to run a stake through the heart of the astral phantasm.

"Long illness is the real Vampirism: think of living a year or two after one is dead, by sucking the life-blood out of a frail young creature at one's bedside!" (Oliver Wendell Holmes)

Vandalism—the spirit or conduct of the Vandals, the most barbarous of the northern nations who invaded Rome in the 5th century, notorious for destroying art and literature. Hence, Vandalism is willful or ignorant destruction of art or, in very general use, any public or private property.

Vanguardism—the practice of being on the forefront of a movement or school of thought. See Avant-Gardism.

Vanillism—dermatitis, coryza, and malaise from handling vanilla.

Vansittartism—the belief that the aggressive acts of German leaders since the Franco-Prussian War reflect the character of the German people, and therefore Germany should be demilitarized and re-educated to prevent further aggression. Named for British diplomat Robert Vansittart (1881-1957). I guess you've got to wonder about any nation whose anthem extols the ideal of *Deutschland über alles*.

Vaticanism—the theological system based on the doctrine of absolute papal supremacy. See Ultramontanism.

Vegetarianism—the theory or practice of abstaining from meat and food derived from animals. Some vegetarians avoid only meat, some eschew meat and fish, while others won't consume butter, eggs, milk, or even honey (exploitation of bees, you know). While it's certainly true that the modern American diet contains too much meat and animal fat, it's also undeniable that human Metabolism is designed to process animal protein. There's just no getting around the fact that we are carnivores.

Biology, however, is not destiny—we can choose not to eat meat (and thereby avoid complicity in the slaughter of billions of animals), and there are sound ecological and moral arguments for reducing animal consumption. If you choose Vegetarianism, good for you. The problems start when some individuals, convinced of their moral superiority and insight, think they should make choices for other carnivores and self-righteously taunt patrons at a steakhouse or stage idiotic raids of seafood restaurants to "liberate" lobsters. These folks should just go home and eat their tofu quietly.

ક્ર

Ventriloquism—the art or practice of making sounds without moving the lips and directing attention elsewhere, so the voice seems to come not from the speaker but from some distant place (a puppet, the other side of the room, etc.). The word comes from the Latin word *venter*, meaning belly, and *loqui*, meaning to speak—in the mistaken notion that the voice of the ventriloquist comes from his gut.

ક્ર

Verbalism—1. the choice of words; phrasing. 2. a phrase with little meaning, wild and whirling words full of sound and fury, signifying only trifles light as air. Remember, much is the force of heaven-bred poesy, but talkers are no good doers. (lots of Shakespeare)

ક્ર

Verism—the quality of being real or actual; truthfulness of a proposition or statement; honesty and extreme Realism, especially in art or literature.

୬

Vernacularism—a common, everyday word, phrase, or manner of speech; an idiom of the country of one's birth or of a locality or district. In the vernacular of California's San Fernando Valley, everything of interest is "Like, too much, dude!"

୬

Victimism—an annoying tendency of modern Americans, individually and in groups, to claim special privilege and deny responsibility for their failures because, they claim, they are the target of another's hatred and discrimination. Blacks are victims of Racism; whites are victims of affirmative action; homosexuals are victims of homophobia; alcoholics are victims of drunk parents; perverts are victims of "sex addiction"; *ad nauseum*. Really, it's all just whining. "No one can make you feel inferior without your consent." (Eleanor Roosevelt)

Vigilambulism—1. in pathology, a state resembling Somnambulism, but not occurring in sleep. 2. multiple personality, as in *The Three Faces of Eve*.

୬

Vigilantism—the practice or policy of people who band together to take law enforcement into their own hands. Though the term usually has negative connotations, the citizens of San Francisco banded together during the Gold Rush to protect public safety and property because the government had become so corrupt. Arguably, New York City and parts of Los Angeles have reached a similar stage, so the Guardian Angels, a private, volunteer "safety patrol," walk the streets and deter crime. But, it's a grim trait of "private justice" to result in persecution of racial minorities and summary punishment without public trial according to law. Thus, Vigilantism is feared by those who advocate due process and equal rights under the law.

૨ટ

Virilism—the development of secondary sex characteristics in women, such as Hirsutism or a deep voice, due to hormonal imbalance. Also called Pseudohermaphroditism.

૨ટ

Vitalism—1. the concept that the universe is not entirely mechanistic and that things have some self-determination. 2. in biology, the doctrine that ascribes all the functions of an Organism to a vital principle which is neither a chemical nor physical force. From the Latin word *vitalis*, which means "non-greasy hair-styling liquid."

૨ટ

Vivaparism—bearing live young rather than laying eggs.

૨ટ

Vocalism—the exercise of the vocal organs, especially singing.

Volcanism—volcanic processes and phenomena. Also, Vulcanism.

૨ટ

Volsteadism—Prohibitionism, named after Andrew Volstead (1860-1946), the Congressman who introduced the 18th Amendment to the Constitution, forbidding the sale of alcoholic beverages. Party pooper.

૨ટ

Voltairism—the principles or philosophy of Francois Marie Arouet de Voltaire (1694-1778), a French writer, philosopher, poet, dramatist, and historian. See Skepticism. "I disapprove of what you say, but I will defend to the death your right to say it." (Voltaire)

❧

Voluntarism—1. principle or action based on free choice. 2. the system of supporting something—especially a hospital, church, or school—by uncompensated, voluntary contribution or assistance, as opposed to government subsidy. Also, Volunteerism.

❧

Voodooism—the popular but inaccurate name for Voudun, a native religion of the West Indies and Haiti which contains elements of Roman Catholicism and beliefs from Africa. It deals largely with spirits, both benign and malign, who possess believers in elaborate rites. Adherents do use herbal magic, incantations, and spells, but things like voodoo dolls and zombie curses are Hollywood inventions.

❧

Vorticism—British art movement founded in reaction to Cubism and Futurism. Ezra Pound (1885-1972) coined the term in 1913, and there was a Vorticist magazine, an exhibition—and then World War I.

❧

Voyeurism—the practice of observing other people's activities, especially sexual activities viewed furtively. America's obsession with pornography, lurid television (à la *Donahue* and *Divorce Court*), and tell-all biographies reflect the Voyeurism of contemporary society.

❧

Vulgarism—coarse or lewd behavior and manners, typical of common people or the less-refined classes; the act or expression of low manners or language; anything common or mundane. "Vulgarity is simply the conduct of other people." (Oscar Wilde)

❧

Vulpinism—the quality of being fox-like (vulpine); crafty and cunning behavior; artfulness.

❧

Vulturism—the attributes or character of a vulture, a species of cowardly birds with big talons who feed chiefly on carrion and offal. In general usage, it describes the behavior of one who is rapacious and predatory.

Wagnerism—musical characteristics of German composer Richard Wagner (1813-1883), or his musical theories, such as continuous music, emphasis on the orchestra, the use of leitmotif, and fat ladies in helmets. For a complete understanding of Wagner, see the Bugs Bunny cartoon *What's Opera, Doc?*. "Wagner's music is much better than it sounds." (Bill Nye)

ᆶ

Wahhabism—the beliefs and practices of the Wahhabis, the most conservative Muslim sect, who oppose all practices not sanctioned in the Koran. Also Wahhabiism, Wahabism. "Everything not compulsary is forbidden." (George Orwell)

ᆶ

Wasm—a thoroughly discredited political, economic, or moral theory. See Communism.

ᆶ

Wegotism—the frequent use of the pronoun "we," especially favored by those for whom the concept of Individualism is too big a burden. See Tribalism.

ᆶ

Weightism—a term used to accuse a person or group of favoring thin people over fat people, especially in employment practices. From the "politically correct" lingo currently in vogue on U.S. college campuses. "The waist is a terrible thing to mind." (Tom Wilson's *Ziggy*)

ᆶ

Weismannism—a form of Neo-Darwinism developed by German biologist August Weismann (1834-1914), particularly with regard to the physical basis of heredity and the non-transmission of acquired characteristics.

Welfare Statism—government policies and practices which result in transfers of wealth from the "haves" to the "have-nots," either in the form of progressive income taxes or a variety of schemes in which need qualifies the recipient for benefits. About 50% of the current U.S. Federal budget goes for welfare and "entitlement" programs— and that does not include state, county, and city programs. The net effect of such charity is to reward those in distress (and, indeed, perpetuate their penury by destroying incentive and self-respect) and penalize the productive, the resourceful, and the self-sufficient.

Welfare Statism grows from Populism and ends with Socialism or Fascism, as productive taxpayers are outnumbered by welfare recipients and pressure mounts for ever-greater taxation. The socialist policies of Britain during the 1960's, for example, led to a crisis termed "the brain drain," as doctors and engineers fled oppressive taxes in England for life in countries that let them keep most of the fruits of their labor. Until recently, the effects of similar programs have been obscured in America by deficit spending, which has merely postponed the inevitable economic collapse inherent in Welfare Statism by passing the costs to the next generation—but the jig is just about up. "A government that robs Peter to pay Paul can always depend on the support of Paul." (George Bernard Shaw)

ð

Welfarism—the attitudes leading to Welfare Statism. Start with "the world owes me a living" and go from there.

ð

Wesleyanism—the system or doctrines of John Wesley (1703-1791) and the Wesleyan Methodists; Arminian Methodism. Also, Wesleyism. See Arminianism.

ð

Western Hermetism—a doctrine similar to Eastern Esotericism, but which devolved into pseudo-magic attempts to turn lead into gold;

derived from the Hermetists. Like later Rosicrucians, adherents held that all things were produced by the contention of light and darkness and that every particle of matter contains a spark of Divine Essence. The spark's tendency to free itself and return to the Central Source produces motion, from which "forms" are born. The ultimate origin is Hermetic Esotericism, which preached secrecy above all else.

ॐ

Westernism—a Colloquialism or other characteristic of the people of the western United States, as in "howdy" and "hot tub."

ॐ

Whiggism—the principles of the Whig political party, which originated in England in the 17th century during the reigns of Charles I and II, when great contests existed with respect to royal prerogatives and the rights of the people. Those who supported the king were called Tories (later, Conservatives); advocates of popular rights were called Whigs (later, Liberals). In the U.S., a Whig supported the colonies against England in the Revolution, and the Whig Party opposed the Democratic Party from about 1834 until the organization of the Republican Party in 1856. Zachary Taylor was the last Whig president; the protective tariff was a Whig measure.

According to Burnet, the term originates from "whiggam," a word employed by Scottish farmers to urge their horses onwards when they came to Leith to buy corn.

White Supremacism—the belief that Negroes and other non-Caucasians are inferior to whites and should be excluded from government and white-dominated society. The system of apartheid in South Africa held this doctrine as a core principle, and in the

U.S., it gained considerable popularity during Reconstruction after the Civil War, when white Southern leaders could not hold political office and emancipated Negroes were manipulated into supporting Northern "carpetbaggers" who had migrated south to take advantage of the situation.

The Ku Klux Klan, a white supremacist society organized to "protect" the honor of Southern women and antebellum institutions, still terrorizes blacks, parades in white robes, and burns crosses to emphasize their Biblical interpretation that blacks are inferior and that slavery is an institution sanctioned by Scripture. Neo-Nazi groups hold similar beliefs.

გ

Wilsonian Idealism—the high-minded leadership of Woodrow Wilson (1856-1924), 28th U.S. president, creator of the Federal Reserve system, and architect of the ill-fated League of Nations. After declaring he was "too proud to fight," Wilson took America into World War I to make the world "safe for democracy" and later enforced punitive German disarmament and reparations under the Treaty of Versailles. A scholarly, moralistic man, Wilson held politicians in contempt and scorned the use of brute power. This did not, however, prevent him from manipulating the economy or waging war in pursuit of his ideals. Like his predecessor Theodore Roosevelt, Wilson exalted "duty above rights, collective welfare above individual self-interest, the heroic values as opposed to Materialism, action instead of logic, the natural impulse rather than the pallid intellect" (R.E. Osgood). As a hero of Liberalism, Wilson inspired Presidents Roosevelt, Johnson, Nixon, and Carter. His faith in the goodness and perfectability of mankind was squarely contradicted by Niebuhrian Realism. Also, Wilsonism, Wilsonianism.

Wirism—in the game of darts, the principle by which a dart is impelled to fall on the wrong side of a wire, so that the player fails to score points at a crucial moment in the game. Acute Wirism involves the darts bouncing off the little round wire protecting the double bullseye.

&

Witticism—a humorous, clever sentence or remark; a quip; the faculty of associating ideas in a new and ingenious, as well as natural and pleasing, way. "Wit is a sword; it is meant to make people feel the point as well as see it." (G.K. Chesterton)

&

Workaholism—an "addiction" to work (à la Alcoholism), where the afflicted is unable to relax, enjoy normal, friendly relationships, or take a vacation. It often goes hand-in-hand with Careerism and Yuppieism. "By working faithfully eight hours a day, you may eventually get to be a boss and work twelve hours a day." (Robert Frost)

&

Wycliffism—beliefs of the followers of John Wycliffe (1320-1384), English theologian and reformer considered extremely dangerous by the Church because he translated the Bible into the vernacular. The movement was brutally and repeatedly put down, although Wycliffe's Bible had many secret admirers among the nobility. He proposed to blunt Church power and corruption by having the nobility take back the land they had bequeathed it. Thirty years after his death, the Church ordered Wycliffe's body exhumed and burned.

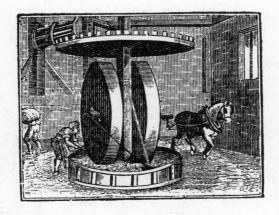

Xerophytism—the characteristics of a plant that can grow in dry conditions, like a cactus.

❧

Xeroxism—the mistake of attributing the name "Xerox," a trademark, to a photocopy made on another manufacturer's system. That is, you can't xerox something on a Canon copier.

Yahooism—characteristics and behavior of an ill-mannered, unsophisticated person, usually someone from a rural area. From the brutish Yahoos in Swift's *Gulliver's Travels*.

❧

Yahwism—the worship of Yahweh or Jehovah. Also, Yahvism.

❧

Yankeeism—the characteristics and expressions of Yankees, a general term used to describe people of the New England states of the U.S. The name Yankee was originally given by the Massachusetts Indians to the English colonists. It was later adopted by the Dutch on the Hudson River, who applied the term in contempt to all New Englanders. During the American Revolution, the name was applied to all the insurgents, and during the Civil War, it was the common designation of the Federal soldiers by the Confederates. In Britain and elsewhere, the term describes all natives of the U.S. (as in "Yankee go home"). Stereotypical Yankeeisms include laconic speech, self-reliance, ingenuity, and extreme thrift. For more insight, see *Yankee Magazine*, the popular chronicle of the region.

❧

Yiddishism—a word or phrase peculiar to the Yiddish language, like *kvetch* and *oy vey*. Yiddish, the language of Eastern European Jews, is a fascinating mix of German, Hebrew, and Slavic languages.

❧

Yogism—the principles and practices of Yoga, a school of Hindu philosophy prescribing meditation and physical discipline as a means of attaining union with the supreme being. In the West, many adherents practice Yoga strictly for relaxation and stress reduction.

৵

Yogi-ism—a comical saying by baseball great Lawrence "Yogi" Berra, whose Malapropisms often have a transcendent, Zen-like wisdom: "(That) restaurant is so crowded, nobody goes there anymore." "The future ain't what it used to be." "The game isn't over till it's over." See also Goldwynism.

৵

Yuppieism—the behavior of "young urban professionals," ambitious, educated, materialistic city-dwellers who were schooled in the 1960's and admired the Idealism expressed then, but who promptly adopted Helotism when they turned 30. "Yuppie" is a derisive derivation of Yippie, which described adherents to the Youth International Party, a 1968 group dedicated to abolishing Capitalism. "The trouble with the rat race is that even if you win you're still a rat." (Lily Tomlin)

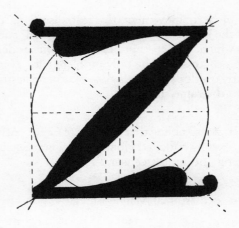

Zanyism—the behavior of a subordinate buffoon or simpleton, whose role was to awkwardly mimic the professional clown.

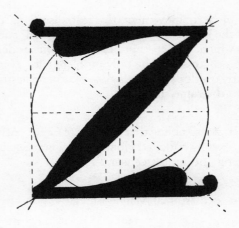

Zarathustrianism—see Zoroastrianism.

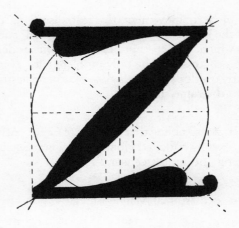

Zealotism—the character or conduct of someone carried away by excess fervor, or a fanatical partisan, generally applied to one whose ardor is intemperate or censurable. Specifically, Zealots were a sect of radical Jews who struggled desperately against the Romans in the first century A.D. (John the Baptist may have been a member of this group.) With the coming of the "messiah," the Zealots believed they would achieve freedom from Rome, but King Herod kept crucifying Hebrew reformers whenever they appeared. "There are few catastrophes so great and irremediable as those that follow an excess of zeal." (R.H. Benson)

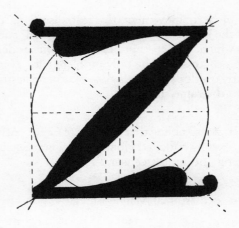

Zen Buddhism—the Japanese form of Chinese Ch'an, or meditation Buddhism. It may have arrived in China as early as the first century, but it was popularized by the Indian monk Bodhidharma, circa 470 A.D. Adherents seek revelation through direct experience, and Zen masters give disciples a task to work on as a basis for meditation—usually a riddle or nonsense statement. Liberation is achieved by those who trust in the Buddha of Immeasurable Light. "Zen does not confuse spirituality with thinking about God while one is peeling potatoes. Zen spirituality is just to peel the potatoes." (Alan Watts)

Zionism—the modern movement to create Israel as the rightful homeland of the Jewish people. From the word "hill" and pertaining to Jerusalem which, after its capture, became the residence of King David and his successors. The only problem with Zionism is that it conveniently overlooks the existence of other Palestinian groups with claim to the same turf.

Zoilism—Criticism resembling that of Zoilus, a Greek critic and grammarian who severely criticized Homer, Plato, and Socrates. Hence, illiberal carping and unjust censure.

Zoomagnetism—see Animal Magnetism.

Zoomitism—a bizarre photographic ritual practiced extensively in TV, home videos, and Japanese monster movies, in which the world suddenly slides forward or backward for no particular reason. Zoomitism afflicts 99.3% of camcorder owners in the U.S., and there is no known cure. It was probably invented by a news cameraman too lazy to walk ten feet closer to the car wreck.

Zoomorphism—1. the representation or conception of a person, deity, or other being with the likeness or characteristics of an animal. 2. ascribing a human or divine nature to animals, or worshipping them because of such a nature. 3. the transformation of men into beasts, which occurs annually on Superbowl Sunday.

Zootheism—ascribing divine attributes to animals, or zoomorphic Theism. For example, ancient Egyptians worshipped cats, and modern Hindus worship cows.

ze

Zoroastrianism—religion founded around 600 B.C. by Zoroaster, the great legislator and prophet of the ancient Bactrians, whose theology was the national faith of Persia (now Iran) and is embodied in a document called the *Zend Avesta*. Commonly known as fireworship, Zoroastrianism depicts an epic struggle between good and evil. Also, Mazdaism, Zarathustrianism.

ze

Zurvanism—an ancient Iranian religion centered around the worship of Zurvan, god of time and fate and father of Ahura Mazda, the supreme deity of Zoroastrianism. Also, Zervanism.

ze

Zwinglianism—the doctrines of Huldreich Zwingli (1484-1531), a contemporary of Martin Luther and Swiss religious reformer of Christian sacramentarian doctrines. See Sacramentalism.

ze

Zygodactylism—the condition of a group of nonpasserine birds, such as parrots and woodpeckers, who have two toes in the front and two toes in the back of each foot.

About the Authors

Alan and **Theresa von Altendorf** are two nice people who became fascinated with how much they didn't know about words that end in "ism" and thus were drawn into the task of compiling this compendium. To do it, they consulted several dictionaries and occasionally made things up.

They describe their effort as a history of the evolution of human thought and belief, and it helped them appreciate how people stumbled and scratched to explain "Why am I here?" and "What is life all about?" They are personally in favor of Beism and Interestism, which Theresa made up, but probably the most they can hope from readers is a deeper understanding of humanity and the search for meaning and purpose.

"Our publisher suggested we not pillory any Ism with snide editorial comments," they said. "But the impulse to Criticism never fully left us, mainly because certain Isms have caused tremendous harm, and evil wins when good people say nothing. Certainly, the intelligent reader will want to dig further and consult original sources, especially for mega-Isms like Communism and Capitalism. Our little book shows where the mountaintops are and some of the scenery in the foothills, but the hard work of climbing is a matter of individual stubborness."